T0244516

SISTERS IN SCIENCE

Also by Olivia Campbell

Women in White Coats

SISTERS IN SCIENCE

How **FOUR WOMEN PHYSICISTS ESCAPED NAZI GERMANY** *and* **MADE SCIENTIFIC HISTORY**

OLIVIA CAMPBELL

PARK ROW BOOKS

PARK
ROW ™
BOOKS™

Recycling programs
for this product may
not exist in your area.

ISBN-13: 978-0-7783-3338-8

Sisters in Science: How Four Women Physicists Escaped
Nazi Germany and Made Scientific History

This publication contains opinions and ideas of the author. It is intended for informational and
educational purposes only. The reader should seek the services of a competent professional for
expert assistance or professional advice. Reference to any organization, publication or website
does not constitute or imply an endorsement by the author or the publisher. The author and the
publisher specifically disclaim any and all liability arising directly or indirectly from the use or
application of any information contained in this publication.

TM is a trademark of Harlequin Enterprises ULC.

Park Row Books
22 Adelaide St. West, 41st Floor
Toronto, Ontario M5H 4E3, Canada
ParkRowBooks.com

Printed in U.S.A.

This book is dedicated to all the women academics murdered by the Nazis. Their absence haunts this book; the rippling impact of their loss affects us all. May their memories be a blessing and remind us of the importance of fighting fascism and unfettered hatred in all its forms.

SISTERS IN SCIENCE

INTRODUCTION

David Hilbert could solve some of the most complex mathematical equations ever conjured, but he simply couldn't wrap his head around the views of his fellow faculty members. In the spring of 1915, Professor Hilbert attempted to recruit a former student to teach alongside him at the University of Göttingen, Germany. This person had been teaching math for seven years at the University of Erlangen, but Hilbert coveted their brilliance for his own department.

And brilliant they were. This mathematician would go on to create modern algebra as we know it. Fellow Jewish academic Albert Einstein would come to refer to them as "the most significant creative mathematical genius." If Einstein is calling you a genius, you know it must be true.

But some of Göttingen's professors didn't care how brilliant this potential addition to their university was; all that mattered was that Emmy Noether was a woman, and that meant she couldn't be a university lecturer.

Silly girl. Didn't she know that universities were for men? That math was for boys? Why, what would the mostly male student body think?

"What will our soldiers think when they return to the university and find that they are required to learn at the feet of a woman?" the faculty demanded.

Hilbert was livid. He knew Noether's astonishing mathematical mind could be nothing but a great gift to the students of Göttingen. "I do not see that the sex of the candidate is an argument against her admission as privatdozent [lecturer]," he fumed in response. "After all, we are a university, not a bathhouse!"

A similarly incensed Einstein offered to intercede on her behalf, but in the end, he didn't need to. Hilbert hired her anyway under the auspices of being his assistant. She even began giving lectures, although her work went unpaid, of course.

Today, such work would be called volunteer, but at the time, women had to grin and bear such positions as a way to get their foot in the door. Apparently, it was audacious for women to expect remuneration for their work in academia.

"It wouldn't have done any harm to the Göttingen Feldgrauen [soldiers] if they had been sent to school with Fräulein Nöther," Einstein quipped. "She seems to know her craft well!"

Within a few years, Noether showed the world just how well she'd mastered her craft. In 1918, she solved the mathematical problem presented by Einstein's new theory of relativity that even the man himself hadn't been able to puzzle out. Her theorem was pivotal to the development of modern physics and forever altered our conception of the universe. Surely, this would prove she was good enough to be a professor.

Finally, in 1919, Noether became the first woman in Germany *allowed* to achieve habilitation, the official certification required to teach at the university level. To mark the occasion, the stuffy

Göttingen faculty conceded "a woman's mind is capable of being creative in mathematics only in exceptional cases."[1]

Noether's experience is the perfect illustration of what it was like for most women in Germany attempting to make inroads in the boys' club of academia in the early twentieth century. Brilliant women were long seen as remarkable, singular cases, not as an example of what women in general were capable of when given the same education and opportunities as men. Your genius was neither here nor there; only your gender mattered.

Math and science were especially difficult disciplines for women to crack. While lone women occasionally fought their way into some of these more analytical subjects, it wasn't until the first decades of the 1900s that we finally saw a major push for women to be more widely accepted in science professions.

While Noether paved the way for women mathematicians in Germany, Lise Meitner, Hedwig Kohn, Hertha Sponer, and Hildegard Stücklen were among those who helped usher in what was essentially the first generation of women physicists.

Tragically, their careers were cut short just as they were getting established. When Hitler took power in 1933, he ruthlessly stomped all over this progress by enacting policies excluding Jewish people and their supporters from civil service employment, and essentially barring women from such work. The Nazis also restricted the number of women who could enroll in universities and forbade women from pursuing certification to teach at universities.

"During the National Socialist years, women were de facto excluded from academic careers,"[2] explains economics professor Elisabeth Allgoewer.

Most of the fifty-six women who'd fought tooth and nail to become lecturers or professors in Germany by the early 1930s lost their positions. Hedwig, Lise, Hertha, and Hildegard all lost their jobs as a result of Nazi policies.

Nazism became a dark force spreading across Europe. Just as

the goal of the darkness is to snuff out the light, the goal of the Nazis was to snuff out anyone who wasn't a straight, able-bodied member of their invented master race—as well as anyone who stood in the way of that goal.

The force grew darker and more violent with each passing day; emboldened by every edict it passed restricting rights, by every atrocity it perpetrated against civilians that went unpunished, by every inch of land outside Germany it invaded. As the Nazi empire increased, so did the need for Jewish people and Nazi opponents to find refuge elsewhere.

Hundreds of thousands of people found themselves desperate to flee to safer shores. As shafts of light desperately defying the dark, these persecuted people sent out calls for help to influential individuals and organizations around the world. Often, an international job offer (and the funds and finesse to sneak out of the country quickly) meant the difference between life and death.

Yet the confluence of sexism and anti-Semitism in German academia meant most women scholars were not advanced or experienced enough to appear like good candidates for such jobs abroad. Not to mention that most universities had little interest in hiring women in the first place, especially in science and math disciplines.

What would it take for Hedwig, Lise, Hertha, and Hildegard to make it out of Hitler's Germany alive? Hope, of course. Persistence, certainly. Well-placed connections never went amiss.

Mostly, it would come down to the indefatigable dedication and resources of a vast network of aid workers, acquaintances, and colleagues: the tirelessness of veritable strangers doing everything in their power to see you safely out of Nazi territory. For organizations tasked with assisting scholars with escape, women invariably took a back seat to men. If they were to make it out, they'd have to help each other.

SECTION 1:
WOMEN SCIENTISTS
ENCOUNTER NAZISM

1

Hedwig Scrambles for Sanctuary

Time was running out for Hedwig Kohn. "Deportation Poland a MATTER of weeks,"[3] the short, desperate telegram read. It was May 7, 1940, and if Hedwig didn't find a country to immigrate to by the middle of June, she was headed for a concentration camp.

"The gestapo presses her; if she has no country to go to, she will be transported, by force, probably to Poland, and that means practically death,"[4] her former colleague Rudolf Ladenburg pleaded to aid agencies on her behalf, from the safety and comfort of his desk at an Ivy League American university.

Concentration camps were proliferating at an alarming pace. By August, the Nazis would have built the Groß-Rosen camp just thirty-five miles southwest of Hedwig's hometown of Breslau, Germany (now part of Poland). The camp would eventually imprison 130,000 people, 40,000 of whom would be murdered.

Hedwig's typically optimistic outlook was being severely

tested. The petite fifty-three-year-old physicist with a youthful, cherubic face and twinkling eyes had been desperately searching for a way out of Germany ever since she lost her job nearly seven years ago. In that time, her situation, like that of many other Jewish Germans, had gone from financially desperate to potentially deadly.

Hedwig's problems started back when the Nazis passed the Law for the Restoration of the Professional Civil Service shortly after assuming control of Germany's government.

April 7, 1933: The Law for the Restoration of the Professional Civil Service enacted

The civil service law was a massive clearing out of the Nazis' racial and political enemies from public offices. All public sector employees were required to provide "certification" of their racial purity and political alignment with the Nazis.

If the government wasn't satisfied with the response, you would be fired. All universities were state-controlled, so nearly all Jewish professors and researchers found themselves newly unemployed—essentially unemployable—after the law was passed. Nazism wasn't just a way; it was the only way.

Hitler had decided that people of Nordic and Germanic heritage, especially those with blond hair and blue eyes, were the master race (provided they were able-bodied, mentally fit, and heterosexual). He named this race Aryan. Everyone else was "Untermensch" (subhuman), aliens on German soil, including Jewish individuals regardless of whether they had German heritage or not. You were considered Jewish, aka a member of one of the "racially impure" backgrounds, if you had at least one Jewish grandparent.

When firing civil servants, the Nazis didn't solely target those with Jewish heritage; being politically unreliable or even just being a woman could also cost you your position.

All four of Hedwig's grandparents were Jewish, and she proudly considered herself a German Jew. Therefore, her twenty-year tenure at the University of Breslau Physics Institute and status as only the third woman in Germany to qualify as a physics professor apparently meant nothing in the face of her Jewish heritage. The law saw Hedwig unceremoniously fired.

At the University of Breslau, Hedwig had taught classes in atomic physics, optics, and heat radiation, supervised grad students, and was a research assistant. She specialized in spectroscopic analysis; using spectroscopy, Hedwig could coax materials into giving up the secrets of their composition.

All atoms and molecules have unique emission and absorption spectra depending on the amount and configuration of their electrons. The amount of energy atoms absorb or release when their electrons move between energy levels is reflected in their spectra.

Mapping a material's spectra can help identify its composition at the atomic, molecular, and macro levels. Spectroscopic analysis is a widely applicable tool; it's used in cancer treatment, food science, water safety, medical diagnostics, forensics, and astronomy. Hedwig's work was particularly useful in commercial lighting.

Unfortunately, no amount of pleading allowed Hedwig to maintain her position. The director of the University of Breslau Physics Institute, Clemens Schaefer, was away when questionnaires about the racial background and political activity of the institute's assistants were sent out by the Nazis after passing the civil service law.

While Hedwig freely admitted to having Jewish relatives on the racial background portion, Schaefer's substitute, who was tasked with filling out the political section, only disclosed that he didn't know anything about Hedwig's political leanings.

When he returned, Schaefer intervened on Hedwig's behalf to better spell out his knowledge of her political inclinations.

He hoped that this would allow her to keep her job despite being Jewish.

His long-winded letter, sent June 22, 1933, defends Hedwig as a German patriot. He did his best to offer the Nazis morsels they might swallow.

"I can attest to the pain she felt inside during the Marxist revolution of 1918 and the deep outrage with which she viewed the events. I can therefore state with certainty that she was and is thoroughly anti-Marxist," Schaefer insisted, hoping to appeal directly to their fears that Hedwig was a political enemy, a communist sympathizer.

He asserted he'd known Hedwig for over twenty-three years now, and suggested that instead of being fired outright, he could simply allow her assistantship to elapse for a while. Schaefer also appealed on an educational basis, defending Hedwig's position because of her importance to her non-Jewish students.

"She has inspired the doctoral theses of five (Aryan) students, whom she is currently supervising. If Dr Kohn were now to be removed as lecturer and assistant on the basis of the Civil Service Law, the greatest damage would be incurred."[5]

Schaefer declared that it would essentially be impossible for these students' thesis research to continue without Hedwig's comprehensive and unique specialist knowledge.

This impassioned plea made no difference. It didn't matter that she was anti-communist or a brilliant scientist responsible for the education of several students (no matter how "Aryan") or anything else. All that mattered was that she was Jewish. At the time, Schaefer didn't realize the Nazis were actively seeking to remove the influence of Jewish scholars on Aryan students.

Hedwig was one of 1,200 Jewish people fired from faculty positions as a result of the civil service law across Germany. The Nazis knew educators were doing the important work of shaping the young, pliable minds of the nation's people, so they went about ensuring they had the "right" people using the "right" ideas to do this shaping. To further complicate matters, her teaching license was revoked—she wouldn't be allowed to teach anywhere else in Germany.

At the time, Germany had over 6,000 university faculty members in total; additional firings came in waves, so the Nazis eventually fired or forced out over 20 percent of the nation's faculty. Thousands more staff, scholars, and students were also ejected from higher education institutions. All told, across Germany and across all job sectors, the Nazis fired roughly 30,000 people.

While Jewish heritage was the main reason people were fired, it was not the only one. Those with Jewish spouses, gay people, members of certain religions, such as Catholics and Jehovah's Witnesses, and those seen as politically or ideologically opposed to the Nazis or who were allies of Jewish people were also removed from their positions.

Many women were also fired simply for being women. Next, the Gestapo began issuing special IDs to Jewish and Polish students to separate them out.

Hedwig's employer was among the three universities hardest hit by the civil service law. The University of Breslau's staff was nearly halved. It and the universities of Berlin and Frankfurt accounted for over 40 percent of Germany's expelled faculty members thanks to the large Jewish communities in these cities and their historic institutions' openness to hiring Jewish professors.

By the end of 1933, nearly half of all Germany's fired academics had fled the country. Out of a job and with nowhere else to turn, some dismissed civil servants died by suicide.

Upon her firing, Hedwig immediately got to work penning pleas for assistance to help her find a job outside of Germany. In addition to reaching out to the British Academic Assistance Council, Hedwig wrote to her former colleague Rudolf Ladenburg, who had recently joined the faculty at the prestigious Palmer Physics Laboratory of Princeton University in New Jersey.

Rudolf immigrated to America in 1931 and had since become the de facto go-to resource for scientists pushed out of work by Hitler's wrath. Rudolf compiled an assistance application for each scholar who contacted him and sent it to the newly formed US Emergency Committee in Aid of Displaced German Scholars.

The organization could help find money to fund positions at American institutions for academics on the run from Hitler. Competition for these awards was incredibly steep since thousands more displaced scholars applied than there was funding to assist.

In November 1934, Rudolf placed Hedwig's name second of twelve on his latest list of displaced German scientists he was recommending to the US Emergency Committee for assistance.

"She did some very good research work and had quite a few young physicists working under her direction. She gets no salary now. I can recommend her very heartily as a teacher as well as a research worker,"[6] Rudolf wrote about Hedwig.

Such a personal recommendation from a prominent figure in American physics education was an incredible blessing, something few refugee academics could boast. Enclosed with the list and letter were Hedwig's CV, a list of her research publications, and testimonials from no less than five professors who had worked with her.

Rudolf wished he could have secured Hedwig a position at Princeton with him, but the school employed only male professors for the all-male student body at the time. (Hannah Arendt, another Jewish scholar who fled Hitler's Germany, would become the first woman to lecture at Princeton in *1958*, and only then as a visiting professor.)

Rudolf then penned a letter to twenty-five of his fellow émigré scholars, many of whom had only recently escaped Nazi Germany and found positions at American universities. The letter, written in German, asked if they would consider donating a small portion of their salary (he suggested between two and four percent) for two years to help support the many scientists still awaiting rescue. Hedwig was among the twenty-eight scholars listed.

Rudolf was right to bank on the likelihood that people would be more comfortable donating if they knew their dollars were going directly to others in the same profession—even if they were on tight budgets because they'd just fled themselves.

The resulting pot of funds Rudolf collected became the German Scientists Relief Fund. It aided quite a few scientists by providing sums of around $300 to $800 to help cover travel costs to get out of Germany or to bolster incomes so that foreign universities didn't have to shoulder the burden of an entire salary themselves.

Larger aid organizations were inundated by thousands of applications, only a small fraction of which they could fund. But the German Scientists Relief Fund was a small outfit that could help a targeted group of scholars, a ragtag startup of scientists helping scientists. But would it be enough?

2

Hedwig Discovers Science

Hedwig was born on April 5, 1887, in Breslau, then one of the largest cities in the German Empire. Today, the town is called Wrocław and falls within the boundary of Poland. She was Helene and Georg Kohn's second child. Their oldest child, Kurt, had just celebrated his second birthday the month before Hedwig was born.

Georg made a good living as a wholesale cloth merchant, while Helene brought the perks of being a member of the wealthy Hancke clan of Breslau. The family were members of the town's vibrant Jewish community, nearly 20,000 strong in 1900.

Her parents immediately recognized that Hedwig was a bright girl and prioritized her education just as equally as they did their son's, and she was lucky to have such support. While basic elementary education covered ages six through fourteen or fifteen, they agreed that Hedwig would benefit from schooling beyond that.

Advanced schools, known as gymnasiums, were university preparatory schools that specialized in modern languages, classical literature and languages, or natural sciences. The curriculum at science schools improved rapidly during the late 1800s and early 1900s, with "Nature Observation" transforming into "Science of Nature," and classes in chemistry, mineralogy, and biology added. This suggests a shift toward the analytical.

At the time, girls were not welcome at traditional gymnasiums but had their own separate girls' institutions—höhere Mädchenschule—that focused on home economics and studies in history and culture meant to foster patriotism. During Hedwig's school years, girls' education in Germany underwent an incredible metamorphosis, thanks to pressure from politicians and women's rights activists.

First, girls were finally granted permission to take the university entrance exam, the Abitur. Next, Germany got a new head of its Ministry of Education. Since its previous leadership felt women should be "companions to their husbands and skillful German housewives" rather than "scholars,"[7] a changing of the guard could only be an improvement.

The ministry appointed an officer dedicated solely to girls' schools and implemented a new four-year preparatory course for the Abitur at Hedwig's local girls' school in Breslau. (Boys got nine years to cover the same ground.)

When the education minister went to check on this experiment in November 1900, he discovered students and teachers alike struggling to adapt to the intense pace of the course. In 1902, it was decided to spread the course over six years.

As Hedwig's school class shows, the rigorous nature of the studies whittled away at the number of girls pursuing the Abitur—with less early training in some subjects, many found themselves underprepared.

After three years, only half the girls Hedwig had begun the course with remained enrolled at the school. But Hedwig persisted. Unfortunately, the difficulty of the courses wasn't the only issue—finding good teachers was a problem as well.

The man brought to Hedwig's school to teach science was "very bad," Hedwig explained "it was very hard to get anyone to go to a girls' school for this purpose. As a result, the ten girls who took the matriculation examinations with me, all feeling deficient with respect to the science examination, marched themselves over to the well-known teacher from the Konig-Wilhelm Gymnasium and arranged to have special instruction from him."

This science teacher at the boys' school that the girls sought out for tutoring happened to be particularly brilliant. "I think many of the physicists who came from Breslau may have been deeply influenced and attracted to the science by him," Hedwig remembered. "I, too found him a considerable source of inspiration."[8] Several other alumni of the era went on to become famous physicists, including Max Born and Richard Courant.

Hedwig and some of the girls from her school took private lessons together to ensure they were ready for the Abitur. Hedwig easily passed the exam in the spring of 1906. But women still weren't officially allowed to enroll in universities in Germany's largest state, Prussia. They had to apply individually to the Ministry of Education to request a special permit to attend university. (As of 1900 and 1904, respectively, women could attend university in the smaller German states of Baden and Württemberg.)

After being exposed to such an amazing science teacher, Hedwig was inspired to study physics at her hometown University of Breslau. It was a brief tram ride away from her family's house, so she could continue to live at home if she attended.

Instead of going through the rigmarole of applying for a permit, she decided instead to only audit classes and not be considered an official student. Like a caterpillar building a chrysalis, Hedwig had to have faith that soon, things would be changing

for the better. Education for women was finally becoming a social and political priority.

Luckily, she only had to wait a year before women were allowed to enroll as official students at Prussian universities. She
was elated to be able to join the University of Breslau as an official student.

Surprisingly, Hedwig was not the first woman science student
to grace the halls of the University of Breslau. Clara Immerwahr
earned the distinction of the school's first woman PhD in 1900
after completing her chemistry degree magna cum laude. The
school made her study for two semesters longer than the male
students, but eventually conceded to granting her a degree. The
townswomen flocked to Clara's thesis defense to catch a glimpse
of "our first female doctor."

Perhaps young Hedwig was among them as a schoolgirl; she
surely would at least have heard about such an incredible achievement. Soon, Hedwig would be able to offer a similar example.

3

Women Make Inroads in Science

Throughout the late 1800s, German women had been forced to watch from the sidelines as foreign women were allowed entry into their universities first. In 1893, Americans Margaret Elizabeth Maltby and Mary Frances Winston, along with Brit Grace Emily Chisholm, enrolled at the University of Göttingen. All three were frustrated that they couldn't earn terminal degrees in their native countries. Margaret studied physics, while Mary and Grace tackled mathematics.

Margaret became the first woman to earn a physics PhD in Germany when she graduated in 1895; Mary was the first American woman to earn a PhD in math at any European university. Foreign women were then expected to return to their home countries; they would not be permitted to stay and upset Germany's traditional gender roles. German women who wanted to attend university mostly went to Switzerland.

In the US, physics—originally called natural philosophy—was

once considered a woman's subject, readily taught at finishing schools and women's seminaries. As with most other sciences, physics slowly transformed into a boy's club as the profession progressed and began requiring advanced degrees.

Women fought valiantly for the right to attend college in the US but often were forced to be satisfied with separate women-only institutions. The first American graduate schools had been modeled on those in Germany, which did not allow women students.

If women were to be able to earn an education, it would have to be separate, at least for a while. It was the only way women could ensure they wouldn't face sexism and harassment just for attending college classes. In the case of sciences, they remained largely confined to disciplines considered appropriately "feminine," such as botany, anthropology, zoology, or nursing.

Isabelle Stone became the first woman to receive a PhD in physics in America in 1897. But allowing women to matriculate at higher education institutions didn't mean they'd be welcome in the professions. When these educated women tried to get jobs or join science societies, men again saw it as women invading their turf.

Under the auspices of the professionalization of the sciences, men barred women from further encroachment by ensuring that for a long time, women could not join professional societies and could only hold positions as men's assistants.

When scientific organizations ostensibly acquiesced to accepting women members, they would often use tactics like encouraging smoking after meals at events to subtly tell women they were not welcome. Until the 1920s, it was considered inappropriate for women to smoke alongside men or be around smoking men. An invitation to an event that mentioned a "smoker" would follow a meal was a hint to women to stay away.

"The introduction of the German Smokers was long a bar to women being present at the banquets of the Physical Society, but finally a number of the younger women joined," remarked Sarah

Whiting, an early woman physicist in America, when looking back on her first years of attendance at these meetings in 1907. "I was not quite sure we were welcome, for men had not then as now gotten over the idea that blue smoke and the presence of ladies at banquets were incompatible."[9]

In 1906, the first edition of *American Men of Science* described the lives of 4,131 scientists, of whom 149 were women; the 1910 edition listed 204 women. Happily, by 1921, the number of women scientists worthy of note had more than doubled: 450 of their biographies were included.

Most of them worked in academia—the number of women scientists who'd achieved the rank of assistant professor more than tripled—yet most of the institutions employing them were women's colleges.

Women physicists, in particular, were relegated to the halls of separate lady-only higher education establishments. Of the twenty-four women physicists listed in the 1921 edition of *American Men of Science*, nineteen worked at women's colleges. Many men still had trouble seeing women as effective physicists.

"The women's experience thus reflects a basic inconsistency in these years: American society became far more willing to educate women in science than to employ them and were almost adamantly opposed to advancing or promoting any but the most extraordinary,"[10] notes Margaret W. Rossiter, a renowned historian of women in science.

In Germany, things started to change when women were finally granted the right to attend university across the country in 1908. Within six years, about 4,000 women were enrolled.[11] Unfortunately, the 1908 declaration did not grant women permission to take the exams required to work in certain fields. Progress always seemed to have limits.

The First World War also provided an important catalyst for women to obtain jobs in areas they would not normally be considered for. While men were away fighting, women entered scientific industries and other professions to help pick up the slack. Many women jumped at the chance to finally prove their scientific and technological aptitude.

Between 1913 and 1918, the number of women employed in the engineering field went up 544 percent in Germany.[12] At the Kaiser Wilhelm Institute's lab for physical chemistry (KWI-PC) in Berlin, for example, it wasn't just that women were needed to fill men's posts: the war had created new posts. As the need for gas masks grew, so did the KWI-PC.

In 1914, the KWI-PC staff had less than thirty people: five scientists, ten assistants, and thirteen volunteers and students. By 1917, it had massively ballooned to 1,500: 150 were scientists, and the rest support staff, most of whom were women employed as gas mask testing technicians.

Overall, between 1907 and 1925, the number of employed women in Germany increased by 35 percent (while the female population only increased by 15.5 percent).

To women's chagrin, this wartime work was largely considered a temporary necessity and failed to push the needle very far on the wider acceptance of women scientists. Their interest in pursuing science, engineering, or other analytical subjects was still considered unnatural. But women like Hedwig were helping to chip away at these disparities and stereotypes, showing the world that women could make incredible physicists.

4

Hedwig Embraces Physics

At the University of Breslau Physics Institute, Hedwig quickly developed an interest in spectroscopy. She spent much of her time peering through the observation tube of a spectroscope, her thick mop of dark, beautifully wavy hair pulled back and puffing out around her head like a halo.

Hedwig Kohn in a laboratory at the University of Breslau Physics Institute, 1912.

A spectroscope, also called a spectrograph, is a tabletop instrument that looks a bit like three small telescopes pointed at intervals around a prism at the center. In the same way a prism splits white light into a rainbow, the device breaks light from a single material down into the component wavelengths that make it up to reveal its chemical composition.

At the end of one tube, Hedwig would place a light source, typically a Bunsen burner. At the end of another, she would secure what she wanted to study. To examine the makeup of metals, for instance, she would sprinkle them into a flame. The light from behind both tubes would pass through an adjustable slit and a lens onto the prism, which then refracted its wave components.

Looking through the observation tube, Hedwig would see a sharp image of the spectrum as a strip of interrupted rainbow, ranging from violet on the left to red on the right. Since electromagnetic radiation occurs at specific wavelengths, each metal's emission and absorption spectra are punctuated by black lines. The positions of the lines would reveal the chemical composition of the material in question.

It was an exhilarating time to be discovering a passion for spectroscopy, but it wasn't exactly a new science. Spectroscopy first gained popularity well before Hedwig was born. In the 1820s, scientists began analyzing chemicals by introducing them to flames and then examining the resulting light dispersion—at least as far as instruments would allow.

"Whenever the prism shows a *homogeneous* ray of any color to exist in flame, this ray indicates the formation or presence of a *definite chemical compound*,"[13] inventor and photography pioneer William Henry Fox Talbot announced in 1826 (emphasis in original).

Talbot went on to identify the spectra of gold, silver, and copper, while others documented those of lead, tin, mercury, zinc, and cadmium.

However, attempts to analyze the spectra of every chemical

to create an exhaustive compendium quickly ran into problems. For one thing, the spectra of the material couldn't always be distinguished from that of the flame.

This major problem was fixed by Robert Bunsen's invention of the Bunsen burner in 1855. With its low-luminosity hot flame, scientists could now analyze spectra with minimal background interference.

In the intervening years between the invention of the Bunsen burner and Hedwig's first day at the University of Breslau at age 20, much progress had been made in the realm of flame analysis of chemicals: Bunsen and Gustav Kirchhoff discovered spectral lines were unique to each element. A pneumatic nebulizer was created to introduce liquid samples into flame.

The elements helium, cesium, rubidium, thallium, and indium were discovered in rapid succession via their spectral lines. Eventually, the first commercially available quartz prism spectrograph was developed. The splitting of spectral lines by a magnetic field was then uncovered. It was important progress, and there was the hope that a scientist like Hedwig could continue making fantastic findings by building on these extraordinary advances.

At the University of Breslau Physics Institute, Hedwig met experimental physicist Rudolf Ladenburg. Only five years older than Hedwig, Rudolf earned his PhD in 1906 (the year Hedwig passed her university entrance exam) and then became a professor a mere three years later.

He was descended from another eminent Jewish family in Breslau, a family of scientists. Rudolf and Hedwig's relationship would soon grow from professor–student to colleagues and vital friends.

Rudolf was excited to assist Hedwig with her dissertation experiments. Her focus was on trying to find out whether the excitation temperature was the same as the kinetic temperature after introducing metal vapor into the flame.

Rudolf and Hedwig spent a year puzzling over her investigations into the emission lines of the alkali metal vapors glowing in the Bunsen flame. Until now, Hedwig believed the answer to these questions had been assumed rather than proven.

To understand the true nature of the light emissions of gases in glowing flames, numerous investigations had been undertaken, but none to Hedwig's exacting standards.

"Kirchhoff himself assumed the requirements of his radiation law were fulfilled for these gases. However, he has not provided any rigorous evidence for this assumption...even the most recent works do not carry out the quantitative testing of Kirchhoff's law."[14]

Kirchhoff's law of thermal radiation defines the equivalence between the emission and absorption of an object under thermal equilibrium. Like water flowing through a pipe, everything that goes in must come out. To agree with Kirchhoff's law, gases would have to emit radiation only at the expense of heat and convert all absorbed radiation into heat.

Solving this puzzle required knowledge of the laws of black body radiation and their experimental realization. Knowledge that Hedwig possessed thanks to the work of her mentor, Otto Lummer, on black bodies.

A black body is a perfect absorber and emitter: an opaque body that absorbs all radiation and then reemits it after reaching thermal equilibrium. It was a concept—the closest thing in nature being a black hole—but could be created in a lab using a hollow sphere painted black inside, with a tiny observation hole.

For her experiment, Hedwig explained that "in the spectrometer, one observes the continuous spectrum of a light source whose rays pass through the glowing gas to be examined. Depending on the intensity of the light source, the spectral line emitted by the gas stands out bright or dark from the continuous spectrum."[15]

The culmination of Hedwig's research on this was her doctoral thesis, *On the Nature of the Emission of Metal Vapors that Glow in Flames.* It offered the first confirmation that Kirchhoff's law of radiation also applied to the emissions of hot gases in flames, that "radiation emitted by incandescent bodies, such as metallic vapors, could be treated as thermal radiation."[16]

This finding was useful for various industrial applications, so her thesis enjoyed frequent citation for several decades. It remained both noteworthy and relevant, two rare and sought-after qualities in a research paper.

After earning her doctorate in physics in 1913, Hedwig stayed on at the University of Breslau Physics Institute to become director Otto Lummer's auxiliary assistant. An assistantship was an incredible endorsement of Hedwig's skills. And it was truly exceptional to be offered such a position as a young woman. Happily, within six months she was promoted to a full-time assistant.

This spoke to Lummer's acceptance of women in science and to the University of Breslau Physics Institute's welcoming atmosphere for women in general. It was one thing to accept women as students, and quite another to ask them to stick around permanently, and even pay them for the privilege.

Hedwig helped Lummer complete research for an expanded edition of one of his previous books, *Foundations, Goals and Limits of Illumination Technology.* Even though most of the experiments were performed by Hedwig—including the measurements that formed the basis of Lummer's conclusions—she was not listed as an author or contributor. Her dissertation and papers coauthored with Lummer are cited, and she is thanked in the acknowledgments for helping prepare the material.

This is just one example of how the extent of women's contributions is erased from the historical record. Still, it wasn't unusual for the time, so Hedwig likely never expected coauthorship credit.

The Physics Institute was a close, congenial group. Every year, the entire institute took a field trip to the woods of Mount Ślęża in Zobten, an hour southwest of Breslau. There was hiking and a picnic and always a group photo to mark the occasion.

Photos from the 1919 excursion offer proof that women were welcomed at the institute: four women in long, pale dresses appear alongside the dozen suited men, surrounded by lush evergreens.

University of Breslau Physics Institute annual excursion to Zobten, 1919. Standing (left to right): unidentified, Martha Schubert, Clemens Schaefer, Arnold Eucken, Erich Waetzmann, Eberhard Buchwald, Gertrud Dlugosch, Hahn, Guenter Thilo, Rudolph Minkowski, Wilhelm Moser, and Martin Rusch. Sitting (left to right): Egon Lorenz, Hedwig Kohn, Elizabeth Benedict, and Rudolf Ladenburg.

But it wasn't all sunshine and team building, of course. Toward the end of 1916, Hedwig found herself overwhelmed. In addition to her own responsibilities, she was also doing the work of the five assistants who'd been called to service in the First World War.

"As a result of the lack of assistants for the regular affairs of the Institute, such as lectures, problem sessions etc., there was so much to do that we often even had to be called upon at night," Hedwig reported.

This meant by the time the war ended in 1918, she was experienced in supervising interns, overseeing student theses, and even lecturing on physics.

One student she guided, Margarete Guckel, was particularly

interested in Hedwig's research into improving the longevity of arc lamps. Their work together culminated in the pair being granted German patent No. 443407 for a "Gasgefüllte elektrische Bogenlampe"—an arc lamp filled with many inert gases. This was a crowning achievement for any research scientist and a particularly expertise-affirming accomplishment for two women scientists.

5

The Long Road to Hedwig's Habilitation

Despite this experience with mentoring advanced students and teaching classes, Hedwig didn't earn her habilitation until well into her career. Had she been a man, she would've likely gotten it much sooner. Habilitation, or *venia legendi*, is required to teach at the university level in Germany. It's essentially a second dissertation, a post-PhD certification that proves you have the depth of knowledge and expertise necessary to teach in your field.

Hedwig first attempted habilitation in 1919 at Lummer's urging. She knew her several years of supervising students should be more than enough experience to pursue the certification. And besides, fellow Jewish academic Emmy Noether had just made history by becoming the first woman in Germany to achieve habilitation (after years of haranguing and proving herself with unpaid work).

Hedwig marched into the dean's office, laying out her qualifications to pursue habilitation. In response, the dean pointedly read aloud the regulations regarding habilitation at the University of Breslau:

"Only a young man may apply." He looked up from the text and asked her: "Miss Doctor Kohn, does that apply to you?"[17]

Where Hedwig's colleagues embraced her and her fellow women scientists in the Physics Institute, the wider university remained stuck in the patriarchal past. Deflated, but undeterred, she returned to her assistantship at the lab.

Again, she had to be patient. And again, she was confident that sooner or later she would be allowed to earn her habilitation, just as she had eventually been permitted to become an official university student.

What men could freely pursue, women had to wait for men to permit them access to. The next time she approached the dean, she resolved to be armed with a research paper he couldn't dismiss so easily.

Determined, she began planning an ambitious experiment. She was interested in investigating whether Einstein's theories on the photoelectric effect in the solid phase were true for the gas phase, too. It was one of quantum theory's puzzles.

To truly test this, however, she would need a fancy new high-luminosity spectrograph with quartz lens components, which would have to be made to order. Such a specialized gadget was required to perform ultraviolet photoelectron spectroscopy. The spectrograph, which normally cost 4,000 marks (about $700 at the time), was now 6,000 marks in 1919 thanks to postwar inflation.

Like many researchers in Germany, Hedwig turned to the newly established Kaiser Wilhelm Institute for Physics (KWI-P) for funding. This meant she got to deal directly with Einstein himself since he was the institute's first director. For a time, the KWI-P only existed on paper; it was actually just the attic of Einstein's apartment.

The KWI-P was part of the Kaiser Wilhelm Society for the

Advancement of Science. At its height, the organization boasted thirty-two institutes. In addition to physics, as of 1919, there were establishments for chemistry, physical chemistry, biology, biochemistry, occupational physiology, the brain, experimental therapy, German history, coal, and iron.

Hedwig excitedly regaled Einstein with a summary of her proposed project and funding needs in September 1919. A few months later, she sent him a more detailed official funding application along with a supporting letter from her supervisor, Otto Lummer.

She told Einstein she wanted to see "if the photoelectric effect, i.e., ionization, occurs only under irradiation with the light of the ultraviolet limiting line $n\infty$ of the [spectral] series of the unexcited atoms. This should be the case from the perspective of Bohr's atomic model."[18]

Hoping to sway Einstein and the KWI-P's board of directors in their favor, Lummer explained that the apparatus would be of use beyond Hedwig's work. Lummer could use it to expand his study of the dispersion of light emitted by gases.

The many letters exchanged among Hedwig, Lummer, Einstein, and the KWI-P board of directors regarding her application reveal much fretting about the spectrograph's ever-increasing costs and growing frustration with the delay. And each hesitation only made things worse since the price just kept going up.

At the KWI-P Board of Directors' meeting on April 22, 1920, Hedwig was granted 7,000 marks. But by the time final purchase approval came through in 1922, hyperinflation was nearing its apex: the cost of the spectrometer had increased by 1,550 percent. It now cost 66,000 marks!

Add to this the fact that Hedwig had now been waiting for this key piece of equipment for several years; other scientists had been conducting investigations of their own on the topic in the meantime. Still, her shiny new spectrograph finally arrived in her lab, and she was able to begin using it in 1923, four years after her initial request.

Hedwig's opportunity to write a habilitation-worthy thesis finally arose when Lummer asked her to contribute to the book he was editing, *Müller-Pouillet's Textbook of Physics*. This second edition of the text would focus on radiant energy.

Hedwig would pen three chapters: one on photometry, the next on determining temperature with radiation measurements, and the third on lighting technology. This work could show-case the depth and breadth of her knowledge. Authoring or con-tributing to a book was an important step in every researcher's career.

Tragedy struck the Physics Institute—and the textbook proj-ect—in July 1925, however, when Lummer died unexpectedly at his desk, just a few months shy of retiring. The first half volume of the book was already at the press, but there was a scramble to find a new editor for the unfinished second half.

Collaborators came and went on the project, causing delays. This meant much revision was needed to keep each section up to date.

When *Müller-Pouillet's Textbook of Physics: Second Volume, First Half, Second Part* was finally published in 1929, the book had bal-looned to a 1,708-page behemoth. Still, it was worth the wait. The work became an indispensable text for German physicists for decades to come.

Hedwig's chapters totaled 270 pages (long enough to be a book in their own right) and would remain the definitive intro-ductory texts on these topics until well into the 1960s, as well as remaining alive in citations until the 1970s.

Now, this was a substantial habilitation thesis indeed! And the school couldn't forbid her application any longer: women throughout Germany had been granted the right to pursue habil-itation in 1920 less than a year after Hedwig first applied. Once again, her patience and faith in the rules of academia changing in favor of women had been quickly rewarded.

When Hedwig finally presented her first official lecture as a member of the University of Breslau faculty on May 5, 1930, she had just turned forty-three. While she may have been about a decade older than most of Germany's habilitation recipients at the time, the auditorium was no less festively decorated than usual.

Her lecture, "The Dualistic View of the Nature of Radiation and Matter," went smoothly. And with it, she joined a very small club: women in Germany qualified to teach physics at the university level. She had raised the club membership to three.

Even after her habilitation, though, Hedwig was still not considered a professor, just a *privatdozent*: an unsalaried lecturer. This was standard practice in Germany. A nonappointment-grade position akin to an adjunct, a privatdozent would offer private lectures that students paid for directly.

It was in this limbo that privatdozents would remain while waiting for a professorial appointment to materialize. Many women remained at this entry level for much of their careers, struggling with the associated income insecurity.

What led to Hedwig's decade-long delay in reapplying for habilitation is not certain; perhaps it was the wait to receive her new equipment, or maybe the lack of habilitation-thesis-worthy research she was able to conduct after receiving it. It very well may have been that she was merely busy with her work.

Overall, Hedwig's time at the University of Breslau Physics Institute consisted of heady days of fruitful scientific collaboration. Hedwig and Rudolf, along with colleagues Arnold Eucken and Fritz Reiche, formed a physics think tank of sorts at Breslau in the 1920s, getting together regularly to discuss their research problems. Of the four, all but Arnold were Jewish.

These were no dry scientific conversations. The room was positively electric; you could practically see the sparks flying as these brilliant minds bounced ideas off each other.

Sitting around a table together, Hedwig's squeaky voice brimmed with curiosity and enthusiasm as she talked about her latest discoveries. Her scientific excitement, wry smile, and sharp sense of humor were a wicked combination and proved positively contagious.

Together, these colleagues helped birth the burgeoning field of modern quantum physics. Hedwig saw Rudolf in particular as a true thought leader in the discipline, saying he possessed keen "quantum mechanical intuition."[19]

Niels Bohr's development of the first quantum model of an atom in 1913 cracked open a whole new dimension for their work to inhabit. The Breslau group tried again and again to uncover the key to quantum mechanics using the correspondence principle. The principle, recently formulated by Bohr, stated that quantum calculations should agree with classical calculations for measurements like large orbits and large energies.

The findings came fast and furious. Thanks to Hedwig's dissertation research confirming that radiation emitted by incandescent bodies was thermal in nature, Rudolf was able to develop the first quantum interpretation of optical dispersion in 1921. Optical dispersion is the spread of light into a rainbow of colors when passing through a prism.

Rudolf's was a radical reinterpretation of the existing model, so radical that theoretical physicist Werner Heisenberg—now widely known as the father of quantum mechanics—called it one of the most important steps toward quantum-theoretical mechanics at the time.

Rudolf's interpretation laid the foundations for Heisenberg to create the theory of matrix mechanics, which offered the first logical formulation of quantum mechanics.

As for Fritz Reiche, he published an entire textbook on quantum theory. These were massive moments in the history of physics, and Hedwig was right there, in the middle of it all, learning, contributing, furthering.

This was how it went for so many scientific findings—one discovery led another scientist to their own realization, which then led to an even bigger aha! moment for still another.

Unfortunately, such chains of findings rarely gave credit or due to the people or ideas further back in the thread. Not to mention that most early women in science spent much of their careers as assistants, with their bosses claiming any and all findings as their own. But credit for her contributions would soon become the least of Hedwig's concerns.

Hedwig's time as a Breslau faculty member was cut regrettably short by Hitler's rise. Yet in the three years she enjoyed as a lecturer, she oversaw two additional doctoral students and authored three papers.

One of these papers she considered her favorite work: a seven-page study about how taking inverse measurements on spectral lines could determine the total absorption and "the occupation numbers of excited atomic states," published in one of Germany's top physics journals, *Physikalische Zeitschrift*.

She was not the only one who enjoyed the article; it regularly popped up in the Citation Index until 1987. Hedwig didn't know it then, but her favorite paper would be her last German publication for a long time.

While Rudolf had gotten out of Germany in 1931, both Fritz and Hedwig were fired in 1933 and still languishing under Nazi occupation in 1940, desperate for an escape route.

Who knows what amazing advances Hedwig might have been able to uncover with her atomic spectroscopy research had she been able to stay in her cheery, collaborative lab at Breslau? The Nazis robbed Hedwig—and the world—from ever finding out.

6

Science Amid Panic for Lise

The founding member of the exclusive club Hedwig belonged to—the "women in Germany qualified to teach university-level physics" club—was Lise Meitner. Born in 1878 in Vienna, Austria, Lise was finishing up university just as Hedwig was entering it. She earned her doctorate at the University of Vienna in 1906. Since her only job prospects in Austria were as a high school teacher, Lise moved to Germany right after graduating and began working as a lab assistant at the University of Berlin.

A slip of a woman with a gentle voice and pensive brown eyes, Lise had developed an impeccable reputation as a scientist. She'd been heading the physics department at the Kaiser Wilhelm Institute for Chemistry (KWI-C) in Berlin for sixteen years when Hitler came to power in 1933.

She was surely headed toward the zenith of her career, having spent the past several decades producing a steady stream of significant studies regularly published in top journals.

Lise loved to bury herself in her work. Politics, gossip—these were messy businesses that muddied things and complicated the world. Physics, on the other hand, made things clearer. It could illuminate the very nature of how the universe worked.

Her mentor, Max Planck, called physics scientifically incontrovertible. For Lise, there was incredible solace to be found in the consistency and objectivity of the laws of nature. It provided a balm amidst the growing unrest across Germany.

In 1934, Lise became transfixed by Italian physicist Enrico Fermi's latest experiments. She went so far as to say she harbored a "consuming interest" in his findings. Why, he may have even extended the periodic table by two elements, she surmised. He'd begun bombarding elements with newly discovered "neutrons."

The norm was to shoot alpha particles at elements, but what new things could be discovered using neutrons?

Lise was so intrigued, in fact, that she simply had to do some tests of her own. But after performing a few neutron experiments by herself in her KWI-C lab, Lise could already tell that something incredibly exciting lay on the other side of her digging.

But she also recognized that two heads were better than one— especially if that other head was a chemist—so Lise excitedly recruited her friend and longtime coworker, Otto Hahn, into her investigations.

Eventually, he agreed, although it took some convincing. Otto was concerned that as the director of the KWI-C, he wouldn't be able to devote as much time to the project as it deserved. This was resolved by the pair later bringing another chemist into the fold, Otto's assistant, Fritz Strassmann.

While not quite outcasts, Lise, Otto, and Fritz had grown increasingly unpopular in their professional spheres during the early years of Hitler's rule. Lise was considered Jewish, Otto espoused anti-Nazi opinions, and Fritz refused to join any Nazi-affiliated professional organizations. Yet despite what was happening in their city, they had each other and their work.

Over the next four years, Lise and her team spent their days hard at work irradiating uranium and other elements with neutrons and then identifying the decay products. Lise would use physics to explain the nuclear processes, and Otto and Fritz would conduct chemical analyses.

If their findings proved to be significant, as they hoped, the notoriety might provide some political insulation. Lise understood that they were on the cusp of discovery. Something big. But she couldn't have comprehended just how big. Career-making. World-altering.

One of the first impactful discoveries Lise made during this time was that slower neutrons were more easily captured. Thus, she became one of the first scientists to posit that neutron energy affected the outcome of a reaction. Lise's research calculations showed that a fast-neutron reaction with the element thorium was possible—in theory—but just barely.

If the bombarding neutrons were too slow, gamma emission would occur before alpha emission could be achieved. The reaction of fast neutrons with thorium was far more complicated than expected, they announced. Their experiments uncovered three activities each for radium and actinium, all of which were beta emitters.

Decaying radioactive elements produce several types of emissions. Alpha particles are full of energy but are too heavy to get very far from the atom. Beta particles, on the other hand, are negatively charged and much zippier. But the ones that can really go the extra mile are the gamma rays; these can penetrate several inches of even the densest material.

Though uranium had proven a bear of an element to study, they now turned their attention back to it. They knew there had to be something there.

Science rarely happens in a straight line. For the trio at the KWI-C, this research was a matter of fits and starts, dead ends and U-turns. So far, all their findings had been "remarkable," according to Lise, but puzzling. They were impossible to make sense of within the rules of physics and chemistry as they knew them.

While the Berlin team was toiling, Irène Joliot-Curie (Marie Curie's daughter) and Paul Savitch were busy investigating the same things in Paris.

In their bombardment of uranium, Joliot-Curie and Savitch discovered strong activity at 3.5 hours: a substance that was entirely separate from actinium, which they believed had to be a transuranic element despite its chemical properties being entirely unlike all other known transuranic elements, "a hypothesis which raises great difficulties for interpretation,"[20] they admitted.

The Berlin scientists were skeptical. Otto called the Paris team's 3.5-hour product "curiosum."

Soon, Otto and Fritz discovered that neutron-bombarded uranium 235 samples contained an element that was not there before. The element was about half the atomic mass of uranium. Might it be barium? But how? Otto could find no chemical explanation for its presence. Would physics hold the answer?

What actually happened was that the Paris team had discovered a product that followed lanthanum, and the Berlin team one that followed barium, but neither team recognized the true nature of what they'd found yet.

According to chemist and science historian Mike Sutton, the best way to picture this experiment is to envision raisins being shot at a cake. Some raisins will hit the cake directly and be absorbed, leaving the cake a bit heavier overall. Other raisins will graze the cake, braking off tiny crumbs and thereby shaving a few ounces off its weight.

No one ever predicted that a single raisin could "cleave it into two different cakes each about half the size of the original," Sutton explains. "Yet something similar appeared to happen when Hahn and Strassmann fired neutrons at uranium."[21]

As Lise and her team's research progressed over the years from 1934 to 1938, the Nazis grew increasingly intolerant and violent.

Lise realized she could no longer bury herself in her work. The team's soon-to-be groundbreaking research—and Lise's life as she knew it—were suddenly and irrevocably interrupted by one big problem: both of Lise's parents were Jewish.

The civil service law had seen her fired from her professorship at the University of Berlin, but she had managed to hold on to her directorship because the KWI wasn't considered a public institution. Now even that position was in jeopardy.

It made no difference that Lise never really considered herself Jewish. Her parents had chosen to raise their children in the Protestant church—baptism and all. At age 28, she officially converted to the Lutheran church and withdrew from her hometown Jewish community in Vienna.

The Nazis considered your ancestry in their calculations of intolerance, not your religious practices. So, while making scientific history, Lise was also frantically searching for a way to make it out of Nazi Germany alive.

June 4, 1938: First official execution in a concentration camp
June 15, 1938: Mass arrest and deportation to concentration camps of approximately 1,500 men deemed "asocial"
August 8, 1938: Flossenbürg concentration camp opened

By day, Lise made sure to go to work as usual so as not to arouse any suspicion that she was looking for an escape. The mail was being censored by the Nazis, so she entrusted visiting foreign academics to relay messages for her.

Evenings and afternoon teas were spent strategizing with colleagues, scrambling to secure a position that would carry her out of Germany and away from danger.

How was she able to concentrate on her experiments with such a threat looming ever-present in her mind? Perhaps it gave her a distraction, a purpose; something to prevent her from collapsing into a puddle of anxiety and panic.

Lise saw physics as a search for the ultimate truth. It was a vision she would never lose sight of, even in the most trying of times. A vision she would never allow the Nazis to take away from her.

7

Lise Carves Out a Place in Berlin

Lise (whose given name was Elise) first arrived in Berlin from Vienna in 1907 as a painfully shy twenty-eight-year-old with a physics PhD and a mind hungry for more. Lise rented a series of spartan accommodations with shared bathrooms. These rooms sometimes included access to a piano, which she enjoyed playing in her downtime.

A slight woman who stood at only five feet tall, Lise soon developed a presence that belied her stature. As one of only a handful of women in the world with a PhD in physics, she couldn't afford to recede into the background and eventually cultivated a reputation for being bossy (a term likely only applied to her because she was a woman). Still, Lise maintained that she struggled with low self-confidence throughout her life.

It was the possibility of learning from theoretical physicist Max Planck that prompted Lise to ask her parents' permission to go to Germany for a few semesters. Lise needed their blessing since she still relied on their allowance.

Planck was notable indeed. He had unwittingly helped birth the subfield of quantum physics while attempting to solve the problem of black-body radiation that scientists had been noodling over since 1859. A break came in the 1890s when Hedwig's mentor, Otto Lummer, established that classical physics was painfully insufficient when it came to explaining the emission curves of a black body.

Planck picked up where Lummer left off. While trying to explain the emission spectrum of a black body, Planck realized energy can only be emitted or absorbed in integral multiples of discrete, or quantized, units, hence the name quantum theory.

This theory of thermal radiation became known as Planck's constant. Classical physics saw energy as an unfettered flow like a faucet; Planck discovered that it was actually more like ice cubes.

"It was, however, a very long time before quantum theory won general acceptance,"[22] Lise mused. Still, Planck's work had lasting consequences, including leading Einstein to postulate the existence of photons.

When Lise first arrived at Friedrich Wilhelm University (later renamed the University of Berlin, and hereafter referred to as such), she was taken aback by the regressive views toward women. Whereas Austrian universities began admitting women in 1901, women, as a rule, were not yet allowed into Prussian universities.

It was humiliating to have to ask Planck if she could audit his classes. Planck "received me very kindly," Lise recalled, though he was confused why someone with a PhD wanted to take more classes.

"But you are a doctor already! What more do you want?" Planck exclaimed on her first visit. She responded eagerly.

"I would like to gain some real understanding of physics," Lise replied, mustering all her courage to be assertive. This was her life's dream, and by golly, she wasn't going to let shyness stand in her way.[23]

From the rest of their conversation, Lise concluded that while

Planck was perfectly amiable, he didn't hold women students in general in very high regard, but was willing to make exceptions.

In 1897, a decade before Lise's arrival, Planck asserted he was not in favor of women studying science en masse, but he did at least recognize that occasional concessions could be permitted. He laid out quite a high bar for women to clear, with *exception* being the key word.

"If a woman possesses a special gift for the tasks of theoretical physics and also the drive to develop her talent, which does not happen often, but does happen on occasion, then I consider it unjust to categorically deny her the means to study," Planck proclaimed, qualifying his statement by saying that such cases must always be considered exceptions. "It would be a great mistake to induce women into academic study. It cannot be emphasized strongly enough that Nature itself has designated for woman her vocation as mother and housewife."[24]

While Planck's view on women in science may have evolved in the intervening years, even if it hadn't changed dramatically, luckily for Lise, she had apparently met the criteria of an exception in his eyes.

She found that the more she got to know Planck, the more she admired and respected him both as a scientist and as a person. Before long, Planck was inviting her to his home alongside the regular students.

In addition to attending his lectures, Lise was eager to engage in some experimenting herself, and others were interested in collaborating with her. One such researcher was Dr. Otto Hahn. Theirs would prove to be an auspicious relationship for both parties, as well as for the world.

Lise felt comfortable with Otto because he was the same age as her and had a more casual manner. "I had the feeling that I would have no hesitation in asking him all I needed to know. Moreover, he had a very good reputation in radioactivity, so I was convinced that he could teach me a great deal,"[25] Lise recalled.

But since she was a woman, it could not be as simple as two people deciding to work together. They needed approval from the institute for Lise to become a part of the lab. The final word on their collaboration lay in the hands of Emil Fischer, director of the University of Berlin's Chemistry Institute, where Otto worked at the time.

"I went to Fischer to hear his decision. He told me his reluctance to accept women students stemmed from his constant worry with a Russian student lest her rather exotic hairstyle result in its catching fire on the Bunsen burner," Lise explained.[26]

He finally acquiesced after making Lise promise not to go into the chemistry department where the male students worked.

Meaning she could work with Otto, but not in the room where he actually did his experiments. The institute had just moved into a state-of-the-art building, but Lise was confined to a small basement workshop Otto had transformed from a carpentry space into a room fitted for measuring radiation.

It was cramped, and Lise was always careful to keep her hair pulled neatly back at the nape of her neck.

And so, a few months after coming to Berlin, Lise became Otto's unofficial, basement-dwelling assistant. She had to use a separate entrance from the regular employees and students. Plus, there were no restrooms on the basement floor, so when she needed to use the toilet, Lise had to walk to a restaurant a few blocks down the street. For years, she remained in the workshop, unable to learn about any of the radiochemistry research that was occurring in the main lab.

Otto and Lise often worked late until the evenings. They took turns nipping out to the shops before closing time to buy a cold supper of salami or cheese. Once their day's work was done, they would go their separate ways, and walk (or bike) home alone.

Having a woman around the lab—a female scientist coworker, not a secretary or cleaner—was quite a novelty. What's more, they worked together, just the two of them, for long hours.

Though Otto and Lise truly were never more than friends, they felt they had to watch how they behaved together outside the lab so no one could accuse them of having anything but a professional relationship. It wasn't Lise's fault that she wasn't permitted to work in the general chemistry department out in the open.

"They always were in a hurry," their colleague James Franck laughed when recalling Lise and Otto's early efforts in their basement workshop. "Because they had to be, of course, [working] with radioactive decay. When they came to the laboratory they rushed down [Luisenstraße Street] and came out of breath."

Lise and James were both fresh from their PhDs when they met; he was an assistant to Heinrich Rubens in the physics section, and she was an assistant to Otto in the chemistry section (despite Lise being a physicist).

James didn't like his given name, so he typically went by his surname, Franck. He would become a close, lifelong friend to Lise, and she would later describe him as "one of the most noble and kind people I have met in my life."[27]

Franck and Otto were among the few young men at the institute who looked past Lise's gender to welcome her as a colleague—a true member of the fraternity—and respect her as the gifted scientist she was.

"Admittedly, the assistants in the Chemistry Institute had no particular love for women students,"[28] Lise remembered. They often made a point of greeting Otto, but not Lise. One time, when introduced to one of Otto's former professors, who had read some of her papers, he was astonished to discover "L. Meitner" was a woman. This wasn't the only time such an assumption was made.

Since Lise's work with Otto in the Chemistry Institute was unpaid, to make ends meet she regularly contributed to a natural science periodical under the byline "L. Meitner."

This work caught the eye of an encyclopedia editor, but upon discovering she was the author, he fumed he "would not think of printing an article written by a woman!"[29] Lise also translated science articles from English to German for $10 a pop.

She lived on a very tight budget but had definite priorities when it came to spending. She spent as little as possible on food to be able to afford concerts and cigarettes. Otto preferred cigars and beer as his poisons of choice.

Luckily, Lise didn't have to wait very long for women to be granted the right to enter any university and pursue any degree of their choosing in the German state of Prussia. The decree came through about a year after she came to Berlin.

This gave her the ammo she needed to convince Fischer to officially allow her free rein in the Chemistry Institute so Otto and Lise's collaboration could truly begin in earnest. Finally, she escaped her belittling banishment to the basement.

Lise Meitner and Otto Hahn in Emil Fischer's chemistry lab, 1912.

From there, Lise's persistence finally paid off when she was offered her first paying position in 1912: grading papers as Planck's assistant at the University of Berlin. This appointment made her the first official female scientific assistant in Prussia.

8

Lise Finds the Rhythm

In 1913, Lise and Otto were excited to move their research partnership into the sparkling new Kaiser Wilhelm Institute for Chemistry (KWI-C). The building was purpose-built for chemical experimentation in Berlin's Dahlem district, outfitted with state-of-the-art equipment. The KWI-C and its sister institute, the KWI for Physical Chemistry and Electrochemistry (KWI-PC), formed the core of the new Dahlem research campus. Lise soon moved into the on-campus apartments created for staff.

The timing couldn't have been better. A fresh start was needed if their measurements were to detect even the tiniest amounts of radioactivity. Their basement lab had developed a sort of background cloud of radioactive dust over the years, an accumulation of spilled liquids and leaked gasses. Lise and Otto vowed not to make the same mistake in their new labs.

To avoid replicating this problem, they outlined strict protocols for handling radioactive substances: chemical and physical measurements would be performed in separate rooms, those handling radioactive substances must refrain from shaking hands with anyone, and there must be a barrier between them and everything they touched.

To achieve this last one, rolls of toilet paper were hung next to all the labs' telephones and door handles.

Lise would eventually become known throughout the KWI as being particularly persnickety about keeping her physics sections clean. But it was worthwhile—thanks to her efforts, Lise's labs remained untainted enough to study very weak activity for decades.

At the KWI-C, Otto was promoted to junior assistant of the radiochemistry section, netting an annual salary of 5,000 marks (roughly $36,000 in today's money). Lise held the title of "guest" and was unpaid. Before long, she and Otto were both named associates (though her salary was less than his), and the Hahn-Meitner Laboratory was officially christened.

Otto received 66,000 marks (about $478,000 in today's money) for his discovery of mesothorium, a radioactive element that proved effective in treating cancer. Lise hadn't yet arrived in Berlin when Otto made the initial discovery years earlier, but she was key in its refinement, having since helped him purify several hundred milligrams of the substance for medical use. He gave Lise 10 percent of the royalties.

The following year, 40,000 more marks came in. Their work on mesothorium had proven not just fruitful, but lucrative. And it was for a noble cause. Playing a part in helping eradicate cancerous growths gave their science a deep sense of purpose; it made it all feel even more worthwhile.

"I love physics with all my heart. I can hardly imagine it not being a part of my life. It is a kind of personal love, as one has for a person to whom one is grateful for many things,"[30] Lise enthused.

The start of World War I, however, interrupted everyone's

work. Lise felt called to duty and went to serve in a medical capacity. She was placed at the front as a volunteer X-ray nurse technician from the summer of 1915 to the autumn of 1916 in her native Austria.

Because she was stationed at a military hospital near the Russian front, it was then that she encountered the horror and inhumanity of war up close. These battles would prove particularly gruesome. She soon found herself back in Berlin, forever changed by what she had seen.

In 1917, Lise was asked to create and lead a radiation physics department in the KWI for Chemistry. It came with a raise that saw her salary now roughly equal to Otto's. Up to this point, she had coauthored twenty-one papers with Otto and one paper with Franck, and had written ten papers herself. Lise was beyond ready to head up a division of her own.

The following year, Franck was named head of the physics division at the KWI for Physical Chemistry. The young friends were going places, moving up the ranks, and establishing themselves as scientific forces to be reckoned with. The staff of these sister institutes were close given the overlap in their subjects.

What's more, Lise finally saw the resolution to the research she and Otto had been working hard on for several years. They were on the hunt for the elusive radioactive element they believed was the precursor to actinium.

Lise had returned from her war service before Otto, so she had gotten back down to work without him. She regularly wrote long letters to Otto detailing her experimental setups and subsequent findings. He was occasionally allowed short periods of leave to assist this research.

Finally, in mid-January 1918, she'd done it. Lise wrote to Otto excitedly that while the activity was weak, it was decidedly measurable. "We can now think of publishing very soon,"[31] she chirped.

The paper was submitted in March, with Otto as the lead

author. Although he'd been away for the latest research, which had been extremely fruitful, he did play a key role in the experiments in the years leading up to that point.

"We have succeeded in discovering a new radioactive element, and demonstrating that it is the mother substance of actinium," they declared. "We propose, therefore, the name of protactinium."[32] It became element number 91.

One of the highlights of Berlin's physics community was the weekly Wednesday physics colloquium. All the latest findings were presented and discussed there. Originally, it was a group of about thirty people, but it soon grew into an exceptional intellectual hub that scientists of every discipline flocked to from all over the world.

"From the very first years of my stay in Berlin, I remember lectures on astronomy, physics, chemistry," Lise mused. "It was quite extraordinary what one could acquire there in the way of knowledge and learning."[33]

Max von Laue, professor of theoretical physics at the University of Berlin, organized the colloquium. He would choose three or four scientific papers and then ask for volunteers to speak on them.

Laue sat in the front row with Einstein, Planck, Haber (director of the KWI for Physical Chemistry), and other notable speakers and guests. In subsequent rows sat young Lise, Otto, and Franck alongside fellow future scientific heavyweights like Hans Geiger and Gustav Hertz.

Over the years, guests included Werner Heisenberg, Eugene Wigner, and Leo Szilard. Laue would become another close friend to Lise; their chats became a regular weekly appointment.

Lise vividly recalled Franck's colloquium lectures; in particular, ones on what were then called "metastable states" of atoms and the connection between ionized energy and quantum theory. Franck was particularly interested in investigating quantum theory; it seemed to hold potential as a new and exciting area to explore.

His colleagues didn't always understand the appeal, though. When Franck and Einstein discussed the topic, Einstein shook his head and said, "In the principle of relativity, everything is so clear. But in quantum theory it is horrible. What a mess it is in."

"You are certainly right," Franck responded. "But you see, as an experimentalist, I am of the opinion that it pays to fish in muddy water. And with the principle of relativity, for the time being we cannot make any experiments. The astronomers can, but we can't."[34]

After initial skepticism, Einstein began to find quantum ideas intriguing, and his research in the area meant he went on to become one of the fathers of quantum theory.

Despite the incredible brilliance of Franck, Lise, and Otto, some concepts could still go over their heads. For instance, they found themselves scratching their heads when Danish physicist Niels Bohr introduced his correspondence principle at the weekly physics colloquium.

"I must confess that when James Franck, Gustav Hertz, and I came out of the lecture, we were somewhat depressed because we had the feeling that we had understood very little,"[35] Lise admitted.

The trio decided to invite Bohr to lunch in Dahlem "bonzenfrei"—without bigwigs—in this case, the bigwigs being the professors. Fritz Haber, director of the KWI-PC, let them use his villa provided they allow him and Albert Einstein to join. Also in attendance was Hedwig's colleague, Rudolph Ladenburg.

"We spent several hours firing questions at Bohr, who was always full of generous good humor, and at lunch Haber tried to explain to Bohr the meaning of the word 'Bonze' (bigwig)," Lise recalled. In a photo of the event, Lise's short stature and pretty dress stand in stark relief amongst the towering sea of men in three-piece suits.

Berlin "bonzenfreie Kolloquium" organized by Lise Meitner, April 1920: Left to right: Otto Stern, Wilhelm Lenz, James Franck, Rudolph Ladenburg, Paul Knipping, Niels Bohr, Ernst Wagner, Otto von Baeyer, Otto Hahn, George de Hevesy, Lise Meitner, Wilhelm Westphal, Hans Geiger, Gustav Hertz, and Peter Pringsheim.

Slowly but surely, Lise was proving her genius and being accepted into the jovial, close-knit KWI family. Making the most of what they had in difficult postwar inflation years brought them all even closer.

For Lise's forty-second birthday in November 1920, Franck's new assistant, Hertha Sponer, used potatoes to craft a little "farmer's wife" for Lise and placed it at her door carrying a basket filled with delicacies. And Lise "put together something resembling a birthday meal."[36]

Hertha would always look back on this time fondly: "I count that year in Berlin among the most beautiful memories of my youth,"[37] she told Lise.

After a long day investigating the very nature of the universe in their labs, they often got together for evenings of music and merriment. "You see, we were really a kind of fraternity, everyone in the laboratory," Franck remembered. "We went in the evening to the theatre together."[38]

Every Wednesday after the colloquium, Lise went home with

Franck for lively evenings of music and conversation. "We had a nice group of people together. My wife was a pianist, so we had music at home," Franck said. Einstein also treated the group to his musical talents by playing for them. Lise excitedly introduced them to the Brahms *Lieder*. "And the whole time we were all together always, in one way or another. It was a group of friends."[39]

Planck instilled in his employees the ethos that creative pursuits were just as vital as scientific ones. Planck himself played piano at a nearly professional level.

Science alone cannot solve the mysteries of nature, he asserted, because "we ourselves are part of nature and therefore part of the mystery we are trying to solve. Music and art are, to an extent, also attempts to solve, or at least express that mystery."[40]

"Yesterday I was with Planck," Lise told Otto. "Two magnificent trios were played—Schubert and Beethoven. Einstein played violin."[41]

Lise made friends outside her physics bubble, too. After she struck up a conversation with botanist Elisabeth Schiemann on a local train, it didn't take long before Lise was treated like a member of the Schiemann family; just another one of the sisters.

On Sundays, Lise along with Elisabeth and her sisters set off exploring the countryside; in the summers, they went on longer hiking trips. They even climbed the highest peak in the Bavarian Alps together. Enjoying nature with friends filled Lise with joy. Elisabeth sometimes accompanied Lise to get-togethers at Planck's. Berlin was truly beginning to feel like home.

In 1921, Lise took an opportunity to expand her horizons when she accepted an invitation from Professor Manne Siegbahn to give a guest lecture series on radioactivity at Lund University in Sweden. Her area of specialty was one that the country had done little research into thus far. In addition to sharing her expertise, she looked forward to learning more about the university's work with X-ray spectroscopy.

Besides Siegbahn, Lise made another important friend in Sweden: Dutch doctoral candidate Dirk Coster. Both Siegbahn and Coster would become key allies for Lise outside of Germany in the troubled years to come.

The following year, she achieved her habilitation to become the first female physics lecturer in Germany. It was a truly incredible feat, since before 1925, only twenty-five women had earned habilitation at German universities.

In response to this crowning achievement, Einstein called her "our Madame Curie," claiming her brilliance for Germany.

Her most impressive accomplishment to date came in 1926 when Lise became the first female full professor ("professor extraordinarius") of physics in Germany. In addition to a boost in respect and professional eminence, such a title came with tenure, something any academic would dream of.

Lise had finally come into her own. The once bashful girl had become an assertive professor and accomplished research scientist with discoveries that captured widespread attention.

A portrait taken by her sister-in-law in 1928 shows Lise leaning on her elbow, casually holding a lit cigarette that is nearly burnt down to her fingers, a slender wisp of smoke escaping from its end. She exudes an alluring sense of self-possession and self-assuredness.

© PHOTOGRAPH BY LOTTE MEITNER-GRAF (COURTESY THE LOTTE MEITNER-GRAF ARCHIVE).

Lise Meitner portrait taken by her sister-in-law, Lotte Meitner-Graf.

The years before Hitler's rule were incredibly stimulating at the KWI-C. Collaboration was at its peak.

"There was really a strong feeling of solidarity between us, built on mutual trust, which made it possible for the work to continue quite undisturbed," Lise mused.

Even though they did not all share the same political views, they were at least united in their desire not to let politics erode their solidarity. "This was a special feature of our circle, something quite exceptional in the political conditions of that day."[42]

With all the rapid advances, fruitful collaborations, and stimulating company, it was an exciting time for Lise. Soon though, everything changed. The music stopped.

9

Hertha and Hildegard

After going as far as she could as a woman studying physics and mathematics in Berlin, young Hildegard Stücklen traveled 160 miles from home to complete her studies at the University of Göttingen in 1912. The daughter of a factory owner, Hildegard's family wasn't Jewish as far as can be surmised; the stylized cursive German script on her birth certificate appears to say her family was evangelical, meaning protestant (most likely Lutheran). She signed letters to friends as "Hilde."

In 1918, another young woman joined Hildegard in Göttingen's physics department after transferring from the University of Tübingen: Hertha Sponer. Tübingen didn't offer physics lectures, so her study thus far had mostly consisted of math and chemistry. Hertha was not Jewish either, but both women were certainly anti-Nazi.

At the University of Göttingen, Hertha was working on *theoretical* physics with Peter Debye, and Hildegard on *experimen-*

tal physics with Heinrich Rausch von Traubenberg and Eduard Riecke.

Theoretical physicists try to explain the interactions of matter and energy by creating mathematical models, while experimental physicists test and study these interactions by performing experiments.

These two women both came to Göttingen in time to see Emmy Noether become the first woman in Germany to achieve habilitation and begin teaching math at the university. As fellow women pursuing what were considered men-only subjects, it must've been incredibly empowering to witness.

Hertha and Hildegard both had cheerful personalities and positively electric smiles. Shy but charming, Hertha had chestnut hair that rippled in waves when she pulled it back, her eyes like deep blue pools. She could easily be considered beautiful. Hildegard was taller with more elongated features, but still cut a striking figure.

COMPETENCE CENTER TECHNOLOGY-DIVERSITY-EQUAL OPPORTUNITIES E. V., BIELEFELD.

Hertha Sponer as a student at the University of Tübingen, around 1917.

The University of Göttingen had a female student population of less than 10 percent, fewer than most other German universities at the time. Hertha and Hildegard must have been a sight to behold in their labs and university halls—far from the "beasts of knowledge who wear flat shoes,"[43] as was claimed by detractors of women in academia.

In April 1919, just shy of her twenty-eighth birthday, Hildegard earned her doctorate. Her thesis pondered the enigmatic topic of "the question of the apparent shape of the heavens."

Using strikingly clear language, she begins by laying out what she means to investigate: "We see the sky, whether cloudy or clear, not as a hemisphere that arches over the observer at the center, but as a flat dome. The phenomenon has been known since antiquity; we find historical overviews of the problem as well as numerous attempts at an explanation."

But the problem proved less a matter of hard science than of perception. She concludes that her paper sought "to prove that the apparent shape of the celestial vault is a thoroughly psychological problem and cannot be traced back to physical conditions."[44]

Robert Pohl had taken over as Hildegard's thesis advisor after her previous supervisor, Eduard Riecke, passed away in 1915. In her paper, she thanks Pohl for inspiring her to do this work.

Pohl was a new professor at the University of Göttingen, as he had been forced to wait for the First World War to end before relocating from Berlin.

It's strange that Hildegard found such inspiration from him since Pohl was notorious for his misogynist belief that women did not belong in science. He and Franck had been among Heinrich Rubens' assistants at the University of Berlin back when Lise was Otto's assistant. Perhaps Pohl was even one of the assistants Lise described antagonizing or ignoring her simply for being a woman.

Unlike Hildegard, Hertha went out of her way to avoid Pohl and his sexism. After her supervisor told her he was planning on leaving the university, she became determined to finish her thesis exam before he left since in his absence, Pohl would've taken over. That meant Hertha had to hurry.

In March 1920, after only four semesters of study, Hertha took the oral examinations for her PhD. She passed easily. Ordinarily, it should have taken much longer. But her first position out of university under James Franck would be the most important of her career, forever shaping the course of her life.

Shortly after earning their PhDs, Hertha, Hildegard, Hedwig, and Lise all became members of the German Physical Society, the nation's top association for physicists. Lise was a member from 1907 to 1937, Hedwig from 1917 to 1937, Hertha from 1921 to 1945, and Hildegard from 1922 to 1932.

They all would've regularly attended annual meetings and other events organized by the society. Since physics was still male-dominated, women at these conferences would've naturally been drawn to one another for solace and support.

Hertha knew both Hildegard and Lise, but whether Hedwig bumped into any of them at these meetings isn't recorded. Even if they had yet to cross paths, before long, these women's lives would become perilously intertwined.

10

Hertha and Franck

Tall and trim, Franck had dark hair that was already receding as a young man, but he maintained a thick, brush-like mustache. With warm eyes and an even warmer nature, Franck was a rarity among men of science: entirely unpretentious, a master at putting people at ease and cultivating a sense of camaraderie.

TRANSOCEAN BERLIN, COURTESY OF AIP EMILIO SEGRÉ VISUAL ARCHIVES, BORN COLLECTION, W. F. MEGGERS GALLERY OF NOBEL LAUREATES COLLECTION.

James Franck, 1925.

Franck had earned his doctorate at the University of Berlin in 1906. He married Swedish pianist Ingrid Josephson the following December, and they had two daughters: Dagmar, aka "Daggie," in 1909, and Elisabeth in 1911.

While serving in the army during World War I, he was seriously injured in a gas attack and bestowed the Iron Cross First Class medal, awarded for courage in combat and going above and beyond the call of duty.

Franck was a lecturer at his alma mater until 1918, when a full professorship opened up there. The same year, he was named head of the physics division at the KWI for Physical Chemistry (KWI-PC).

Franck ensured his lab was outfitted with the latest state-of-the-art equipment—stocked and refurbished using his own money. Given his generous nature, it is fair to assume these resources were shared widely in the institute.

It was well-known that Franck was more open to women scientists than many of his predecessors—early exposure to brilliant female physicists like Lise surely helped solidify this attitude—so it was no surprise when he hired Hertha Sponer as his unpaid, unofficial assistant at the KWI-PC in April 1920.

Fresh from earning her PhD at the University of Göttingen, Hertha brought a youthful energy to the lab. At only twenty-four years old, she was thirteen years Franck's junior.

Hertha helped Franck research the inelastic collision of electrons with mercury atoms. Franck's work showed that under electron bombardment, some atomic complexes were capable of capturing electrons that then became negative. "Such ions, that disintegrate with electron emission and not with light radiation, have met with great interest under the term 'resonances.'"[45]

Hertha teased Franck about the intense expectations he had of his physics assistants. "You insisted that almost all your assistants have some chemistry, didn't you?"

"Yes, that is quite true," he replied. "I did, because I know it was important. One should know a little bit of chemistry."[46] He felt it was especially important at the time since gas discharge and spectroscopy were among the few means of learning about atoms and molecules.

Franck had been particularly transfixed by chemistry as a boy, often doing experiments at home on his own. Hertha, too, was uniquely interested and adept at both chemistry and physics, so they made a great research pairing. She would soon be among the earliest researchers in the field of spectroscopy to understand how her work could illuminate issues in chemistry, making her a trailblazer in interdisciplinary investigations using spectroscopy.

AIP EMILIO SEGRÈ VISUAL ARCHIVES, LISA LISCO, GIFT OF JOST LEMMERICH.

Hertha Sponer in the laboratory, around 1920.

Hertha and Franck didn't stay in Berlin for long, however. In 1921, Franck wholeheartedly accepted an offer from his long-time friend Max Born to join him at the University of Göttingen, where Born had created a chair of experimental physics position just for him.

Born was building one of the foremost centers for physics in the world. The role would give Franck far more responsibilities than he currently had, a welcome challenge.

While Franck's desire for more academic freedom might have been what compelled him to take the position, Franck was also Jewish, and it's likely that the increasingly loud anti-Jewish sentiment in Berlin was also a motivating factor.

Jewish scientists and other scholars were quickly becoming favorite targets of bloviating anti-Semites. Some of the arguments espoused then against Jews, especially Jewish thinkers, sound just as ludicrous as today's anti-intellectualism.

A few months after Hertha came to the KWI to work with Franck, one of the intuition's most well-known Jewish scientists, Einstein, was specifically targeted.

First came a barrage of newspaper articles accusing Einstein of plagiarism and deriding his publications and ideas as anti-German machinations. This attack on his character and intellect culminated in a massive rally against the theory of relativity at the Berlin Philharmonic on August 24, 1920.

At the rally, Max von Laue "was stunned at the way that the discussion of the most difficult scientific issues was treated with a level of complexity befitting a beer hall."[47] Einstein himself was present for the speeches given at the ridiculous rally. It was upsetting, but he understood their motives were purely racial.

"These tirades were the first excesses of the ever-stronger anti-Semitism that was also being directed against physics and especially its theoreticians," Hertha's biographer, Marie-Ann Maushart, explains.[48]

Einstein should've had the last laugh when he was awarded the Nobel Prize in physics shortly after this episode, but that only further inflamed things. Next, Einstein's friend, Jewish statesman and physics PhD Walther Rathenau, was assassinated in Berlin by far-right nationalists. A wave of death threats deluged Einstein, forcing him to flee Germany temporarily.

For Franck and his wife and children, leaving Berlin for Göttingen would allow them to also escape this increasingly hostile atmosphere, at least for a while.

Göttingen was a quiet university town of 40,000 residents, nestled in the countryside. Surrounded by woodlands, it enjoyed greater access to produce and other fresh foods than Berlin did at the time, so Franck and his family could enjoy a quieter, more comfortable life with ready access to nature.

Hertha went with Franck, of course: she was his ever-devoted *assistentin*, no matter the location. Besides, the University of Göttingen was her alma mater. Hertha would always remember her time at the KWI fondly, though, and the friendship she had struck up with Lise while she was there. Theirs was a relationship that would grow to transcend careers, continents, and decades.

In a photo to mark the occasion of the farewell party for Franck at the KWI, seven of his male colleagues perch around the sofa where Franck sits between Lise and his wife, Ingrid. Ingrid is looking over at Hertha in the chair next to her, while Franck, seemingly midsentence, glances over at both of them. Between Hertha and Ingrid, Einstein has cheekily inserted himself.

Lise and Gustav Hertz gifted Franck a comedic poem poking fun at his leaving the KWI and some cartoon renderings of the group.

Kaiser Wilhelm Institute going-away party for James Franck, 1920. Standing (left to right): Walter Grotrian, Wilhelm Westphal, Otto von Baeyer, Peter Pringsheim, and Gustav Hertz. Sitting (left to right): Hertha Sponer, Albert Einstein, Ingrid Franck, James Franck, Lise Meitner, Fritz Haber, and Otto Hahn.

Though Hertha was initially only considered a temporary hire, within a few months, Franck secured a budgeted position for her that would be renewed every two years. This ensured she enjoyed financial security and independence, but only because a man believed in her enough to vouch for her and push for it.

In his University of Göttingen experimental physics lab, Franck worked hard to create a casual, familial atmosphere entirely unlike the formal, stiffly hierarchical environment typically encountered in German labs and classrooms.

He invited colleagues for "walk-and-talks" to discuss research while strolling the beautiful grounds and organized group hikes, ski trips, and other team-building excursions. His magnanimity bred not only familiarity but devotion from his colleagues.

Hertha Sponer, James Franck, and colleagues at University of Göttingen, around 1923.

In most of her experiments at the lab, Hertha used a calcium fluoride vacuum spectrograph. A hydrogen lamp would provide the light source, which was focused through an absorption cell with calcium fluoride windows.

Hertha would first evacuate the cell, then fill it with whichever gas she was studying. Each gas was measured at a variety of both high and low temperatures. The unabsorbed light would appear through a slit at the front of the spectrograph. The dispersed light spectrum was then recorded on film.

Over the years, Hertha grew close with Franck and his family. At lunchtime, the pair bicycled to his home to eat with his wife and kids or brought sandwiches to nibble while lounging by the pool.

Hertha practically became a fully-fledged member of the Franck family. She often took his daughters, Daggie and Elisabeth, bicycling and even taught them how to ski, sometimes acting as a babysitter to the children.

Her letters to Franck reflected their growing intimacy. Soon, she switched from "Dear Professor" to "Dear Franck," the informal *Du* pronoun replacing the formal *Sie*. Such a change is much more significant than most English speakers realize.

Hertha decided to pursue habilitation so she could also teach at the university. Her thesis dove headfirst into the study of molecular spectra within the burgeoning field of quantum physics, *Excitation Potentials from the Band-Spectra of Nitrogen*, while the qualifying lecture she presented focused on *Problems and Methods of Vacuum Spectroscopy*.

Of the three physicists who had to approve Hertha's habilitation, one was an old nemesis of sorts, a man staunchly opposed to women in science who did not think women belonged in the role of professor: Robert Pohl.

He required some persuading by Franck; Pohl would only approve Hertha's habilitation and subsequent lecturer application on the condition that her employment at the university would be tied to Franck's. Meaning that if Franck ever left the University of Göttingen, Hertha must leave as well. No Franck, no job.

According to Pohl, a woman's talent and expertise could not possibly stand on their own merits. How he had overseen Hildegard Stücklen's doctorate six years prior while so vehemently against women scientists is a mystery. However, it does seem that Pohl was particularly against women becoming professors.

Still, in October 1925, Hertha was awarded habilitation. She was the second woman in Germany to achieve habilitation in the field of physics, after Lise. At the age of 30, she was the youngest woman to earn a physics habilitation in Germany before WWII.

It was a banner year for Franck, as well: he won the Nobel Prize for Physics with Gustav Hertz "for their discovery of the laws governing the impact of an electron upon an atom."

Before she began her lecturing job, Hertha was off to America on a prestigious grant. She had earned a Rockefeller grant to study molecular physics at the University of California, Berkeley, for a year.

The Rockefeller Foundation had been funding international scholar travel programs for years in an effort to advance science by promoting the free flow of knowledge among nations. A mere seven days after receiving her habilitation, Hertha hopped aboard a ship headed for New York.

Some time out of Franck's shadow would be good for Hertha. It was time for her to start growing as an independent scientist, to go beyond being simply an assistant. Yet in the four years she had worked at the University of Göttingen, she'd become nearly as beloved as Franck himself, and her send-off created quite a scene.

"The bevy of students, friends, and devotees who insisted on providing her an honorary escort to the train station was so large that Göttingen's normal public transportation would not have been sufficient," the local paper reported.

By happy coincidence, a local company let them borrow a large new automobile for the occasion. "Decorated with flags from both the German Empire and the United States, the impressive omnibus drove with over 50 passengers. After a few brief but pithy farewell addresses, the train began to pull out into the dark autumn night amid the sounds of lively folk tunes."

In an incredible display of feminism, the paper also noted: "The voice of each opponent of women in higher education, and particularly those opposed to allowing women to teach at university, must have fallen silent when confronted with this public show of honor that was spontaneously offered."[49]

The article text had apparently been drafted by the organizers of Hertha's send-off and sent to the paper, where it was printed in its entirety.

While she was gone, Hertha would miss several exciting breakthroughs in quantum mechanics back in Europe, but Berkeley was the place to be for a scientist interested in spectroscopy. Hertha learned so much by using the brand-new ten-foot vacuum ultraviolet spectrograph John Joseph Hopfield had just built there. While any access was useful, you could learn the most about how scientific instruments worked by calibrating them when brand-new.

Hopfield described how they used the spectrograph to study nitrogen: the discharge tube was X-shaped, about a meter long and a centimeter in diameter with the horizontal part facing the slit end. A water-resistant transformer excited the discharge.

Nitrogen was passed over red-hot copper filings to remove oxygen, then over phosphorus pentoxide to remove the moisture. Next, the nitrogen was sent through a valve into the discharge tube and pumped out through the receiver.[50]

Since lenses could interrupt the light beam and absorb UV radiation, Hopfield left tiny holes in the end plates to allow a narrow beam to pass through. Hertha sent off a report to *Nature* describing her findings:

"We filled the whole spectrograph with carefully prepared nitrogen and used Lyman's capillary method for the continuous light source. The plates show a band system with frequency differences which have the same values as those of the final state of the first positive group, proving definitely that the first positive group is going out from the first excited state of the molecule."[51]

Having a single-author paper in such a prestigious journal was a big feather in Hertha's cap.

Her other main research partner while in California was Raymond T. Birge. The Birge–Sponer method they developed together—to calculate the dissociation energy of diatomic molecules—interpreted spectroscopic data using a clever mix of physical chemistry and molecular quantum physics. It was a significant publication: the only method to calculate this quantity for many years to come, and one of the most notable findings of Hertha's career.

"She was a pioneer in applying spectroscopy observations to problems in chemistry," one of Hertha's future colleagues explained. "At the time the field of Quantum Chemistry was becoming very important and developing rapidly. She acted as a liaison between these disciplines."[52]

Hertha Sponer in America, April 1926.

Hertha's trip to America helped her discover new ideas, new ways of thinking, and new collaborators. It encouraged her to be more independent of Franck, both personally and professionally. It was also quite culturally illuminating, helping introduce her to American customs and academia. She returned to Germany with a firm grasp of English and a burgeoning professional reputation.

To add to her achievements, Franck had arranged for Hertha to pen a volume on vacuum ultraviolet spectroscopy for the *Structure of Matter* textbook series he was editing for publisher Ferdinand Springer. She signed a contract, agreed to a deadline of May 1927, and received an advance of $40. It was incredibly exciting, an honor even, to be tasked with writing an entire volume on her own.

11

Women in the Interwar Era

Hertha, Hildegard, Hedwig, and Lise all benefited from the improvement in women's rights brought about by Germany's Weimar Republic government. The Weimar Constitution of August 1, 1919, declared, "Men and women have the same fundamental rights and responsibilities." Women earned citizenship rights, the right to vote, to hold elected office, and to freely pursue higher education, certifications, and careers. What's more, women faculty members now enjoyed legal rights as civil servants.

"There was a growing desire for new things and a belief that they were possible,"[53] Lise mused about women's growing participation in the workplace.

Psychologist Alice Rühle-Gerstel was one of these progressive "new women" of the 1920s. She was a German Jewish feminist who closely charted the course of women's changing role in German society as it was happening, writing about the ups and downs she had observed in the decade leading up to the Nazi era. She superbly described it this way:

Women began to cut an entirely new figure. A new economic figure who went out into public life as an independent worker. A new political figure who appeared in parliaments, demonstrations, and gatherings. A new physical figure who cut her hair and shortened her skirts. A new intellectual-psychological figure who fought her way out of the fog of sentimental ideologies and strove toward a clear, objective knowledge of the world and the self.[54]

Even under the rule of such progressive politicians in Weimar-era Germany, it was not all smooth sailing for these independent "new women." For one thing, the government granting women rights does not mean that sexism at large suddenly disappears.

As our women scientists have shown, many positions offered to women were still volunteer or low-pay roles, especially at first. In some cases, women were given preference for jobs solely because employers could pay them less.

The end of World War I saw men return to reclaim their jobs, and the jobs the war had created for women became redundant. In addition, the Weimar government ordered employers to lay off women in a triage-like manner, based on urgency and need, to facilitate the integration of soldiers back into the economy.

At the KWI, not every woman's wartime position was temporary, however. Dr. Marie Wreschner remained at the KWI, even earning her own office and phone line.

"Wreschner would spend 1920 to 1933 as a scientific affiliate of the Institute, joined at times by Vira Birstein, Erika Cremer, Thea Knipping, Deodata Krüger, Hilde Levi, Emilie Schalek, Hertha Sponer, and Margarete Willstätter," noted the one-hundred-year commemorative history of the institute.

But while they were permitted—or perhaps tolerated—these women had yet to gain a true foothold at the institute: "aside from von Wrangell, none of the women at the Institute would hold an official position underwritten by the Kaiser Wilhelm Society."[55]

In the UK, things were also progressing slowly, notes science historian Sally Horrocks: "Female scientists who started their careers in the years after the First World War were a small minority in a relatively new profession that was concentrated in Europe and North America."[56]

A perfect example is biochemist Kathleen Culhane Lathbury. Though she was employed by one of the UK's top pharmaceutical companies during the interwar years, Lathbury was given rote tasks far below her skill set. Once, when the results of her experiments disagreed with those of her male coworkers, she was written off as incorrect. Of course it turned out that it was the men who were wrong. What's more, she wasn't allowed to enter the staff cafeteria.

"For women in the chemical industry, magnificent health and a thick skin are more important than a knowledge of chemistry," Lathbury observed. She was livid to discover that the male graduate "is usually given quite a dignified position from the beginning," while, the women who had worked alongside him at university had no such luck. She was "hard up and constantly humiliated."

Lathbury laments that even if women were able to find intellectually satisfying work, "she will be expected to attain results from the ground floor for which her male equivalent is given the help of a little altitude."[57]

As progressive as the Weimar government sounded, "compared to the USA, Germany must still be regarded as extraordinarily backward in terms of women's access to studies, doctorates and lectureships during the Weimar period, and the gap was not made up in terms of the proportion of doctorates,"[58] noted Ulla Knapp, a German economics professor who specialized in women's historical role in the labor market.

America enjoyed more opportunities for scientific women. Astrophysicist Cecilia Payne-Gaposchkin moved to the US after she realized her only job prospect in the United Kingdom was as a secondary school teacher. In 1925, she became the first person to earn an astronomy PhD from Harvard University's women's school, Radcliffe College.

It's important to remember employment data is only one aspect of this story. To see rising numbers of women working in previously male-dominated industries and assume it means women received equal opportunities to men in professions and that they were treated equally is a mistake.

While the inter-war period saw an increase in the number of women employed in science across Europe, their exclusion from certain disciplines or professional groups and segregation from male scholars persisted.

What's more, women scientists' career trajectories were vastly different from their male counterparts. Disparities in pay, promotions, tenure, job security, and institutional support remained.

This observation also applies to America, according to historian Margaret W. Rossiter: "Outstanding women frequently held lowly titles and were recognized only belatedly, as in their obituaries, decades after their achievements."[59]

Back in Germany, these "new women" quickly ran up against countless barriers before they could become the norm. Many Germans had trouble letting go of their ideals about women's role in society.

With progress comes inevitable backlash, often in the form of regressive backsliding. Change can be scary. Accepting that women were equal to men would mean changing a lot of things about the way the world currently worked. Society was not quite ready to make these changes.

The latter half of the 1920s saw a revival of obsolete ideals of femininity. Maternity continued to be elevated. The slogans "Kinder, Küche, Kirche" (children, kitchen, church) and "Die Frau gehört ins Haus" (women belong in the home) persisted, clearly spelling out to women they had no business in public life.

"The 'new woman' was also the target for nationalists who

believed that her selfish reluctance to have children endangered the future of the German race," writes historian Helen Boak.[60]

The loss of millions of young men in the war meant there was a "surplus" of young single women. For many of them, seeking a job was out of necessity, not an attempt to assert their female equality. Still, they were viewed as threatening the status quo of the male-breadwinner nuclear family (despite the fact that there were few eligible bachelors).

Conservative thinkers of the era encouraged women to return to more traditional paths. "Since the task of every woman culminates in motherhood and therefore the preservation of the population, any job a woman may have must take a back seat to family life," German educator and theologian Magdalene von Tiling asserted in 1925.[61]

Even though teaching was an acceptable profession for women, "professor" was considered a much more peculiar career aspiration. Most women were still expected to quit their jobs if they got married; schoolteachers were required to. If they did have a husband and/or kids, then they were clearly neglecting their homemaking duties by working.

Their potential as child-bearers was another double-edged sword for women academics. Having children would render women less capable of fulfilling their professional duties, and less reliable, so female faculty members were required to pledge their celibacy (a decree that wasn't overturned until 1950).

Conversely, childless women were accused of taking a job that rightfully belonged to a married man who needed to provide for his family. And women who didn't have kids were deemed selfish. There really was no winning.

When they weren't accused of being beasts who'd turned their backs on their feminine natures and abandoned their womanly duties, single women in academia were labeled as shameless flirts who only entered lecture halls to secure husbands.

But such rhetoric didn't scare away everyone. In the '20s and

'30s, women made crucial steps toward normalizing their presence in academia. By 1933, 10,595 women had earned a doctorate in Germany.

What's more, the Weimar Republic's laws declaring women constitutionally equal to men made an indelible impact on many young Germans. And trailblazing women academics also played a part in helping open minds and show younger generations what women were capable of achieving when given equal support and opportunities.

Unfortunately, calls to return to the regressive ideal of women as homemakers would soon become even louder under Hitler. Just as the first women to become lecturers and researchers were settling into their careers during the interwar period—providing mentorship and a model for other women—the Nazis tore them down.

12

Hildegard Comes into Her Own

Whether she knew it or not, by pursuing advanced education and living independently from her family or a husband, Hildegard Stücklen could be counted as a "new woman" of the era. After graduating, she traveled even farther from her hometown of Berlin, taking a job and seeking additional schooling at the University of Zürich, Switzerland.

In 1921, she spent a year at the Delft Institute of Technology in the Netherlands. Following that, Hildegard's star started to shine brighter. She returned to the University of Zürich, resuming her research assistantship and beginning to teach classes.

It was in the lab of physical chemist Victor Henri that Hildegard discovered a passion for spectroscopy. Henri had become a professor at the University of Zürich at around the same time that Hildegard arrived there. Henri was not just an innovator in spectroscopy and photochemistry but also dabbled in experimental psychology and physiology.

During Hildegard's time in his lab, Henri discovered proof of the phenomenon of predissociation, which is when a molecule transitions from a stable excited state into an unstable excited state.

After four years with Henri, Hildegard moved on to another lab at the school, researching gas discharge as an assistant to fellow German experimental physicist Edgar Meyer.

Hildegard also began regularly publishing her findings, an important aspect of establishing yourself as a reputable scientist. Her paper "On the Influence of Water Vapor on the Spark Potential," published in the *Annals of Physics* in 1921, was the first of multiple articles she would write on the topic of spark potential over the next several years.

In 1924 came an investigation into the absorption spectrum of neutral and ionized cadmium in underwater sparks, and the following year, a look at the line and band absorption spectrum of copper.

For *Das Handbuch der Physik* (*The Handbook of Physics*), where most contributors only penned a single section, Hildegard authored an astonishing three different sections. Published by Julius Springer Verlag, the ambitiously exhaustive, twenty-four-volume series sought to capture the present state of experimental and theoretical physics in its entirety.

For her chapters, Hildegard outlined dependent discharge between cold electrodes, ionization by glowing bodies, and flame conductivity, all of which appeared in Volume 14: *Electricity Movement in Gasses.*

Still, despite holding positions as both a university lecturer and a research assistant, she had to rely on translation work to make ends meet.

While in Switzerland, Hildegard was excited to meet Lise, who regularly visited for conferences and programming. This was likely at the Swiss Physical Society's annual physics conferences in the late 1920s or early 1930s. In photos from scientific conferences throughout their careers, most of these women physicists only appear alongside two, maybe three other women amidst dozens of men.

Before long, Hildegard met another important woman scientist, someone who would change the course of her career: Emma P. Carr.

Emma was named chair of the chemistry department at Mount Holyoke College for women in Massachusetts a mere three years after earning her PhD. In the intervening sixteen years between becoming chair and meeting Hildegard, she had built an impressive research program at the school that focused on examining the ultraviolet spectra of hydrocarbons.

Emma was invited to help prepare absorption spectra data for the International Critical Tables alongside Victor Henri in Zürich and Jean Becquerel in Paris. She accepted and asked Henri if she could work in his laboratory while performing this work.

Emma entered Henri's lab for a temporary research trip in February 1925. Going from a small women's institute to a large male-dominated university may have been a shock, but the fact that there was another woman in Henri's lab helped Emma feel more at home. She worked closely with Hildegard, and the pair quickly become fast friends.

Emma found the facilities at the university impressively state of the art, but at the same time, often strangely lacking in what she would consider basics in a lab.

"The equipment in luxuries is splendid, but in everyday necessities nil—when I asked for a funnel they said, 'Oh, we make those when we need them,'"[62] Emma reported.

Still, the school was another hub of physics brilliance. While Emma and Hildegard got down to work sharing spectroscopic tips and techniques, Erwin Schrödinger was next door developing what would become his namesake equation, which describes the probability waves that govern the motion of small particles.

Emma headed back to Mount Holyoke too soon, but the women's friendship and professional relationship was far from over.

Hildegard completed her habilitation thesis in 1931: "About a simple method for determining the intensity ratio of two neighboring spectral lines." This earned her a promotion from lecturer to privatdozent, or senior lecturer, in physics at the University of Zürich.

Emma and Hildegard's friendship and shared research interests translated into another transatlantic trip. This time, Hildegard did the traveling.

Just like Hertha, Hildegard took a temporary leave of absence to accommodate a transatlantic fellowship trip right after achieving habilitation. They both knew a once-in-a-lifetime international scholarship opportunity when they saw it. In the long run, this fellowship would prove incredibly important for Hildegard's future.

"It was in order to do research in spectroscopy that I have been asked by Prof. Carr to come over from Zürich for one year (1931/32),"[63] Hildegard explained. She would spend a year measuring spectra and teaching American students at Mount Holyoke College for women.

On her travel papers from Switzerland to America, Hildegard's profession is listed as "doctor," likely because she had a PhD. She enjoyed a fruitful year among students and professors in Massachusetts. She returned to Switzerland full of ideas; her passion for spectroscopy deepened.

13

Might Hertha Be More than an Assistant?

Though acceptance of women scientists grew throughout the careers of these women, progress in the area was never quick enough. While at the University of Göttingen in the mid-1920s, Hertha began publishing in research journals exclusively using the moniker "H. Sponer." This was likely an effort to render her authorship not immediately recognizable as female.

It was a painful lesson in misogyny that most women scientists must learn at some point: at the beginning of your career, for men to read your work and take you seriously, their view couldn't first be colored by gender.

But encouraging a "gender-blind" reading of your work was also a double-edged sword. It made it much more difficult to develop your reputation as a woman scientist. (Truly, are there any swords that don't prove double-edged for women?)

When a job opened up in early 1929 to take over Alfred Stock's section at the KWI for Chemistry (KWI-C), Hertha's name was tossed around as a potential candidate for the post. By this time, Hertha had filled in for Franck on several occasions while he was away. She and Franck had also begun publishing papers jointly, a nod to the fact that she was beginning to be seen more as a collaborator than an assistant.

Despite this, Lise, who was also at the institute, made it known that she thought Hertha was not ready for a leadership position. Lise wrote to Franck to report on a meeting between herself, Otto Hahn, and Fritz Haber, the director of the KWI for Physical Chemistry.

"Haber suggested Miss Sponer. That's not some sort of bad joke on my part; my words are accurate. Hahn rebuffed this suggestion politely but very firmly; such an idea is as totally inappropriate as it is insulting to us," Lise fumed to Franck.

After Lise told Haber that Hertha definitely wasn't far enough in her career to take over an independent research group, "surprise [was] written all over his face."

"But I heard from Franck how interested you were in Miss Sponer's career path," Haber responded.

"Now I regret having talked with Franck about Miss Sponer at all," Lise resolved.[64]

In Lise's early years of heading up her own department, she wrote to her friend Elisabeth Schiemann about what, at first blush, appears to be skepticism of women scientists:

"Things are going a little haywire in our laboratory; we are building and that prevents continuous work and my current employees aren't the best either. Two 'feminini generis' in particular give me a headache. Otherwise, I'm fine."[65]

While women are not immune from expressing sexism, it's doubtful that Lise was speaking against women in the lab outright based on their gender. What is more likely is that she simply knew from experience that they would be subject to more scrutiny and higher expectations than their male peers.

Perhaps Lise wanted to prepare Hertha and others to be above reproach scientifically, or maybe she worried that less-than-extraordinary female physicists might tarnish the reputation of all women scientists. Or maybe Lise's female assistants were simply annoying. Women can be just as annoying coworkers as men.

Lise didn't publicly participate in feminist movement machinations—honestly, she had enough on her plate—but she did occasionally write and speak about the advancement of women's rights, especially later in life. During a visit to the US, Lise gave a series of lectures at Bryn Mawr College. One stunning presentation was not about physics, but about women.

The lecture was published in *Physics Today* the following year, titled "The Status of Women in the Professions." In it, Lise offers an incredibly well-researched, engaging look at the historical evolution of women's rights in education and professions. When researching for the speech, Lise found that the issue was much deeper and wide-reaching than she imagined.

She asserted that the question of the position of women prior to the feminist movement could not be answered without considering the sociological and sexual-psychological aspects of our Western culture.

Her talk eloquently spans women's fight for rights from biblical times to the present, and she notes how women were always met with antagonism when they attempted to gain rights in work or education.

"The professional training of women encountered great opposition in nearly all the professions," Lise proclaimed. "The motives for the opposition were essentially the same everywhere, and the influence and aftereffects of old habits and traditions can be clearly seen. The game was always the same. There were sharp adversaries and passionate advocates of the emancipation and higher education of women."[66]

In the case of Hertha rejoining the KWI as a department head or as Haber's assistant, Lise seemed more upset about Franck's potential involvement in the suggestion than about the suggestion itself. She pleaded with Franck to clarify what had happened:

"I don't know if you share Haber's opinion that Miss Sponer's accomplishments entitle her to such a position. I cannot come to grips with the thought that Haber, having heard you clearly explain to him how inappropriate it would be to bring in Miss Sponer, could have had the gall to make such a suggestion."[67]

Franck, of course, clarified that he had no intention of letting his dear Hertha go. "I do not share Haber's opinion that Miss Sponer should be the head of a research group at your institute; I hold such an opinion to be preposterous," Franck told Lise.

He said he merely happened to mention to Haber that Lise was worried about Hertha's career advancement: that Lise felt if Hertha remained Franck's assistant forever, it would not be in her best interests professionally and could lead to "intellectual dependency."[68]

Franck assured Lise that he understood her agitation, but was hurt by the suggestion that he would go behind her back and encourage Haber to make such a suggestion, noting that even if he considered Hertha a genius, he wouldn't recommend her for a job that Lise felt should be filled differently.

Was Hertha aware that her good friends Lise and Franck had been discussing her career progression and need for greater independence, not just professional, but intellectual? Did she have any idea of the hubbub she had caused at the KWI? Unlikely on both counts.

Franck may have known that Hertha needed to be allowed to spread her wings professionally, but he was not ready to lose her charming personality and keen intellect in his lab just yet. The characteristic Hertha possessed that Franck most cherished was one he lacked: organization. Besides, he knew Hertha would have far less freedom as Haber's assistant. Franck often left Hertha in charge while he was away.

The KWI institutes were indeed a breeding ground of scientific breakthroughs, so an official invitation to a new position may have tempted Hertha. Still, the University of Göttingen had developed into quite a hotbed of physics innovations itself.

Thanks in part to Franck and Hertha themselves. And besides, the countryside was much less stressful than the city.

What Franck and Lise seem to have forgotten is that Hertha was an independent, self-possessed woman. And she was in control of her own career. Given that she had published more than a dozen scientific papers by this point, if she had wanted to find a job where she would have more responsibility, she most certainly could have.

She was happy where she was, basking in Franck's glow and working on developing a luminescence of her own.

Part of that professional advancement included publishing a book. Or at least, Hertha hoped so. Despite initial plans for her volume on vacuum UV spectroscopy for the *Structure of Matter* series being scrapped, she wasn't ready to give up on writing a book for Ferdinand Springer. Hertha asked the publisher if her text might exist as a standalone book aimed at university students. They agreed that this sounded like a good idea. Hertha said she could submit the book by October 1, 1930.

Yet when October came and went, she told Franck that June or July 1931 would be a more obtainable goal. The publisher checked in with Franck at the end of January 1931 to inquire as to where their promised manuscript was. He asked them to push the submission deadline back to October 1931.

Hertha sent the publisher a groveling letter blaming the fact that the research for the book was bloating beyond expectations; there was much more she wanted to include in the book than she initially anticipated. Even though she had requested and been granted a leave of absence for the winter 1930–1931 semester, the book was nowhere near finished.

"Missing the deadline is incredibly embarrassing to me," Hertha admitted to her publisher. "I had hoped to complete the book during a three-month break from my duties. Unfortunately, that did not work out."[69] She told them the research she needed to cover was heftier than anticipated and that writing a book was much harder than she'd expected.

In February 1932, Springer's editor reached out again. Would an attempt at passive-aggressive humor inspire Hertha to hurry up and complete the project?

"He would like you to know that his belief in the book can now be compared with that of an ancient myth, and he has not spoken with you about it because he does not, as a matter of principle, deal with the occult."[70]

This was not to be the last of Hertha's precious, if not always high-priority, book project. Clearly, she believed authoring a book was an important accomplishment for a scientist to achieve. But she just wasn't very good with deadlines and was too fastidious to turn in anything but a perfect manuscript. An entity that, of course, does not exist.

Hertha felt pulled in too many directions. She complained that she felt working on the book meant neglecting her research responsibilities in the lab. Yes, three months had obviously not been enough time to complete work on a heavily researched science text, but the project was dragging on even by the publisher's standards.

It was dangerous for a woman to be behaving so unprofessionally as to repeatedly miss deadlines. Women who were among the first had to set an example to ensure others would be given similar opportunities. One wrong move and a publisher might swear off women authors altogether.

If you're the only woman and you fail, you fail for all women, observed Stephanie Shirley, a German Jewish refugee who fled to England as a child and became a pioneer in the field of IT. "They say, 'Well, we tried one of those and she was awful.' Whereas, if you succeed, the presumption is that, 'We had her and she was good; we'll try another one and see if it works again.'"[71]

Hopefully, Hertha understood the wider potential ramifications of her failure to produce a manuscript.

14

Lise and Physics Under Hitler

Like many other Jewish academics in Germany, the development of Lise's situation from uncomfortable to desperate was a slow, insidious progression. The Nazis didn't care that Lise didn't consider herself Jewish. Her parents were Jewish, so therefore she was Jewish, and in turn, an obstacle to be overcome on the path to creating a pure white race.

January 30, 1933: Adolf Hitler appointed chancellor of Germany

At the end of February 1933, the Reichstag—the German parliament building—went up in flames. Hitler claimed the arson was perpetrated by communists trying to overthrow the government. He used the incident as an excuse to crack down on political opponents, declare a state of emergency, and strip all citizens of most of their civil liberties.

Historically, there's been debate over whether the Nazis themselves may have been involved in starting the fire as a ploy to earn public sympathy for their power grab.

February 28, 1933: Reichstag Fire Decree abolishes the right to speak, assemble, protest, and due process

Lise did not see Adolf Hitler as nefarious at first; few did. Hitler understood the political importance of appearing fair, of eroding democracy slowly and methodically. You couldn't just bluster into office and begin spouting off your plans for racial cleansing.

"It was harmonious and dignified throughout," Lise told Otto of the March government transition ceremony, which she listened to on the radio. Her friend Elisabeth and Otto's wife Edith had come over so they could listen together. Otto was away, guest lecturing at Cornell University in New York, and while he was gone, Lise substituted for him as temporary director of the KWI-C.

The ceremony, featuring Hitler, President Hindenburg, and former Crown Prince Wilhelm, had been orchestrated by the Ministry of Propaganda to portray a smooth passing of power. "Hitler spoke in a very moderate, tactful, and conciliatory way," Lise said. "Hopefully it will continue this way."[72]

Above Lise's head at the KWI-C, a newly unfurled swastika flag flapped uneasily in the wind.

Franck was more wary and more prescient than most. He told Lise: "After all the anti-Semitic agitation, the National Socialists, as I see it, cannot do the same part of what they have always preached."[73]

Of course, Franck was correct. While Hitler was declaring "We are sincere friends of peace" at the podium in Potsdam, twenty-five miles away in Oranienburg, the first concentration camp, Dachau, was opening. That evening, the Nazis would drag their first prisoners there: forty of their political opponents. Next, Hitler ensured he could pass any laws he pleased.

Through the Enabling Act of March 1933, the Reich government was now permitted to issue laws without parliamentary oversight. Though some recognized how dangerous the Reich was, it's difficult to say just how many, since it was well-known at the time the risk of putting those thoughts to paper, in letters to friends or otherwise, for fear of repercussions.

Between the Fire Decree and the Enabling Act, Hitler quickly assumed dictatorial power. Though Hitler immediately ordered the imprisonment or execution of his political opponents upon assuming his dictatorship, he worked up to more widespread persecution and murder of Jewish civilians and other adversaries, first taking away rights and livelihoods, and then gradually ratcheting up the violence.

Taking baby steps toward genocide gave everyone time to get on board. This made each step—each revocation of rights and freedoms and increasing violence—seem like a reasonable extension of previous actions.

The Nazis were never going to play nice, despite their initial attempts at lip service to that effect. Their ultimate goal was a racially "pure" Aryan nation that took up as much land as they could conquer. And they would happily kill anyone who stood in the way of that goal.

Jewish people were the focus of Hitler's hateful eradication campaign, but they were not the only targets of the Nazis: Roma, Sinti, Slavs, those of African descent, communists, political dissenters, members of certain religions, and gay men were also targeted.

The mentally and physically disabled were deemed "undesirable," while sex workers, alcoholics, and the "work-shy" declared "asocial." Political opponents and those who were allies or defenders of any of these targeted groups also had to be removed.

All these people posed a threat to the tidy world order of Hitler's imagining, so these "worthless" citizens were slowly swept out of society to make room for the "valuable."

It was eugenics with an army; a racial superiority complex with heavy weaponry.

Hitler had been sowing the seeds of anti-Semitism since the 1920s as head of propaganda for the Nazi party. The indoctrination of youth by the Nazi party throughout this time had proven wildly effective.

Well before Hitler rose to power, "antisemitism was the prevailing *Zeitgeist*, notably among university students, that dominated campus life," explains Luise Hirsch, a scholar of Jewish history. Jewish students were increasingly "openly harassed" by students and authorities alike, relegating them to "a precarious existence in the fringe of German society."[74]

Hitler knew that to control a society, you first had to control what its people were being taught in schools. One of his first acts as leader was to implement laws to achieve his dual goals of *saeuberung* and *gleichschaltung*—or cleansing and coordinating—the country's education system.

The views of professors and teachers had to "coordinate" with those of the Nazis. Schools and universities had to be purified of both Jewish thought and Jewish thinkers.[75]

This initial purge was achieved by the 1933 civil service law. Students at several universities insisted their schools fire even more professors than required. They threatened to disrupt lectures unless every non-Aryan and their sympathizers were removed from their positions, and their books and papers removed from the library.

At the University of Berlin, where Lise taught, students demanded the dean post signs on every building with declarations like, "Jews can only have Jewish thoughts. If a Jew writes in German, he is a liar," or else resign. Students gathered in Berlin's Opera Square to "purify" Germany of "foreign" thought by burning over 25,000 books.

What's more, Hitler appointed his favorite racial scientist, Dr. Eugen Fischer, as the university's new dean. Fischer created dozens of new courses in race science. Before long, his "science" was providing what Nazis considered a justification for their eugenics program, including the forced sterilization and murder of hundreds of thousands of physically disabled and mentally ill people.[76]

Even at the KWI, Nazism wasn't exactly a new feature. Lise's chief lab assistant was an ardent Nazi. As was the guest chemist who'd joined the KWI-C in 1921 on the institute's top floor, Kurt Hess. Otto's chief assistant was also a Nazi, and he went so far as to take up the mantle of "party steward" for the Nazis at the institute.

In April 1933, a Berlin newspaper published a list of the civil servants slated for firing by the Nazis. That summer, another list appeared with yet more faculty members facing dismissal from the University of Berlin, and Lise's name was on it.

The reason? Because she had not been a "regular" employee before World War I. It was obvious she was being targeted because she was Jewish and a woman.

Lise's colleagues Otto Hahn and Max Planck pleaded with the government on her behalf, noting she would have been a regular employee if only women had been allowed to pursue habilitation back then. It made no difference. Lise—Germany's first woman physics professor—lost her professorship in September because she was not considered a regular employee before World War I, her military service was "*not at the front*," and she was "100% non-Aryan."

The initial loopholes in the Nazi's policies, such as being exempt if you served in the military, were already being adjusted and tightened to ensure they only covered the smallest number of people possible.

Thus began a long wave of anti-Semitic firings. Over the coming years, roughly 250 faculty and staff were fired from the University of Berlin. Additionally, several students and researchers were also ejected, and numerous doctorates were withdrawn.

These weren't all Jewish scholars; some were simply opponents of the Nazis or supporters of their Jewish colleagues. Several of those kicked out were deported, and the rest were largely forced to leave because all job opportunities had dried up. In the end, the Nazis had cleared out about a third of the university staff.

Lise was alarmed by the firings, notably her own. Yet she still had her position at the KWI-C to provide her with a salary. While she got along well enough with most of her coworkers, the institute wasn't without tension.

"Even here it is obvious who values people and who does not. And I was not surprised that my house-partner is of the latter type," Lise worriedly told Otto of her neighbor, none other than fervent Nazi Kurt Hess.

His assigned apartment on the institute grounds was right next door to Lise's. She still hoped for the best, but felt it was becoming clear that things were quickly deteriorating. "Anyone who cares about Germany should be worried about what will become of it all."[77]

The Nazis never had any intention of allowing those they deemed ethnic aliens or their allies to live free and prosper in their land. Though she was fired from the faculty of the University of Berlin, Lise held on to her position at the KWI-C for dear life, hoping to be able to weather the Nazi era and come out on the other side.

15

Hertha Loses the Protection of Her Mentor

When the Law for the Restoration of the Professional Civil Service was enacted on April 7, 1933, Hedwig had just celebrated her forty-sixth birthday two days prior. Hildegard was forty-one, and Hertha only thirty-seven. At fifty-four years old, Lise was the oldest of the four women by more than a decade, and her former colleague James Franck was fifty.

While they all stood to lose their careers thanks to the Nazis, Lise and Franck had gotten much further in theirs by the time Hitler took power. It would be understandable that they'd be more resistant to leave Germany, more set in their ways. They had so much to lose.

Despite this, rather than using his World War I military service to buy him some more time at his job, in April 1933, Franck chose to resign from the University of Göttingen just before the Nazis officially dismissed him, in protest of the blanket firing of Jewish civil service workers.

He refused to put his genius to work for this racist state. It wasn't a decision he made lightly. Lise reported that it was "very hard for him not to be allowed to set foot in his institute."[78] While he didn't know how bad it was about to get, he already foresaw the depth of Nazi hatred and refused to be a tool to further their goals.

"We Germans of Jewish descent are being treated as aliens and enemies of the Fatherland. Our children will never be allowed to regard themselves as Germans," Franck announced in the local newspaper, adding that while those with war service such as himself could apply for special permission to keep their jobs, he refused to serve such a hostile government.[79]

His resignation was a big deal since he was a Nobel laureate and a decorated war veteran. Some worried his very public resignation had the opposite of the desired effect, noting that his display was fueling anti-German sentiment internationally.

When the paper reported on Franck's resignation letter, it noted that he hoped to remain in Germany doing scientific research at a non–civil service job. Hoping to stay in Germany hardly sounds anti-German, but that's not how several colleagues saw it.

A letter signed by forty-two of Franck's fellow lecturers at Göttingen claimed his resignation was tantamount to an act of national sabotage. Franck would've been in a better position to fight Nazi policies by maintaining his position of power, some asserted, and besides, things weren't *that* bad.

"My decision for publicity," Franck later explained, "was in order to give many young Jews the feeling that they were not simply being left in the lurch."[80]

Franck was following in the famous footsteps of Einstein, who, the previous month, had resigned from the Prussian Academy of Sciences. Einstein publicly denounced Hitler's regime after it began suspending civil liberties, declaring:

"As long as I have any choice in the matter, I shall live only in a country where civil liberty, tolerance, and equality of all citizens before the law prevail. These conditions do not exist in Germany at the present time." Einstein had been staying in America as a visiting academic, and, after a few months in Belgium and England, returned to the US for good in October 1933.

Einstein, Franck, and fellow Nobel laureate Erwin Schrödinger were among the small group of scientists who chose to resign in protest of the firing of their colleagues. It was an option reserved only for those eminent enough to know they could easily find a job elsewhere.

American institutions couldn't wait to snap up the best (male) physicists Germany had to offer. The California Institute of Technology—Caltech—recruited Theodore von Karman and courted Einstein. Princeton, where Einstein ended up, also secured John von Neumann, Eugene Wigner, and Hedwig's former colleague Rudolf Ladenburg. Hans Bethe landed at Cornell University. All told, a dozen Nobel laureate scientists immigrated to the United States between 1930 and 1941.

Other countries also got in on the opportunity to import some geniuses. To help build up its universities' science departments, Turkey snagged several astronomers, physicists, and other scholars. Similarly, émigré scientists were brought in to help grow Hebrew University's burgeoning physics department. After accepting a position at the University of Saskatchewan, Canada, Gerhard Herzberg went on to earn a Nobel Prize in Chemistry.

Germany was losing its greatest minds to Nazi anti-Semitism and misogyny.

Before Franck left Germany, he and Hertha published a final joint paper, which they coauthored with colleague Edward Teller, in the *Journal of Physical Chemistry*: "Remarks on the Predissociation of Triatomic Molecules." It was a research path all three would have liked to continue down, but Teller was also Jewish. With the help of the International Rescue Committee,

Teller successfully fled Germany to work at Niels Bohr's lab in Copenhagen.

A "departure tea" was held for Franck at the Physics Institute. A somber affair, Hertha gifted him an artfully lit black-and-white profile portrait of herself.

In it, she is looking toward the light, her ear and hair deeply in shadow. She does not smile and wears no makeup. Her wavy hair is pulled back in a low, loose bun; a blurry necklace hangs above the V-neck white lace collar of her dark dress. She signed the photo and expressed her hope that she remains in his thoughts: "So you won't forget me." As if that were even a possibility.

"The Francks depart on Saturday. Their leaving is going to be horribly difficult for me," Hertha confessed to her friend Werner Heisenberg. He had been a physics lecturer at the University of Göttingen alongside Hertha in the 1920s. "The Institute will truly be desolate."[81]

In November 1933, the Francks were off to Denmark, where he would join his old friend Niels Bohr's lab. By now, Franck and Bohr were both "Bonzen" (bigwigs), at least in the science community. The Franck family had no difficulty leaving Germany. They were lucky to get out early; the Nazis had yet to begin restricting the movements of Jewish people.

Franck's absence had a profound effect on the University of Göttingen physics department. "There was a large vacuum afterwards. Nobody trusted anyone anymore," one employee reported. "There was no cooperation anymore. Physics at Göttingen was in ruins."[82]

Most of Hertha's professional circle had been via Franck, so the circle was now largely closed off from her and in disarray from the loss of so many colleagues thanks to Nazi anti-Semitism.

His departure also left her vulnerable to attacks from some of the sexist faculty members. When Franck left the University of Göttingen, Hertha's favorite misogynist, Robert Pohl, temporarily took over his position.

Had her colleagues not been sexist, Hertha might have been promoted to take Franck's position instead. Had she been a man, she almost certainly would have become his successor. Alas, she was a woman, so instead of a promotion, Hertha received threats of dismissal.

For women academics across the country, the loss of a boss or colleague who was acting as their guarantor because of their gender quickly translated into the loss of their job as well.

After the Nazis fired the father of modern biochemistry, Carl Neuberg, for being Jewish, his KWI department was shuttered. Neuberg was a rare supporter of women scientists, so his forced departure left his assistant Maria Kobel in a similar situation as Hertha.

As soon as Pohl took over for Franck, Hertha found herself perilously unprotected. She saw the writing on the wall; she knew Pohl's tolerance of her was already wearing thin. So, it was little surprise when, a mere three months after Franck's departure, Hertha's name appeared on the latest list of those relieved of their duties at German universities.

Of the University of Göttingen's 253 faculty members, a total of 56 would be fired or forced out by the Nazis over the course of their reign. Among them were scientific luminaries Emmy Noether, Edward Teller, Max Born, Gustav Hertz, and Lothar Nordheim. Even Franck was listed if only to give the Nazis the hollow satisfaction of saying they'd fired him even though he had already left. The entire leadership at the University of Göttingen's Institute of Theoretical Physics was gutted.

The mini professional bio that accompanied Hertha's name on the list of fired faculty noted that she was an "exceptional teacher," and that she'd made important contributions to determining the heat of dissociation of molecules from their band spectra.

Hertha's write-up also spelled out—in no uncertain terms—what women scholars across the country now faced: "no prospect of university professorship in Germany as a woman."

To argue against her firing, Franck provided Hertha with a certification of her allegiance to the German nation, though how much weight the word of a Jewish scholar carried with the Nazis is debatable.

Even though Hertha had been a dedicated research assistant for thirteen years and a lecturer for eight, and had published an impressive twenty-six papers in peer-reviewed science journals, Pohl handed down her official dismissal on December 30, 1933. Pohl noted it was on the grounds that Franck's successor might want to fill her position as chief research assistant "differently."

On the surface, the reason was that Franck's successor might not specialize in spectroscopy, but Hertha read between the lines and understood they intended to fill her position with a man.

Moving her to another role was out of the question due to Professor Pohl's "rejection by principle of women teachers. Pohl is against women entering the academic career path."[83]

"I would be happy to give the reason for the termination. But perhaps my antipathy for Pohl would be too obvious,"[84] Hertha harrumphed to Franck. The institute secretary told Franck that Hertha was "putting on a brave front and took her dismissal with a certain grim humor," and that she was trying to keep Hertha distracted with movie theater outings and walks.

As for her teaching, Hertha would be permitted to finish out the current academic term, which ended in October 1934. But lecturing didn't cover her bills; the chief assistant job was where her salary came from, so this arrangement would leave her unable to make a living for nearly a year. With no husband, no family wealth, no savings to speak of, and no other source of income, she'd be out of money by the summer.

"The Nazis believed that women should not be teaching physics and doing research at a university," noted Hertha's future colleague Horst Meyer. "She could have stayed, but at most she could have taught high school. So, she looked for a way out."[85]

Teaching basic science to young boys or girls would be a huge demotion for someone like Hertha, who had worked long and hard to earn her habilitation to teach at the university level. It would be significantly less fulfilling than her current career.

Hertha quickly concluded she had no future in Germany. Countless women academics faced similar prospects of being forced to look abroad if they wanted to continue their careers in research and university lecturing.

16

Roadblocks for Hedwig

Hedwig was one of the many German Jewish academics who found themselves hoping to find a job abroad after they were fired by the Nazis. For displaced scholars looking to land in America, a major stumbling block to immigration was that a basic prerequisite for US university jobs was having spent the previous two years teaching at the university level. The clock started ticking the moment they were fired; any time Hedwig spent in Germany after losing her lecturer job meant time spent not teaching.

Given the deeply ingrained institutional and cultural sexism that saw women forbidden from applying for the licensure or examinations required to become professors in Germany until well into the 1900s, this policy ended up being deeply sexist. And that sexism proved deadly in many cases.

Women had only been allowed to apply for habilitation in 1920, and even then, universities continued to make pursuing habilitation extremely difficult and academic atmospheres hostile to women.

The roadblock of habilitation, which had only been instituted in the nineteenth century, "solidified the deeply patriarchal academic structure," explains Britta Ohm, a social anthropology scholar at the University of Bern, therefore "immensely complicating the possibilities of women to change the evolving modern university system."[86]

Many universities refused to hire women even after earning habilitation—especially in math and science departments—merely on the grounds of their womanhood. If women were hired as lecturers at all, they were typically employed only on an unscheduled or temporary basis.

Women were often brought on as unpaid staff, and when they were paid, it was less than men. Only full professorships included the benefits of a reliable salary, research funding, conference invitations, and the subsequent inter-university networks these fostered.

By 1933, of the 10,595 women who'd earned a doctorate in Germany, only 56 had achieved habilitation, and a mere 27 had advanced beyond lecturer to be hired as the German equivalent of an associate professor. Two—that's right, two—had achieved full professor status (Lise was one of them).

As mere private lecturers, reliant on student fees for their income, women's opportunities for advancement and reputation-building in the scientific world were extremely limited. Women's ability to participate and progress in the scientific community often depended on finding a male mentor (which often took the form of a husband scientist).

To add to the harm, in 1933, the Nazis explicitly denied women the right to seek habilitation. This legislation was short-lived and was rescinded the following year, but the Reich found another way to keep women out of university professions: it now required applicants to have participated in teaching academies that women were not allowed to attend.

Nazi policies ensured that as a woman, it was nearly impossible to earn a living as an academic, professor, or researcher in Germany. Shut down just as they were getting started, women only accounted for one percent of the faculty at German universities when most of them were fired or forced out by the Nazis. "Women who did not share the Nazi worldview were also driven out of their jobs," explains historian Michelle Mouton.[87]

All these elements conspired to compound the harm to women who'd been fired as a result of Nazi edicts. Women academics were less likely to have positions that garnered the attention of the wider scientific community and the sort of notoriety that for many men translated into immediate job opportunities outside of the country.

At the very least, women often simply lacked the teaching experience needed to look like good candidates to international hiring institutions. No job to pull you out of Germany often translated into a death sentence for dismissed scholars.

To be a woman and Jewish was doubly dangerous. Throughout the 1920s, men who would go on to become active in the Nazi movement were often the ones in charge of the hiring, promotion, and firing at universities. They routinely overlooked Jewish scholars for key jobs and promotions they deserved.

Hedwig couldn't afford to sit around waiting for an American job offer to rescue her. Would such an offer ever even materialize? She wasn't married. Her mother had died in 1926 and her father in 1932, so she didn't have parents to support her.

Luckily, she didn't have to face this predicament alone. She had her older brother, Kurt, who was all that was left of her immediate family. After their parents passed away, Hedwig and Kurt continued sharing the apartment in Breslau they grew up in, now joined by their cousin Emma.

Kurt was also having a terrible time. When the civil service law was passed, he was working as a state councilor in Breslau and had been slowly building a reputation as a respected lawyer in the region's highest court for the past five years.

He didn't lose his job right away but instead was demoted and transferred to a district court in the region of Schweidnitz twenty-seven miles southwest of Breslau. Kurt was required to find housing closer to his new position, which meant they couldn't afford to keep their parents' apartment.

Hedwig and her cousin Emma were forced to move to a smaller apartment. Within a year, Kurt's demotion had become an official firing. He landed back in his hometown with no job, no job prospects, and no pension. It was up to Hedwig to support them.

However, Hedwig and her colleagues believed she only needed a temporary solution for what they assumed was a temporary problem, and they encouraged her to persevere during this brief period of professional hardship under Nazi control.

Hedwig and her family were proud to be Jewish Germans. They never imagined it would soon become a designation hunted to virtual extinction. The general presumption was that the Nazis were mostly more bluster than an actual threat, and that soon enough they would be replaced by the next political party, just as had always happened.

But the civil service law was just the beginning. When yet another new Nazi policy aimed at curtailing the education of Jewish people was announced, over in Göttingen, Hertha wrote to tell Franck about it.

An amendment to the civil service law declared that any "non-Aryans" who hadn't registered for exams before August 1, 1933, were prohibited from taking them. Hertha was concerned for the two Jewish doctoral students she'd taken under her wing after Franck's departure:

"I expect that the amendment will shortly be extended to doctoral exams and see a dark future for Jaf [Jaffé] and Oe [Oeser]."[88]

Hertha's predictions were correct. It only got worse from there. Jewish scholars soon lost their right to pursue habilitation, obtain doctoral degrees, and even enroll in university. Edicts and decrees restricting the rights of Jewish Germans appeared at a sickening pace.

April 25, 1933: Law against Overcrowding in Schools and Institutions of Higher Education declares Jewish students should make up no more than 1.5 percent of the total student population of any school or university

July 14, 1933: Political parties other than the Nazi party banned

December 13, 1934: Proof of "Aryan" ancestry required to qualify for tenure at universities or pursue habilitation

September 15, 1935: Nuremberg Race Laws render Jewish people no longer full citizens of Germany and ban marriage/sexual relations between Jewish people and "Aryans"

April 15, 1937: Institutions forbidden from granting doctoral degrees to Jewish people or renewing their existing doctorates

Over the course of just a few years, the rights of Jewish people to receive an education, to practice their profession of choice, to move freely in public—to simply exist—were systematically stripped away.

17

Women in Nazi-Era Germany

One of Hitler's campaign promises was that he would solve the unemployment crisis by opening up hundreds of thousands of positions. Positions that happened to be occupied by women and Jewish people. Nazi rhetoric insisted ethnic aliens and women were taking jobs that rightfully belonged to Aryan men. Hitler assured the nation he would fix this.

Traditional patriarchal ideals had been woven into the fabric of Nazism from its inception, and the work of spreading the belief that women belonged in the home and not in public spaces began long before Hitler took power.

Once his rule began, the Nazis were now officially empowered to create policies and initiatives to support these ideals. That meant a swift, ruthless reversal of the rights women had been granted under the Weimar Republic.

In their "History of Equal Rights in Germany 1789–2007," scholars at Bielefeld University in Germany explain that during Nazi rule, "women were deprived of the right to vote and the opportunity to be admitted to postdoctoral qualifications at colleges and universities; banned from taking up certain professions (including scientific and technical professions)."

Women's societies were subject to "forcible coordination" to bring them into alignment with Nazi ideals. International Women's Day was eliminated in favor of Mother's Day, and a massive propaganda campaign promoting motherhood was undertaken.[89]

Nazi Propaganda Minister Josef Goebbels made it sound like they needed to save women from themselves, announcing their plan to "liberate women from women's emancipation." The Nazi version of emancipation meant blockading any educational and professional avenues that had recently been opened to women.

Two of the Nazis' goals—reducing male unemployment and growing their Aryan race—had a single fix: restricting women's roles in public. Again, the propaganda hounds were on it, spinning motherhood as a woman's highest calling, and the domestic sphere where she could best serve her nation.

Nazis were specifically concerned with ensuring women were not competition for men in the workforce. Men were the breadwinners; if a woman got a job, she was taking it from a man. That meant career women were not just peculiar; they were a threat to the very fabric of society.

The Nazis viewed women's employment as a "deformity of capitalism," and saw the rights the Weimar government had granted to women as a "confusion of a rootless liberalism," Gertrud Bäumer wrote in the feminist journal *Die Frau* in 1933.[90]

First on the chopping block: the 7,000 married women with public service jobs. The Nazis declared female civil servants could be fired without cause if their husbands were employed by the state. And if one such unceremoniously fired civil servant later found herself divorced or widowed, she had no right to claim her job back.

The new law also allowed women to be paid less than men and

barred them from permanent state employment before the age of 35. Women's constitutionally protected equality no longer existed.

Financial depression amplified men's calls for the exclusion of women from the professions. "The overcrowding hysteria of the early 1930s made gender into a divisive issue, exaggerating the numerical impact of female inroads into main domains," historian Konrad Jarausch notes.[91]

Women were forced out of certain professions and excluded from training programs. Women doctors, judges, and lawyers— Hitler wasn't having it. Orders to give preference to young married men for physician jobs saw as many as 700 women physicians lose their jobs.[92] So many women civil servants were sacked that even the Minister of the Interior called for moderation.

Nazi students were foaming at the mouth to enact this newly sanctioned sexism. At the University of Leipzig, they demanded "drastic reductions—and in some subjects such as physics, chemistry and the like—a complete exclusion of women studying at the university."[93]

Women were already barred from running for elected positions at German universities because it would be too taxing for their "delicate constitution."[94]

The Nazis derided intellectual pursuits as unhealthy for women. Hitler railed that "the goal of female education must be unswervingly the future mother."[95] Such indoctrination started young. School curriculums were changed to reflect Nazi beliefs. An hour each of English and math were replaced by needlepoint.

Before taking the university entrance exam, girls were required to pass a test on "domestic skills and knowledge including cooking, cleaning, sewing and mending."[96] Aryan girls were required to join the League of German Girls. Before they could attend university, women were required to put in six months at the Reich Work Service.

The Nazis continued to step up their efforts to discourage women from pursuing higher education by limiting the number of women who could enroll in universities to no more than 10 percent of the class. For the Nazis' purposes, the rule had the desired effect: the number of women university students in Germany dropped precipitously, from 18,315 in 1932 to 5,447 in 1939.[97]

World War I had hit Germany's male population hard. To truly assert their dominance in the world, the Nazis needed more manpower. What is a nation without people, after all? That meant in the Nazi state, women's role was producing more citizens.

But they only wanted more of a certain kind of citizen. "Racially pure" women were the only ones seen as valuable. They were encouraged to bear as many babies as possible; those who birthed four or more children were even awarded a cross of honor.

The Nazis dangled the carrot of generous loans to any valuable women who left the labor force to get married. Loan payments were paused after the birth of each child; after four children, they were canceled altogether.

Some scholars like to argue that this meant the Nazis revered women, in some perverse way. What it really looks like is that white women of sound mind and body were seen simply as breeders and family caregivers.

"However high a 'value' Nazi leaders placed on women and however much they flattered them, the intention was to deny them free choice and self-determination," writes historian Jill Stephenson.[98] Thousands of Aryan women were punished by the Nazis for seeking an abortion.

"Valuable" women were only permitted to have jobs deemed appropriately feminine, and only if it did not interfere with their main role of childbearing. Those who worked as nurses, childcare workers, and social workers were lauded for using their innate nurturing abilities in the service of the Volksgemeinschaft (an imagined white German utopia).

As for the "undesirables," they were forced to undergo procedures that would prevent them from ever bearing children.

July 14, 1933: Law for the Prevention of Offspring with Heredi-
tary Diseases mandates forced sterilization of people with certain ill-
nesses

The law required anyone suffering from "feeblemindedness," schizophrenia, manic-depressive disorder, Huntington's disease, physical deformity, alcoholism, genetic blindness, deafness, or epilepsy to be forcibly sterilized.

The Nazis viewed such people as "hereditarily unhealthy," and a financial drain on society who would only produce still more burdensome offspring. Any doctors who diagnosed these conditions were compelled to report them.

Roughly 400,000 Germans were sterilized, both men and women. Many died from botched surgeries or complications, most of them women; nearly a hundred women died from forced tubal ligation procedures. What's more, roughly 500 biracial Black children were secretly sterilized by Nazi doctors so they couldn't reproduce.

Of course, women were much more likely to be declared feebleminded because of their lifestyles or sexual proclivities. As many as 80 percent of the women who were sterilized were single; at best, their marriage prospects were severely impacted, and at worst, they were confined to a psychiatric institute, workhouse, or concentration camp.

For women sent to camps, pregnancy could mean an immediate death sentence. If you were discovered to be pregnant upon arrival, you were sent right to the gas chambers. If, somehow, a pregnant person was able to hide their pregnancy until giving birth, the newborn baby was murdered by drowning or lethal injection.[99]

In concentration camps, guards raped prisoners; "brothels" were established in some camps where women were forced into sex work to service male prisoners.

Under Nazism, women were both victims and perpetrators,

depending on their racial heritage, political leanings, health, and other attributes. Nazi rhetoric called women to selflessly devote themselves to others: to dedicate their life to their children, spouses, and communities.

Assisting the Nazis' efforts was part of serving their community. Many helped run programs that taught mothers how to parent and cook and gave out health advice. The posts were largely unpaid and mostly held by older women, single women, or women whose children were school-aged or older.

Many women embraced their roles in assisting the regime, in the birthing and building of a "pure" nation. They had been primed by the teaching of Nazi values that had begun appearing in their school curriculums and communities when they were young.

Plenty of women worked as nurses and even doctors in concentration camps. There, instead of delivering medical care and "doing no harm," they did the most harm: delivering lethal injections and performing horrific scientific experiments, such as intentionally creating wounds and inducing infections to test the efficacy of various treatments.

"The German nurses looked on the misery of the sick with the greatest indifference and even sarcasm and never made any effort whatsoever to help them even though it was possible for them to do so,"[100] asserted Helena Esther Goudsmit, who was a prisoner at the Ravensbrück concentration camp for women.

Women can be just as evil as men. And no gender is more easily indoctrinated than another. Many German women played a key role in embracing and propagating Nazi ideals. They believed in the cause strongly enough to do whatever they were told, to abandon all sense of humanity or compassion.

18

Hertha Struggles to Find a Paying Position

Hertha felt she had to leave Germany out of a sense of solidarity for her Jewish colleagues and friends. She likely harbored a special commitment to Franck. Perhaps she felt that after all he had done for her, she owed it to him to not continue advancing physics in a country that treated him with such disdain because of his heritage. Why should she serve a regime so hateful it failed to recognize even the humanity of her mentor, let alone his genius?

Or perhaps she cared for him more than she was allowed to admit while he was married. "She adored him, you could see it clearly," one of their colleagues later noted. "Whether you want to call that an amorous overtone or not, I'd say that was on the borderline."[101]

After Franck left Göttingen, Hertha wrote to him constantly. At times, it was close to every day. (Hertha's biographer refers to it as a "continuous exchange of letters."[102])

Still, Hertha was also good friends with Franck's wife, Ingrid, and their children; she would never dream of making any romantic overtures toward Franck while he was married. She cared for them too much.

Who's to know whether Franck appreciated this deluge of communication from his dedicated *assistentin* or felt overwhelmed by it? At the time, Ingrid had been diagnosed with multiple sclerosis, and her condition was worsening. Franck himself was prone to occasional fits of depression throughout his life. He was easily affected by the pain of others, whether personal or global, so was greatly depressed by Ingrid's decline.

Hertha's sense of solidarity was relatively unique. The lack of widespread outcry at the mass firing of Jewish scholars was deafening.

At a meeting of all German university presidents five days after the civil service law was passed, Hamburg University's president suggested the only principled course of action would be to protest the expulsion of their Jewish faculty and staff.

Sadly, he was among the minority. Most of those gathered at the meeting insisted such action would be "dangerous and futile."

Many of those who were not thrust out of their positions were happy to carry on, feeling lucky to still have a job at all. Many felt cowed into silence by the specter of swift, harsh retaliation from the Nazis should they speak out against the regime.

The threat of violence is a powerful tool; fear encourages compliance and conformity. Others believed Nazi propaganda regarding the outsized influence of Jewish scholars at German universities.

But not everyone. Some scientists were utterly embarrassed to be associated with their country. Max Planck told Franck he could not bear to attend international science conferences because he would have to hide his head in shame as a representative of German science.

Like most people forced to look for work outside Germany,

Hertha didn't want to leave her home country; she would prefer to stay if she could. She'd built a life she loved, but the foundation of that life had been pulled out from under her. "You know how difficult it is to say goodbye,"[103] she told Franck.

But most non-Jewish women scholars who stayed in Germany had limited options: take a significant demotion by becoming a schoolteacher, leave education entirely, or become active participants in the Nazis' agenda at research institutions. None of these choices appealed to Hertha.

In addition to searching for a new permanent job for himself, Franck did all he could to try to find work for Hertha after she petitioned him for help. He reached out to the Emergency Association of German Science in Berlin on her behalf, but all it could provide was the use of the gas spectrograph and rotary vacuum pump Franck had been borrowing.

Not exactly the sparkly job offer she was hoping would whisk her off to a brighter future.

Franck was just getting started. He reached out to Hildegard's former colleague, Victor Henri, to see if his spectroscopy lab in Belgium had a permanent position available that his former chief assistant could fill.

"There are extremely few prospects for women in Germany," Franck explained to Henri. He talked Hertha up as best he could, saying he "would really get a very valuable co-worker in Miss Sponer." Franck also lamented to Henri that he was not able to continue working with her himself: "to take her along to a place where she could have a suitable position."[104]

Bohr was already doing Franck a favor by offering him a place in his lab. There wouldn't have been another paid position available for Hertha.

Still, that Franck could offer such a glowing letter to a professional colleague speaks volumes about how much Hertha meant to him and shows he recognized that a woman scientist might require a more ringing endorsement than a man. Alas, no job materialized.

However, an invitation for Hertha to present a colloquium lecture in Groningen, Netherlands, soon materialized. Surely this would lead to an offer of a permanent job, Hertha hoped.

All of Hertha's free time was taken up by job-seeking. She was eyeing potential opportunities in Madrid, Spain, via Werner Heisenberg; in Oslo, Norway, via Victor Goldschmidt; and in Groningen, Netherlands.

Goldschmidt—considered the father of modern geochemistry—had been a professor at the University of Göttingen until he was forced to flee back to Norway in 1933 because of his Jewish heritage. While Hertha and Goldschmidt were not in the same department, they would certainly have crossed paths at Göttingen.

Hertha knew she had to stoke several fires at once because she was not sure which spark, if any, would ignite into a legitimate, paying job offer, preferably one that lasted longer than a few months. She reached out anywhere she had a connection: through a former student, a former colleague.

This shows once again how vital it was to develop a wide network of professional contacts, something far more difficult for women than for their male colleagues.

In addition to Franck, Charles W. Edwards, the chair of Duke University's physics department, was trying to secure a job for Hertha. Though she wasn't facing the same threat of physical danger as her Jewish colleagues, she was a Jewish sympathizer. In some cases, this could be nearly as dangerous, especially if it involved loudly speaking out against Nazi machinations or hiding Jewish people or aiding their escape.

Hertha wasn't independently wealthy, nor did she have a husband to provide for her. She needed a job to make a living, and the Nazis were making that virtually impossible for women academics.

Edwards had heard from a colleague at the Rockefeller Foundation that Hertha was looking for work abroad, and another Duke professor happened to have worked with Hertha when she was in California. He vouched for her ability to integrate into American labs with ease. Hertha was charming, intelligent, and spoke fluent English, they reported. It would be such a shame to see her brilliance wasted on anything less than a research professorship.

Duke was sure they'd be more than lucky to snap her up. Yet the US Emergency Committee in Aid of Displaced German Scholars declined to fund the position. Instead, Edwards began working with the Rockefeller Foundation to find money to pay for Hertha to teach for him. At the time, Duke was a new and well-endowed university, an institution vying to quickly build an international reputation.

"I am very much indebted to you for your efforts in securing an appointment for me at Duke University," Hertha wrote to Edwards. "An appointment at your University is quite tempting for me as you mention the possibility that it could become a permanent one."[105]

But not everyone in the US was excited to hear a woman might be offered a physics professorship. The president of Duke, William P. Few, received a scathing letter from Robert A. Millikan warning him against hiring women.

Millikan was a Nobel laureate in physics and president of Caltech. He backed up his warning with the anecdotal observation that "at least 95% of the ablest minds that are now going into physics are men."

It obviously never crossed Millikan's mind that rather than a reflection of women's abilities, this might be the result of women not being encouraged to enter the field, or welcomed or well-supported in it. He was sure the only possible interpretation was that women were simply bad at physics.

Women were capable of doing good work in biology, astronomy, and maybe chemistry, he conceded, but America had yet to produce a single outstanding woman physicist, Millikan insisted.

What's more, female faculty would negatively impact the prestige of the department, Millikan railed. They couldn't possibly attract high-quality students: "I should expect the more brilliant and able young men to be drawn into the graduate department by the character of the *men* on the staff, rather than the character of the women."

Finally, he resorted to rumor-mongering to try and scare Few off hiring Hertha, insinuating that she had gained more power in her lab than she deserved as a woman: "I have heard the report that the general feeling which I have expressed had appeared to some extent in Franck's Laboratory at Göttingen, Miss Sponer having got herself into a larger position of influence on the administrative side of the *research* laboratory than was best for its effectiveness."[106]

Hertha had no idea such a prominent physicist had taken so much interest in trying to keep her out of American academia. She had enough trouble with Pohl in Germany. At least if she did end up at Duke, Millikan would be far away in California.

At the moment, Hertha was just happy to have an old friend to talk to in person about her circumstances. She visited Lise in Berlin in January 1934, staying at Lise's apartment, as she often did. It was a lovely, if anxiety-laden, reunion discussing the sad state of affairs of their jobs, politics, and the deteriorating climate of the country in general.

They sat across from each other chatting, while Lise darned her stockings. By this point, Lise had been let go from her university teaching position but was still holding on to her role at the KWI.

"I'm more than sorry that Hertha is having such difficulty," Lise told Franck. "But how to help her?"[107]

From Berlin, Hertha telegrammed Franck to tell him she would accept a job at Duke if funding for the position came through. Franck relayed the message to Edwards. That funding was a big if. Hertha wasn't comfortable relying only on a "maybe" offer. How long would she have to wait to hear if Duke had funded the position? What would happen if they couldn't secure funding? She needed something definite.

In another long letter to Franck, she explained what it would take for her to be excited about working in America: the possibility to really do physics properly. She was worried this would not be the case.

Might she be asking too much? Many men scholars could be that choosy and get what they wanted. Were women not allowed such audacity? Should women be happy and grateful to get any job at all?

In the midst of all this was Hertha's ill-fated book project, which she still—still!—hadn't given up on yet. After the summer 1932 deadline came and went, she felt contrite enough to apologize to her publisher again but confident enough to articulate that she believed the manuscript was, in fact, nearing completion.

"I am, regrettably, still not done with my book," Hertha acknowledged. "I can see, however, that it is converging in finite time and the manuscript will be in your hands in the near future. Hopefully you are not losing patience with me."[108]

When an American physicist published *Spectroscopy of the Extreme Ultra-Violet*, Hertha worried her book would be redundant, but hoped it would be different enough to be useful. "My book is more directed towards non-spectroscopy readers," she told Franck. "What is really new in my book are the ultraviolet spectrums of the polyatomic molecules."[109]

19

Hedwig Finds Temporary Work

While Franck was helping Hertha find a job, Hedwig's former supervisor was making moves to see her gainfully employed as well. In 1934, Clemens Schaefer, who had taken over Lummer's position at the Breslau Physics Institute, secured a freelance contract for Hedwig at the OSRAM corporation's Research Society for Electric Lighting.

It was research Hedwig had published with Lummer back in 1915 on developing criteria for assessing candidate materials for light bulbs that established her as an important asset to the commercial lighting industry. Only public service jobs were officially affected by the civil service law; Jewish people could still hold positions in the private sector, at least for the time being.

Best of all, Hedwig wouldn't be required to move to Berlin; she could continue to work from the University of Breslau Physics Institute, conducting freelance research using equipment that OSRAM didn't possess. OSRAM's name was derived from two common lighting-filament elements, osmium and Wolfram (German for tungsten).

For OSRAM, Hedwig says she tackled problems in illumination engineering and "design, development, and testing in the field of spectrum analysis, photoelectric photometry, and physiological optics."

Hedwig was given a tiny back room at the institute. It was cramped and hard to locate, but that was part of the appeal. Hedwig didn't want to be too easily found by the Nazi delegations who occasionally stopped by the institute to parade their authority. Should the Nazis find her still working there, they could easily arrest her because she was not restricting her work to OSRAM-related duties.

As Schaefer had noted in his defense of her position, Hedwig's firing from the university was leaving a handful of students without a thesis advisor. Ever the dedicated educator, she felt she couldn't leave them in the lurch, so she chose to continue supervising three students even though she wasn't getting paid to do so. Even if it was potentially dangerous.

Happily, students and colleagues who needed to find her knew where to look. For a time, at least, Hedwig was relieved to find a solution that allowed her to remain part of the University of Breslau Physics Institute community.

The thought of leaving the city she'd grown up in, the university where she'd once been a student, then a lecturer, researcher, and mentor to the next generation of students—well, that was too much to bear. But she knew her options were becoming limited. In the back of her mind, she realized leaving home might be her only chance.

In 1935, another ray of hope shone in. The German Scientists Relief Fund awarded Hedwig a $300 grant to fund a three-month research sabbatical in Arosa, Switzerland, a renowned spa-town with ten mountain lakes. But Hedwig wasn't there for rest and relaxation. Given her circumstances, she likely found it difficult to relax at all.

Her time in Arosa would be spent at the Lichtklimatisches Observatorium (LKO). There was hope that this would translate into a permanent position out of Germany. Permanent job offers in foreign countries were hard to come by; few institutions wanted to hire scientists who weren't already well-known. Women like Hedwig had to rely on first completing an internship or fellowship, during which they could prove their aptitude and suitability for a more permanent role.

At the LKO, she measured the sun's ultraviolet light intensity, or the "spectral distribution of the intensity of sky radiation," using the observatory's ultraviolet spectrograph. The observatory had only been established in 1921, and its founder wanted the best spectrograph his funding could buy.

His meticulous specifications and continuous back-and-forth with the spectrograph manufacturer meant it took two and a half years to build the instrument, which boasted crossed prisms. It arrived at the observatory in 1928 and was presented at a conference the following year. Hedwig was surely excited to utilize this unique gadget.

As a precaution, the observatory's record of visiting scholars lists Hedwig only as "Dr. H.K." in case the Nazis' hounding decided to cross borders. Her planned research did not progress as far as expected, likely because Hedwig was quite preoccupied with finding a permanent position.

During this time in Arosa, her feelings alternated wildly, swinging between deep disappointment and unmitigated hope.

Unfortunately, her hopes were dashed when no job offer materialized. Hedwig, along with some photographic plates of her work, returned to Hitler's Germany, to hiding in her back room at the Breslau Physics Institute, working for OSRAM.

Even though she had an impressive research and teaching record, and many prominent people vouching for her, no American colleges had offered Hedwig a position in the years since Rudolf's appeal. No British schools came calling, either.

Her OSRAM contract was renewed every year until the spring of 1938, when Nazi rules made employing Jewish people impossible even for private enterprise. Out of a job yet again, Hedwig's fate looked grim. Without a way out of the country, her situation would remain bleak.

20

Not Even Switzerland Is Safe for Hildegard

Things in Switzerland were not going much better for Hildegard. When Hitler seized power in Germany, she had just returned to Switzerland after a year in America, where she learned all about its women's colleges and academic culture. Even though she no longer lived in Germany, the ripples of Nazism quickly reached her.

At first, Hildegard felt relieved to be out of the country, lucky to have a job as a university lecturer and research assistant since the situation for women academics in Germany had deteriorated so rapidly. But her luck didn't last long.

In early 1933, thousands of German refugees from the Nazis flooded Switzerland, so the nation decided to tighten its immigration laws. As a result, Hildegard's research assistantship at the University of Zürich was terminated that October.

Her lecturing position was also on the line. She begged the immigration police to be allowed to keep this job at the very least. Unfortunately, her boss didn't formally support her request, so it was rejected by the immigration authorities.

The president of the Swiss Association of University Women, chemist Jeanne Eder-Schwyzer, petitioned the university rector to intervene on Hildegard's behalf. The rector's support saw Hildegard's residency permit and lectureship extended until August 1934.

Knowing her time in Switzerland would soon be up—and not wanting to return to Germany in its current state of hostility to women academics—Hildegard, too, began frantically looking for a job even further afield. She applied for an American Association of University Women (AAUW) fellowship but was rejected.

Franck, as always, was eager to help when he heard about Hildegard's plight. He wrote to the International Federation of University Women (IFUW) in 1934 to inquire about possible fellowships for Hildegard.

After the IFUW's fellowship committee held its meeting, the organization's secretary informed Franck that out of the twenty-five candidates under consideration for the international fellowship for research scientists—"many of these candidates being of quite outstanding ability"—Hildegard was not among the three chosen for fellowships.

The secretary was happy to note that nonetheless, two of the three were "very distinguished German women—Dr. von Ubisch, a brilliant botanist, and Dr. Klieneberger, a bacteriologist, who is said to be doing quite admirable work here in London."

The secretary also pointed out that it could be due to the women's scientific specialties: "I am afraid the physicists are not having the Fellowship this time, but as they have had several of our Fellowships lately it is perhaps the turn of another science."[110]

This is yet another issue fleeing scholars often had to contend with—funding organizations who felt like it was only fair to

financially support a wide variety of disciplines and subspecial-
ties. They couldn't appear to favor one field over another. For
those applying for fellowships, it must have felt like spinning a
roulette wheel. Would it be their field's turn this time?

Hildegard applied to the US Emergency Committee in Aid
of Displaced German Scholars, but, like Hertha, she didn't win
their aid. There was incredible competition for this fund. Several
thousand scholars applied when there was only money to cover
a few hundred. Most candidates could only be aided financially
if they had already been offered a position in a new country.

It was there that Hildegard found herself lucky: she had previously established connections with American academics. Could
her old pal Emma Carr help her find a job in the US? Anything
was preferable to being sent back to Germany, where she'd likely
struggle to find work; the best she could hope for was a role as
a secondary school teacher.

21

Hope for Hertha

At the beginning of 1934, Hertha, meanwhile, still had no confirmation that any of her international job offers were real, meaning that there was funding for them to be actual paying positions. Hertha knew she was in trouble. But unfortunately, her trouble had just begun. Next, she learned she would not be allowed to keep lecturing through the end of term in October, as she was led to believe. Pohl wanted rid of her sooner; Hertha would be forced to step down in July. Losing several months off her original timeline significantly increased her anxiety.

Hertha and her helpers were now forced to speed up their efforts to find a guaranteed position and funds to get her out of Germany.

The German Scientists Relief Fund, created by Rudolf and other previously expelled academics who had landed in America, held aside a pot of funds for Hertha amounting to $737.50. They said if she didn't end up needing it, the money would go to Hedwig. It would take about a thousand more dollars, likely from several organizations, to come close to a year's salary.

Franck turned to the American Association of University Women (AAUW). Esther Brunauer, the director of the organization's International Relations Office, replied that they weren't sure they could raise the necessary funds, but they'd put Hertha's case before the Fellowship Committee of the International Federation of University Women (IFUW).

The IFUW, in turn, subsequently regretted that it had absolutely no funding left for grants and had already awarded all its fellowships. Between 1924 and 1939, the IFUW only awarded 120 fellowships.

It was clear that Esther was sympathetic to each case that came across her desk, that she saw the person behind each application, the lives hanging in the balance.

"I cannot begin to tell you how sorry Dr. McHale and I are," she concluded in her letter to Franck. "I know that if I had any money of my own I would be more than glad to use it for such a purpose."[111]

Hertha continued to tend her nest of potential jobs, which she referred to as unhatched chickens. "The whole thing is an exercise in patience,"[112] she complained to Franck.

"I'm already completely exhausted. It's absolutely incomprehensible to all of us what's actually going on," Hertha wrote on July 13, 1934. "It's like I'm jinxed. My mood can't be described anymore. This futile waiting is taxing my nerves."[113]

Luckily for Hertha's nerves, she didn't have to wait too much longer. "Alea iacta est!" (the die is cast) she wrote excitedly to Franck the following day. The Rockefeller Fund had come through. The Oslo job was a go. "I am very happy after having my morale barometer sink so low."[114]

As is always the case when sitting on two eggs, hoping one will hatch, both inevitably hatch at the same time. Just as Hertha heard about a job offer at the University of Oslo becoming more solid, the offer from Duke University also firmed up.

"Just a word to say that conditions are now quite favorable to securing an appointment here for you. I sincerely trust that this may reach you before you are definitely located elsewhere,"[115] Edwards wrote to Hertha from Duke University.

Ever the diplomatic people-pleaser, Hertha attempted to nurture both hatchlings; that is, she tried to take up both job offers. She told Edwards that she regretted that she had already accepted a post at the University of Oslo, Norway, while she was waiting to hear from him about the Duke position becoming a reality.

She hadn't thought that there was a real chance of Duke becoming a legitimate offer. However, the job in Oslo was temporary and began in September 1934. Might she be able to come to Duke next summer when that post was finished? Would Duke be willing to wait for her?

Also in the spring of 1934, Hertha turned in her book manuscript. Apart from a routine round or two of edits, this should have been the conclusion of the lengthy fiasco. Yet the debacle was far from over.

Unfortunately, the publisher found that the book had too much in common with another one they were about to publish in the same series. They asked Hertha to transform her manuscript into an appendix for that book. She would have to shorten it *significantly*.

Would they have done the same if she was a man? Hertha, to her credit, declined, but offered instead to publish her extensive data tables as a stand-alone volume. While this would be less work than editing down her entire book, it wasn't exactly nothing.

What's more, Springer was now only offering Hertha half the sales profits after the costs had been covered. It would take the sale of about 600 copies to cover production costs, meaning, in the end, it would be far too much work for far too little pay, Hertha concluded. (Her original contract said she would earn 150 marks per page, with a print run of 2,000 copies.)

So, in addition to finishing out her teaching duties, supervising doctoral students, and trying to find a new position before hers expired or she ran out of money, she was also fighting with her publisher and attempting to produce a product they both could agree was publishable.

The project continued to drag on, now nearly a decade after she'd signed her initial contract. Hertha wanted to be through with this book business before she was off to Oslo, but she wasn't sure she could manage that.

"I'm literally hovering over the stuff night and day. But I will take on any amount of work to have the story come to a happy end. At the moment, believing in that happy ending is a challenge,"[116] Hertha admitted to Franck.

"How I'll manage to pull up stakes here in five weeks' time, having delivered the book beforehand, is still a mystery to me."[117]

Hertha ended up having to cancel one of her final University of Göttingen classes in the summer term because only one student had registered. She wasn't exactly going out with a bang.

Low enrollment reflected the perilous political situation. Jewish students likely no longer felt welcome, even though they weren't officially expelled until several years later; all the Jewish mentors were gone, that was for sure. Might students also have been wary of a woman professor thanks to sexist Nazi rhetoric?

Yet it must've been a bit of a relief to have some more time on her hands to prepare to leave the country. Even though her Oslo job was temporary, Hertha was excited to have a confirmed position with a real start date in a new country. A confirmed plan of action was infinitely better than the utter agony of being stuck in waiting-and-wondering purgatory.

The only problem? She didn't speak Norwegian.

SECTION 2:
ESCAPE AND PHYSICS

22

Hertha's Sojourn in Norway

In September 1934, Hertha was feeling lucky to have gotten a new job outside of Germany. She was welcomed into Norway by Goldschmidt himself, her former colleague at the University of Göttingen, who picked her up and brought her to the Mission Hotel. He even took her to the rental agency to find some potential apartments to tour and to the bank to find out if her Rockefeller funds had arrived yet. It was nice to have someone she already knew help her establish herself, but still, she was homesick and desperately lonely.

"Because of all the work and anxiety, I'm not even getting around to bawling my eyes out,"[118] Hertha told Franck. "The old institute is really very bad. The library is crummy too. I will think back often to the good library in Göttingen."

But her missives weren't all complaints. She was excited to report she had already picked up about forty words in Norwegian, and the fresh seafood was glorious: "I'm especially taken with the bowl of lobster and delicious jumbo shrimp. If I weren't so concerned about my slender waist, I'd eat so much more."[119]

The weather ranged from "dazzlingly beautiful" to "cloudy, wet, cold, foggy—occurrences that can happen individually or—and this is the case quite often—unfortunately, all at once."[120]

Hertha's typically bottomless well of persistence and fortitude was really drying up now. She increasingly turned to her old friends. Between August and December of that year, she wrote to Franck about twenty times.

"It's just horrible that you are so far away. I continuously have something I need to ask you."[121]

"Despite the fact that everyone is very nice here," Hertha confided in Franck, "I miss my old friends, and you most of all."[122]

To Lise, she described her loneliness, the difficulty of adjusting to a new country, and her eagerness to move into a place of her own.

"One first has to get used to all of the new and strange things which is not so easy since I am all alone here and without my former friends," Hertha confided in Lise. "Even the best food cannot make up for the fact that I am missing my books."[123]

Hertha was upset that the construction of the new physics institute was running behind schedule. It was supposed to be ready by September, but now Hertha feared it wouldn't be done until January. She chose to see it as a blessing that the new institute was not ready yet, because it meant she had time to work on edits for her book.

Yes, the book project had followed her to Norway. Because printing had been postponed for so long, new findings now had to be incorporated into the text. What a beast it had become.

Even though the new Oslo Physics Institute eventually shaped up to be a beautiful, spacious building, lots of items were still missing, so several of the experiments Hertha had planned would have to be put on the back burner. "I knew that we were spoiled in Göttingen with the marvelously equipped institute we had there,"[124] Hertha told Lise.

In addition, her three rooms at the institute—lab, study, and office for meeting with students—were all on different floors, not adjacent as she had been promised.

This is an interesting perspective: universities, research institutes, and commercial enterprises were all very loud about their reticence to hire scholars sight unseen, but what about the other side of the coin?

Academics were being hired at institutes whose premises they'd never toured, whose teams they'd never met. For academics attempting to escape the dangers of Hitler's Germany, a job offer was the sole lifeline saving them from financial ruin— or worse. If they found their new professional situations less than favorable, there was little recourse.

To add to Hertha's anxiety, multiple Norwegian newspapers ran a story about the country's new female physics professor— why, she'd come all the way from Germany! While such recognition should have been a moment of excitement, Hertha knew it would unintentionally put a target on her back.

Hertha was a suspected Jewish sympathizer, the former protégé of a well-known Jewish scientist. And now she had gone and proved her disloyalty to Germany by not only leaving the country but by taking a scientific job abroad. Her research was now in service of another nation.

The Nazis would be excited to attempt to thwart her career, ruin her reputation, or even harm her if possible. Hertha was besieged by a flood of requests for interviews and photos. She turned down every single one.

The press coverage also attracted the attention of the Anti-Fascist League, who implored Hertha to come to Geneva as a delegate and give a speech. But she just couldn't risk public condemnation of the Nazis at this point. Her fears of potential retribution were warranted.

A call came from a German woman to alert her that this press coverage had not gone unnoticed by the Nazis. They were looking into her case and now considered her hostile to Germany. She explained to the woman that she had no foreknowledge of the article or its contents, but that didn't matter.

Germany's Foreign Office tasked its diplomats with monitoring the activities of German citizens who left the country, and they could easily invalidate Hertha's passport if they wanted to, leaving her stuck in Norway.

She had no plans to stay in Norway any longer than she had to. In fact, she was currently preparing a series of ten different lectures she'd been contracted to present in Madrid, Spain.

She wrote the lectures in German, then sent each to her sister Margot back in Berlin. Margot, who was a languages scholar, would translate the lectures into Spanish. Then Hertha would correct any mistakes Margot had inadvertently introduced into the physics.

Hertha's spirits were raised by a telegram from Duke University. Her wait for their acceptance of her delayed start was finally over. Duke would be happy to have her come for a trial one-year professorship with an annual salary of $3,000. She could begin on February 1, 1936.

Hertha recognized her incredible good fortune to have two job offers: "Others are looking frantically for job openings while I, for the moment, enjoy an embarrassment of riches."[125]

Franck was also making career moves, enjoying offers of riches of his own. In January 1935, he left Bohr's lab in Denmark to accept a position at Johns Hopkins University in Baltimore, Maryland.

Hertha visited the Franck family in Copenhagen that Easter before they left the continent, and Franck stopped in Oslo to bid Hertha farewell before he was off for the United States that summer. Franck's salary at Hopkins? $6,000. Double what Hertha was offered by Duke.

Hertha still harbored reservations about leaving Europe. "In principle, I dread the prospect of America," Hertha admitted. "I wonder if the Duke people aren't somehow hoping that, once I've arrived, I'll be a source of cheap labor for them, and they will try to take advantage of me."

Was offering her half the salary of a man taking advantage? It is difficult to say, but worth noting that Franck was also further along in his career.

Still, the fact that Franck would be in America as well likely helped Hertha feel more comfortable moving there herself. Hertha was also excited to hear that she'd already been assigned a PhD student to supervise at Duke—and she was a woman.

23

Space for the Displaced

It was incredibly difficult for many displaced scholars and other refugees to find people willing to help them abroad because many did not comprehend the severity of the situation. The international community largely believed German refugees needed jobs and freedom from oppression, not an escape from imminent death. And it's true that early on, the Nazi government encouraged Jewish people and political opponents to leave the country. It was only later that they began rounding up and murdering Jewish civilians.

In the wake of the 1933 civil service law, approximately 38,000 Jewish people fled Germany, mostly settling in other European countries. It wasn't an immediate flood so much as an ever-increasing trickle over several months.

Many of these people were later caught in the Nazis' web again as Hitler's fury spread to consume neighboring countries.

As the Nazis' reign of terror spread, the need to whisk refugees out of harm's way went from pressing to urgent to a humanitarian emergency. While masses of people successfully immigrated out of Germany, not everyone was saved.

Throughout the Nazis' increasingly deadly rampage, thousands of people applied to enter safer countries, only to be met with full quotas, more anti-Semitism, and constantly shifting immigration laws. More often than not, if you couldn't organize an international job offer fast enough, you were out of luck.

As has always been the case, there were more refugees than there were visas, and governments prioritized the highly educated as more "valuable" potential citizens. In the wake of World War I and the Spanish flu pandemic, America tightened its immigration policy, and in 1921 an immigrant quota system was implemented.

Only a small number of people were now allowed to enter the US from each country every month, totaling no more than 350,000 in a year. Those quotas were further tightened a few years later, shrinking the total number to 164,667 and barring anyone of Asian descent. In 1929, that number was again whittled down, to 153,879.

America's nationality quotas were derived from complicated calculations based on the number of people of that nationality who already resided in the US as of the 1920 census.

The 1929 recalculations saw the immigration cap of UK citizens rise from 34,007 to 65,721, while the German cap was slashed in half: from 51,227 to 25,957. (At the time, there was no category of "refugee" in America.)

Though the country had always tried to weed out "undesirable" immigrants who would be a drain on public resources, the Great Depression saw President Herbert Hoover decree that immigration applications should be rejected if the person didn't have a way to cover their cost of living.

The rise of the Nazis unfortunately coincided with America's financial troubles. Budget cuts saw colleges and universities firing professors and staff in droves. If there wasn't money for their citizens to stay employed, how were they supposed to offer jobs to foreigners?

Throughout the refugee crisis, the US government seemed to make immigration harder rather than easier. It was not until 1948 that Congress passed the first specific refugee act: the Displaced Persons Act was created to assist the seven million Europeans displaced by World War II.

Another impediment to immigration was that gathering the necessary papers for a visa application could alert the German government to your intentions to flee. Authorities could delay your paperwork requests or deny them entirely.

Funding was the biggest hurdle. In 1933, only 1,241 Germans were granted visas to enter the US, but that was not because few were applying: 82,787 remained on the waiting list since they lacked the funds to qualify.

Where governments failed, nongovernmental organizations tried to pick up the slack. In most cases, securing a foreign visa first required you to secure a job or proof of independent funding. Financial affidavits for visas were largely procured via international emergency aid or education organizations, but proof of a job offer was most likely to garner a visa.

Unfortunately, securing a job offer was even more difficult than securing a visa. Quite the catch-22. Asking a college to hire you sight unseen was a big ask, especially when there was already a shortage of jobs.

Nonprofit aid organizations began springing up for the sole cause of helping people displaced by the Nazis, resulting in a veritable smorgasbord of acronyms.

The lengthily named National Coordinating Committee for Aid to Refugees and Emigrants Coming from Germany (NCC) was created to centralize the relief work of America's private refugee agencies. It was established and largely funded by the American Jewish Joint Distribution Committee (JDC) (an organization itself created to coordinate aid to Jewish people during World War I). The NCC later became the more concise National Refugee Service (NRS).

Several relief organizations arose with the specific cause of helping scholars and other professionals escape Nazi oppression, meaning they received more help than most other groups of displaced Jewish people. Whether intentionally or not, prioritizing aid for scholars reinforced the ableist view that smart people are more valuable and more important to save.

Scholars were considered easier to get out of the country because they were educated and could find jobs, lessening the likelihood of them being financially dependent on the state. Still, their escape was in no way guaranteed, nor was the process simple or short.

When the Nazis created displaced scholars, the Rockefeller Foundation broadened its scope from funding international travel stipends by establishing the Special Research Aid Fund for Deposed Scholars. The fund offered to cover about half the salary if institutions in Europe and the US would employ scholars who had been fired.

The US Institute for International Education established the Emergency Committee in Aid of Displaced German Scholars. As the Nazis spread across Europe, the geographical scope of the Emergency Committee widened along with it, and its name changed to the Emergency Committee in Aid of Displaced Foreign Scholars.

In the UK, the Academic Assistance Council (AAC) was formed, and later was consolidated and renamed the Society for the Protection of Science and Learning (SPSL).

These organizations did what they could to scrape together funds for travel out of Germany or a few months of living expenses and connect displaced scholars with international jobs. Other organizations preferred to assist those who had already been offered a position in a new nation.

The US Emergency Committee, for example, asserted it only assisted in cases where a scholar had already received an offer of employment from an educational institution. This may seem like after-the-fact assistance, but it was structured as such because visas were much more likely to be approved alongside proof of long-term financial stability post-immigration.

In most cases, the Emergency Committee and the Rockefeller Foundation each paid half of a displaced scholar's salary at their new job. There was significant overlap in the 300-some scholars each organization is said to have funded.

These funding bodies largely assessed candidates solely on professional merit, not on financial need. Since women academics had been held back professionally by sexism and gender-based restrictions on advancement, on paper, they appeared to be less-deserving candidates: Less experienced, less senior.

The case of Leonore Brecher, a zoologist who specialized in butterflies, is a perfect illustration of the huge barrier merit-based assessment represented. After being fired from her research position for being Jewish, she reached out to Emergency Committee board member Leslie Dunn for help in finding a job in America, preferably in his Columbia University lab. It was an audacious ask, but why not go for it? It was a matter of life and death, after all.

The Emergency Committee could not help her, Dunn explained, since she had not already procured a US job offer, and so far, only older, more established (and more male) émigré scientists had been successful in getting those. The chances of foreigners finding employment in America "are extremely bad just now," he told Brecher in December 1933.[126]

But Brecher's problems, like those of many Jewish Europeans, were just beginning. She continued pushing Dunn for help.

"I am not very hopeful," he finally responded the following May.[127]

Colleges and universities were looking for Goldilocks: scholars who were established, but not too old. With plenty of work years ahead of them, but not too inexperienced. Eminence mattered more than potential.

There's a reason why so many of the displaced scientists who fled to safety are now household names synonymous with genius: Albert Einstein, Erwin Schrödinger, Enrico Fermi. They were already famous. At the time of their immigration, they were already Nobel laureates.

Of course, male scholars continued to be preferred over women; some colleges even issued blanket refusals to hire women. "There are not many places in the country where a woman scholar could hope to get placed,"[128] a Yale University professor wrote around 1936. Yale accepted women students and research assistants, but would not employ them as professors.

Employers in many fields remained reluctant to hire women throughout the 1930s and '40s, their facilities entirely ill-equipped to handle another gender. Women were still the last resort, to be employed only when there were no male candidates available.

Some companies thought women workers were okay, so long as they weren't foreign ones. Imperial Chemical Industries, the UK's biggest chemical manufacturer at the time, placed job ads for "women chemists of British nationality." So even if a company was open to hiring women scientists, the chance of a displaced foreign woman being hired was slim to none.

Organizations established specifically for women academics understood better than most that women faced steeper odds when it came to securing jobs abroad, especially Jewish women. These groups acted immediately to assist women fleeing the Nazis.

The American Association of University Women (AAUW), along with the International Federation of University Women (IFUW) and its British arm, the British Federation of University Women (BFUW), remained quite active during the Nazi era. Their collective work saved the lives of many women scholars.

In May 1938, the London-based BFUW put forty-one-year-old Austrian Dr. Erna Hollitscher in charge of a new committee that would oversee refugee assistance. Erna was new in town, having just escaped to England after Germany annexed Austria. She held a degree in languages from the University of Vienna. As a Jewish refugee herself, Erna brought a level of compassion and understanding to her role that few others could.

Erna, or Holly as she came to be known, quickly became the soul of the federation's refugee assistance efforts. She would help save hundreds of lives across Europe. Had the federation more funding—and the British less anti-immigrant sentiment—she could have saved many more.

At every refugee scholar assistance organization, each scholar's case had to be considered on an individual basis. It wasn't enough just to be in peril. Refugees had to prove they could bring something valuable to the table in order for a government or relief organization to warrant funding their immigration.

In the US, the only saving grace for many academics appeared to be the provision for non-quota visas. It allowed relatives of US citizens, but also professors and clergy (and their wives and minor children), to immigrate to America outside of the quota caps. "Wives," mind you, not husbands.

But it was more hype than hope for most scholars. Applications from professional scholars weren't approved very often. Non-quota visas were largely issued to relatives of American citizens because they didn't have to prove their own financial stability, just that of those they were related to.

The number of scholars receiving non-quota visas was small, likely because there were so many hoops to jump through. As if it wasn't hard enough to qualify for a regular visa, applicants for non-quota visas were required to submit financial affidavits as well as several declarations of their moral fortitude written by impartial authorities.

There were other qualifications as well. They had to have been working in their profession for the previous two years and plan to continue in that career in America. Scholars also had to be connected to a higher education institution, which meant independent intellectuals were out of luck. As were prep school teachers, and even seminary faculty (though clergy were welcome). Being a librarian or researcher at a university wasn't enough; you needed to be a professor.

In addition, the immigration authorities in their home countries were allowed to approve or reject their applications. The State Department would then do its due diligence of checking up on the applicant's background, references, and professional qualifications. Many higher-ups in charge of creating rules around immigration also believed that most Jewish professors were dangerous socialists.

Americans, Brits, Scandinavians, and plenty of others could be as prejudiced and suspicious as Nazis. They just typically were not as violent about it. A climate of xenophobia and fears of espionage fueled America's resistance to foreign scholars. They would take university jobs from Americans, indoctrinate our youth! Why, they might be spies! These fears eventually gave rise to further visa application restrictions.

As the Nazis' territory and violence grew, refugee numbers jumped. President Franklin D. Roosevelt, who took office in 1933, combined the German and Austrian visa allowance when the Nazis annexed the nation in 1938. Yet of the 27,370 visas now available, only 19,552 were issued in 1938.

In the summer of 1938, President Roosevelt had called an emergency meeting of nations to discuss the growing refugee crisis. The meeting did little to ameliorate the situation since hardly any of the thirty-two participating nations agreed to allow more immigrants.

With America's immigrant quotas unchanged, visa applicants from Germany or Austria could expect, at minimum, a nine-year wait.

On November 9 and 10, 1938, the Nazis perpetrated an organized pogrom against the Jews, destroying 250 synagogues,

wrecking 7,000 Jewish businesses, and dragging 30,000 Jewish men to concentration camps. This Kristallnacht, or Night
of Broken Glass, was the first time the Nazis arrested Jewish
people en masse simply for being Jewish.

America was shocked by the Kristallnacht, but not enough
to offer refuge to those who desperately needed it. Roosevelt's
only concession was to allow the 12,000 Germans who had already entered the US to stay indefinitely. The visa waiting list
of people urgently seeking to flee to America bloated to nearly
140,000 people. It was now several years long.

But Jewish refugees didn't have that kind of time. Refugees
seeking solace elsewhere in Europe, beyond current Nazi reach,
also increased after 1938. They were now desperate for any way
out they could find.

"At the outset most of them were political refugees opposed to
the Nazi regime and trying to escape. [Their] number was rather
small... But after the anti-Semitic trend of the German government, now whole families arrived,"[129] noted an anonymous report
on German immigration to Belgium between 1933 and 1938.

The New School received Rockefeller funding to open University in Exile to create jobs that would garner more visas for
refugee academics. (By 1934, its rescued scholars became known
simply as graduate faculty of political and social science.)

Still, in late 1938, this project also felt the crunch of an influx
of applications. The New School president worried that thousands of refugee scholars were vying for "the ten jobs that are
likely to turn up."[130]

While America had plenty of colleges and universities, and
took in many more refugee scholars than other nations, it could
never hope to accommodate all of the job requests it was receiving. For most of the hopeful displaced academics, university
positions in America never materialized.

24

Hildegard Heads to Massachusetts

The clock was ticking on Hildegard's Swiss visa expiration. Without a solid job offer elsewhere, she would be deported back to Germany, where jobs for women academics were essentially nonexistent. So far, all of Hildegard's fellowship and funding applications had been rejected.

It was her old friend Emma Carr at Mount Holyoke College in Massachusetts who came through in the end. Emma arranged a job offer for Hildegard at her school as a "research instructor" in the chemistry department, beginning in the fall of 1934.

Based on this offer, Hildegard was allowed to emigrate to the United States. Technically, she would be considered on a "leave of absence" from the University of Zürich.

Hildegard sailed on the *SS Albert Ballin* from Hamburg to New York on September 13, 1934. On the ship's manifest, Hildegard's occupation is typed out as "lecturer," but has been crossed out by hand, and "professor" written in its place. Thus, with a slapdash correction, she became the first German woman physics professor exiled to the United States during the Nazi era.

On the ship, Hildegard bumped into her former classmate Melitta Gerhard, who was fleeing the Nazis; she was fired from her German studies lectureship for being Jewish. Gerhard was on her way to another women's college in Massachusetts, Wellesley, on a one-year visiting professorship.

Emma, along with Jeanne Eder-Schwyzer, the president of the Swiss Association of University Women, recommended Hildegard for a National Research Council Rockefeller Fund scholarship to help fund the position.

Their pleading finally paid off when the Rockefeller Foundation produced two grants, for two years each beginning in 1935, for Hildegard to continue in her job at Mount Holyoke.

At the time, a Rockefeller grant was a rare award, one she could be proud of. The Rockefeller Foundation would contribute $925 toward her salary and the college $575. Much of the money from the college was coming from Emma's own pockets.

A salary of $1,500 was on the low side for a research professor of Hildegard's stature—it was half of what Hertha was offered at Duke and a quarter of what Franck was making at Johns Hopkins—but it wasn't entirely unreasonable.

A survey of 25,530 faculty members at 252 colleges and universities across America for the 1935–1936 school year found that depending on the size of the college and the faculty rank, of course, salaries ranged anywhere from $1,000 to more than $7,000, with the median salary of a full-time professor being about $3,600 for a nine-month contract.[131]

Hildegard fit right in at Mount Holyoke. She was incredibly lucky to have a preexisting relationship with an American college that could translate into a job offer. It meant she was familiar with the school and its employees since she'd been a guest scholar there before.

While acclimating to living in a new country may have been

a bit overwhelming, Hildegard at least had experienced this before when she went from Germany to Switzerland. Still, this
was a much bigger leap.

It was surely exhilarating to be surrounded by not only women
but fellow women academics who had similarly dedicated their
lives to scholarship, to becoming experts in disciplines of their
choosing. And while they were siloed away at a women-only
college, it was a sort of educational and professional freedom
women in Germany had been fighting hard to achieve.

A single, forty-three-year-old lifelong scholar, Hildegard was
quite fashionable, often wearing long skirts, a cardigan with big
square buttons, crisp white gloves, and a tightly woven straw
cloche hat with a short brim and pretty ribbon around it and
a flower on the side. It perfectly accented her dark blond hair
and kind blue eyes.

PHOTOGRAPH BY SAMUEL GOUDSMIT, COURTESY
OF AIP EMILIO SEGRÈ VISUAL ARCHIVES, GOUDSMIT
COLLECTION.

Hildegard Stücklen walks down stairs.

Hildegard lived in the modest faculty housing, known as
Dickinson House. It was quite the multidisciplinary dormitory,
housing professors of English, French, physiology, Greek and

Latin, history, archeology, political science, botany, and geology, and even a librarian.

Even though the college was small, the chemistry department was a close-knit group of colleagues with a well-appointed lab. In 1930, Emma had received a $1,500 National Research Council (NRC) grant—which Mount Holyoke matched—to have a new vacuum spectrograph specially constructed. For its dispersive element, the instrument had the highest-quality fluorite prism of any spectrograph yet created.

In their lab, Emma, along with Mary Sherrill and later Lucy Pickett, used this spectrograph to investigate the far ultraviolet region of the spectrum. They'd received the NRC grant because they proved their research included an investigation of biologically important fundamental organic compounds.

"We have been working in a group, with Prof. Carr as physico-chemist, Prof. M. Sherrill as organic chemist and myself as physicist and have studied chemical and spectroscopic properties of organic compounds,"[132] Hildegard reported.

"The work is not precisely exciting, but it will accomplish an important job," Emma noted.[133]

Emma and Hildegard were a professional match made in heaven. The duo published seven joint papers on ultraviolet absorption spectra of hydrocarbons. They even presented their findings at the American Chemical Society's molecular structure symposium at Princeton University in December 1936 and at the spectroscopy symposium at the Massachusetts Institute of Technology.

Hildegard and Emma's MIT presentation was deemed noteworthy enough to mention in the *Science-Supplement*. The report explained that using a spectroscope to determine the molecular makeup of simple hydrocarbons and see how they changed during photochemical decomposition would provide crucial information. It noted that their research "promises ultimately to lead to a better understanding of the energy relationships involved in a carbon–carbon double bond, a problem with significant biological implications."[134]

Understanding the mechanisms behind carbon bonding is vital to illuminating the structure and function of molecules in living organisms. It can help researchers predict and alter molecules' behavior, which can in turn guide them to discoveries and advancements in medicine and materials science.

"Working with Miss Carr was very stimulating," Hildegard said. "And the scientific climate at the institute was extremely pleasant. I really like Miss Carr and can see that our Spectroscopy Department has really made progress."[135]

Students played an active role in the research. Emma explained why their master's program was so unique among small women's colleges when it was instituted.

"The graduate work for the M.A. degree was introduced in 1910," Emma noted. "It was something of an experiment for an undergraduate college at that time but has become a very general practice and we count it one of our most successful ventures."[136]

By 1937, forty-four master's degrees in chemistry had been awarded at Mount Holyoke. In addition to establishing a research tradition for students at all levels, Emma set the precedent for having a lab director who was responsible for maintaining stock of all the lab supplies.

This freed up time for the rest of the faculty, which they could instead dedicate to research. Emma was the first person awarded the American Chemical Society's Garvan Award for women chemists in 1937.

That year, Emma again approached the Rockefeller Foundation for help in boosting Hildegard's salary to a more sustainable level. She was worried Hildegard might begin to look elsewhere for a more lucrative position.

"For the last two years Dr. Stücklen's total salary has been $1,500, a stipend much too small for a person of her distinction in her field and I hope very much this can be increased to

$1,800," Emma told the foundation. "The productivity of the group is just now at its height; if we were to lose Dr. Stücklen now, it would be a matter of some five years before a group could be re-built to the same degree of effective work together which we now have."[137]

She wanted $1,300 from the organization to fund her research duties to add to the $500 stipend the school would furnish for her teaching duties. When word came through about the approval of the grant, the chemistry department erupted in rejoicing.

"I can't stop to be but all day long, happy, happy, happy,"[138] Hildegard chirped to Emma.

Hildegard's extended leave of absence from Zürich ended up lasting for six years when, in the summer of 1939, Hildegard was considered to have vacated her position.

25

Lise Loses Her Life's Work

Lise spent the first few years of Hitler's dictatorship in a sort of wishful denial. She saw what was happening and feared the worst, but didn't want to believe it would ever get as bad as it did.

Lise had built a life she loved that had everything she needed: a perfectly appointed lab, stimulating colleagues, close friends, thought-provoking students, and edifying research. Lise had meticulously cultivated this life in Berlin over three decades; now she was fully entrenched. The thought of being torn away from it all was more than she could bear.

She also didn't want to undertake the hefty task of immigrating to a different country yet again at her age. The year Hitler took power, Lise turned fifty-five. It was difficult enough to move from Austria to Germany when she was young and full of energy. Why would she want to go through the work of establishing herself again?

"I built it from its very first little stone; it was, so to speak,

my life's work, and it seemed so terribly hard to separate myself from it,"[139] Lise confided in an old friend about her department at the KWI.

Lise was able to hold on to her other job as head of the physics department at the KWI-C much longer than her university
position because the institute was a public–industry partnership
and therefore not entirely state-controlled, and because she was
an Austrian citizen, not German. She was also assured her service during World War I would protect her. But all these promises of protection eventually evaporated.

German science journals had stopped accepting the work of
Jewish scholars. The only journal that continued to accept Jewish scholarship was the multidisciplinary natural sciences journal
Naturwissenschaften (*The Science of Nature*), which was Springer's
flagship science offering, and that was only because its editor
was Jewish.

From 1933 to 1935, this was the only publication in which
Lise's work appeared. When prejudiced scholars began boycot-
ting the publication for printing Jewish work, the editor was
fired.

Once they had established a stranglehold on Germany, the
Nazis took their show on the road, slowly spreading across Europe. Hitler's first international target was incredibly troubling
for Lise.

*March 12, 1938: The German Anschluss, or annexation, of
Austria*

Austria largely welcomed the Nazis and their anti-Semitism.
Three days later, as celebrations of the annexation wound down
in Vienna, people began dragging Jewish citizens from their
houses: beating them, stealing from them, in some cases even
killing them. It was a truly shocking display of inhumanity.

When Hitler annexed Austria, Lise lost her Austrian citizenship. In addition, the KWI-C was reorganized to become fully under the government's control. Her only forms of protection for the past five years had disappeared. Would this mean she would lose her position? Would she even be in danger of physical harm? This was when the other shoe finally dropped for Lise. She quickly realized it wasn't just her job that was in peril.

The Anschluss provided a useful opening for Kurt Hess—Lise's Nazi neighbor and colleague—to make his move against Lise. "The Jewess endangers the institute,"[140] Hess insisted the day after Austria's annexation, newly emboldened to speak up as Lise was officially no longer considered an Austrian citizen.

One of Lise's former students informed Otto about Hess's threats and noted that Lise's case had been taken up by the head of Hitler's Reich Research Council. When Otto told Lise, it only heightened her already high anxiety.

The Reich Research Council was created in May 1937 to centralize the oversight of all scientific research in Germany. Science would now only be in service of the state.

Six days after the Anschluss, Otto went to find out if Lise was at risk of imminent firing. He met with the treasurer of the KWI-C's main funder, Nazi *Wehrwirtschaftsführer* Heinrich Hörlein, to discuss Lise's position. *Wehrwirtschaftsführers* were Nazi-appointed liaisons of sorts who worked in positions of power at companies or institutions deemed important to the production of war materials.

The meeting was a mistake. Hörlein demanded Lise leave the KWI at once.

"Hahn says I must not come to the institute anymore," Lise noted in her diary. She was hurt that he had not stood up for her after her decades of work. "He has, in essence, thrown me out." Worse, this told Lise he was ready and willing to throw her under the bus in order to save his institute.

When Otto confided in her that Hörlein claimed the Nazis had horrible things planned for the Jewish population, it sent a chill down Lise's spine. On top of her fear at what terror lay ahead, she was livid that Otto continued to consider Hörlein a "very decent person." If Otto was truly her friend, how could he not feel anything but revulsion toward him?

Otto realized his attempt to head off trouble had backfired spectacularly, but how to help without provoking the ire of the government? "Lise was very unhappy and angry with me that now I too had left her in the lurch," Otto recalled.[141]

Hörlein soon had a change of heart. He contacted them to say he had decided she could stay after all. It was important that Lise knew who held the power here, that she understood she could be fired on a whim for no good reason. It was a relief that Lise could stay at the KWI, but this interaction likely left her decidedly ill at ease.

If she was going to be fired for certain, she wanted to know sooner rather than later. There would be much to do: finding a new position, securing travel visas and transportation tickets, and sorting out her banking and housing situations. Lise hoped above anything to hold on to her current position. It held everything she could want as a scientist.

The KWI's general director (a devoted Nazi staunchly opposed to working women) assured her that the KWI's new president, chemist, and Nobel laureate, Carl Bosch, was adamant that she should retain her position. This did little to assuage her fears since she knew Bosch only held so much power. The government and its rabid police force always had the last word.

She was right to remain concerned. Within a few weeks of Otto's meeting with Hörlein, the Reich Ministry of Education began looking more closely into Lise's case.

Had Otto not raised the question of her continued employment with the higher-ups, Lise's life might have taken an entirely different path. She might have been able to continue flying under the radar at the KWI for longer.

Or maybe Hess's rabble-rousing would have ultimately been

her undoing. Whatever their intentions, the actions of friends and foes alike all seemed to work against her.

The wheels had been put in motion. Merely by coming to the attention of the Ministry of Education, Lise's situation became dire.

She would certainly be fired and possibly deported to a ghetto or death camp since the ministry loved to make examples of the more well-known Jewish scholars and scientists. They were livid that Einstein resigned before they could fire him. He made them realize they would have to act preemptively to prevent another such embarrassment.

Lise finally realized she needed an escape route. Her old friend Niels Bohr, the famous Danish physicist, invited Lise to present a seminar at his institute in Copenhagen. Bohr was an eminent figure in the international scientific community. His assistance shows how respected and valued Lise and her work was.

His letter was carefully worded so as to not only give Lise some hope, but to provide her with written proof of a legitimate professional reason to leave Germany. He asked Lise to come deliver a seminar to the local Physical Society and Chemistry Association on her investigations into the artificially induced radioactive families of radioactive elements.

Bohr also offered a reassurance that they would pick up the tab. "The Physical Society and the Chemistry Association will cover all your travel expenses, and you would give my wife and me special pleasure if you would live with us during your stay in Copenhagen."[142]

Lise also reached out to Franck, who was now securely ensconced in a new job in America. Franck, terrified for his dear Lise, frantically offered her all he could think of: he used his job to vouch his financial support of Lise to the American Consulate in Germany should Lise need to escape stateside.

(This is unlike when Hertha was looking for a position, as he had yet to be hired by Johns Hopkins and could not guarantee financial responsibility for her.)

Franck knew by then that to the US government, money talked: "This is to certify that I, James Franck, propose to give every support to Prof. Dr. Lise Meitner in case she emigrates to the United States," and will ensure she never becomes a public charge in the United States.[143]

He explained that while he was currently employed by Johns Hopkins University with a salary of $6,000 a year, he had just accepted an offer from the University of Chicago. The position would begin that October, and his salary would rise to $10,000 a year. He also described his current life insurance policy holdings, which totaled $24,500. He included policy numbers and had the letter certified by a notary public.

The earliest academics to make it out of Germany did what they could with their prestige and security to assist others. By this point in time, Franck had already helped Lise's nephew, physicist Otto Robert Frisch.

Otto Robert's boss, Jewish Nobel laureate Otto Stern, had resigned in protest of the mass firing of Jewish people, then landed a cushy position in Pittsburgh. But Otto Robert, like so many others, couldn't find a new job without the help of more prominent scholars.

Franck looked to their Dutch friend, Dirk Coster, to see if there might be a place for Otto Robert in his University of Groningen lab. Lise had met Coster during her visit to Sweden when he was a student at Lund University working in Manne Siegbahn's spectroscopy lab.

Coster had quickly gone on to great things; by analyzing zirconium ore using X-ray spectroscopy, he discovered the element hafnium in 1923. While Otto Robert didn't land with Coster, he eventually found a place in London and then joined Niels Bohr's Copenhagen lab just as Franck was leaving it.

Franck was one of the best allies a refugee scientist could

have. Not only because he was a loyal, dedicated friend with a large, deeply empathetic heart, but also because he was a well-known scientist and scholar, now with a hefty salary to match.

He was earning a lot more than other, less famous academics who had fled Nazi territories for America. Many were lucky to get $1,000 to $3,000 per year (which makes their donations to relief funds even more impressive).

Lise preferred to consider moving to America only as a last resort. It seemed so dreadfully far from home. Still, Franck knew plenty of people who were finding themselves turning to their last resort lately.

Even if she'd wanted to go to the US, it was beginning to have its fill of refugees from Germany; waiting lists for entry were bloating far beyond capacity.

A request for Lise to present lectures came from Caltech and the University of California, Berkeley. These might have been enough to get a temporary travel visa to enter the US, but likely not much more.

Other professional acquaintances tried to get her a position in England, which she would have preferred given her many friends and family members there.

The chair of physics at King's College London wrote a glowing recommendation that made its way to the director of Oxford's experimental physics lab, asserting that Lise was "the most distinguished woman scientist to-day. But owing to her having a Jew somewhere in the background she seems to be in danger of losing her post. She has a really magnificent record of work."[144]

But Oxford's head physics professor was militantly misogynist (as well as a eugenicist who despised poor people, Black people, the mentally disabled, and non-heterosexuals). He had no interest in having a female professor on his campus, let alone in his lab.

Girton College—the women's college at the University of Cambridge—was poised to offer Lise a one-year position with room, board, and a small stipend. While it was not the permanent position she would have expected as the tenured professor she was, it was something.

Lise's interest was piqued since Cambridge was home to a world-renowned physics lab, but she was miffed as to why she should be confined to the women's college.

She decided that if she must be forced to leave Germany, Bohr's lab would be the best place to land, at least temporarily. Her nephew was already there, and moving to an institute where she knew people would be very nice.

But as plans for her departure progressed, she was informed by the Danish consulate that they no longer recognized her Austrian passport. Not even a carefully contrived letter from Bohr could get her out of this.

Doors kept cracking open, only to shut again. "Promises are of no use; they are not kept. Possibilities narrowing," Lise wrote ominously in her diary on April 22, 1938.

It was all becoming too much—trying to calmly complete her work every day while quietly panicking as every escape avenue invariably led to a dead end.

She was constantly wondering which way to turn next, calculating who she could trust—and who she couldn't. When you consider this was the backdrop against which Lise was conducting soon-to-be revolutionary scientific work, it's quite simply astonishing.

26

The Promise of German Physics

As evidenced by the work of Lise, Hedwig, Hertha, and Hildegard, physics enjoyed a dazzling golden age from the 1910s through the 1930s, with Germany its beating heart.

Discoveries and advances came in rapid succession: general relativity, the modeling of the atom, matrix mechanics, wave mechanics, the birth of quantum physics, the invention of the particle accelerator and electron microscope, and the discovery of neutrons and antimatter. One eureka moment begot another, then another, with findings swiftly building on the last.

Germany quickly established itself as the cradle of such growth. German literally became the language of science, with scholars all over the world needing to learn German if they were to remain abreast of important scientific advancements.

This prominence, in turn, attracted more top-tier scientists and eager students, furthering German science and bolstering its reputation. This scientific progress also excited the wider public in Germany, increasing interest in pursuing the subject, prompting the proliferation of science programs, and leading to improvements in the quality of science education.

Lise traced much of this momentum back to a pivotal moment in 1913: the discovery of the atom.

"During the First World War, physics had been placed on an entirely different basis, both from the experimental and theoretical points of view," Lise asserted. "The main credit for that rests with Niels Bohr and his work on the structure of the atom." [145]

She explained that while Bohr's work clearly had a decisive effect on physics, repercussions also rippled throughout astronomy, chemistry, biology, and other disciplines.

Franck's work actually influenced Bohr's discovery: Bohr said the "wonderful experiment by Franck and Hertz" was the basis for his theory of the atom. This is how science works: not only the collaboration within teams and institutions but the free exchange of information and ideas among them.

More broadly, the First World War—and the associated increase in employment of women—was a significant catalyst for Germany's rapid scientific progress. During World War I, the German government invested in science as part of its war effort and saw this relationship rewarded.

Fritz Haber, director of the KWI for Physical Chemistry, became obsessed with chemical warfare. His institute quickly abandoned all scholarly projects to focus solely on military research. Haber set to work creating effective gas masks, discovering new toxic gases, and searching for a chemical that would act as both irritant and propellant in grenades.

War can see science used in aid of leaders longing to create deadlier, stealthier weapons. Of course, many wartime scientific creations are also used to defend nations, protect soldiers and civilians, and improve health outcomes in field medicine. No matter their focus, war provides an opportunity for scientists to shine.

Another reason for Germany's scientific dominance was its connection to industry. Discoveries that had clear practical applications were quickly funded and used commercially. Lise and Otto themselves benefited financially from these practices since many of their discoveries had practical uses.

Unfortunately, as research into atomic and nuclear physics was reaching its zenith in Germany, so was Nazism. Already by 1935, one in four physicists in Germany had been fired thanks to the Nazis' anti-Semitic and misogynist policies.

These physicists accounted for 64 percent of all German physics citations at the time, meaning the Nazis swept out the scientists responsible for producing nearly two-thirds of the physics research considered publication-worthy.

Colloquially referred to as "brain drain," the Nazi purge of scientists swiftly ended Germany's international reputation as a hotbed of physics innovation.

Nazi academics quickly stepped into the roles they'd fired Jewish people from to become "lecturers of the new order." Now their racial pseudoscience could flourish, and their backward ideas further spread across the country under the guise of real science.

The Nazis twisted science to a hateful purpose: promoting eugenics, supporting white supremacy, and looking for new, ever more terrible ways to inflict harm and pain on fellow humans.

In addition to stripping Germany of its greatest physicists, Nazi anti-Semitism aimed to control the parameters of the nation's scientific research, explains Philip Ball in *Serving the Reich: The Struggle for the Soul of Physics Under Hitler*.

"Nazi ideology was not merely a question of who should be allowed to live and work freely in the German state—like a virus, it worked its way into the very fabric of intellectual life,"[146] Ball asserts.

The importance of collaboration in cultivating the luster of Germany's golden era of physics cannot be overstated. So, when the Nazis broke up scientific collectives by firing all their Jewish or politically unreliable members, it effectively disbanded the research groups that had made these institutes so renowned.

Just imagine how much further science might have progressed had the Nazis not fired and snuffed out so many incredible minds. Their hatred kneecapped German science and scientific discoveries that could have been used worldwide.

When the Nazi minister of culture asked aloud at an event whether the University of Göttingen's storied mathematics institute had actually suffered after the expulsion of the Jewish teachers, Professor David Hilbert (Emmy Noether's mentor) replied: "Suffered? No, minister, it has ceased to exist."[147]

Perhaps it would have been easier if the international community truly understood what was happening in Germany, and what Hitler's ultimate plan for Jewish people was.

At the time, the Nazis excelled at information suppression and twisting the truth in their favor. They were careful to suppress any negative reports of their activities; censorship and propaganda were rigorously implemented.

What little info did make it into the international news was not yet alarming. The international press largely reported on Hitler's rise to power with neutrality and complacency, the tone of reporting ranging from approving to mild concern.

Imagine American neurologist Bernard Sachs's shock upon visiting Germany in August 1933 and observing of academia: "German conditions are as bad and as damnable as they could possibly be, and no one dares say a word."[148]

Many scholars attempted to alert the international community to the incredibly alarming nature of the Nazis' wanton expulsion of academics.

"Nowhere have the totalitarian dictatorships revealed their intolerance in more striking fashion than in the ruthless manner in which they have laid their heavy hands upon science, literature and art," political scientist James Wilford Garner warned in an editorial in the *American Journal of International Law*.

It wasn't just that these arenas were now controlled by the Nazi government, Garner noted, but also that they had been compelled to play the utterly "degrading role" of promoting political, racial, and ideological propaganda.

Garner explained that it was particularly strange to see this extreme academic manipulation in a country like Germany, where science and scholarship were highly developed, professors venerated, and academic freedom a sacred national institution. Germany had, in fact, "outdone the other dictator-ruled states in the shabby manner in which it has treated its professors, scientists, and scholars,"[149] he asserted.

But Germany's loss was the rest of the world's gain. These scholars fled the Nazis in search of safer shores, bringing their scientific genius with them. Many displaced scientific geniuses found new lives in countries that would soon become the Allied powers. They put their know-how to work to help defeat the Axis powers of Germany, Italy, and Japan that would oppose the Allies in World War II.

After the war, most refugee academics chose to remain in their new countries; only a few returned to Germany. The Nazis had crippled German science for decades to come. Sweeping out nearly all the country's top scientists could hardly have had a different effect.

27

Hertha Lands in America

On January 11, 1936, Hertha sailed for Norfolk, Virginia, an ocean crossing that took eleven days. Next came a five-hour bus ride. She arrived at Duke exhausted, but excited about her new adventure. At least this time, she spoke the language. Again, newspapers hailed her arrival, but at least in America, it was much harder for the Nazis to reach her. She was the second exiled female physics professor to arrive in America during the Nazi era, and the first to arrive at Duke University.

It's worth pointing out that Hertha and Hildegard—the first two displaced women physics professors to successfully flee the Nazis—were not Jewish, and the two still left behind, Hedwig and Lise, were.

Hertha and Hildegard had both managed to find new jobs and funding quicker than Hedwig and Lise. Yes, they faced just as much sexism, but they did not also have to contend with anti-Semitism.

Hertha knew she had been extremely lucky to find a funded position outside of Europe when she did. Many others would not be so lucky.

For Hertha, the good news kept coming. Within a month of her arrival at Duke, additional funds from the Rockefeller Foundation were secured for her salary, and by April, she learned that her position had been made permanent with a $4,000 annual salary.

What's more, at long last, Hertha's book, *MolekulSpektren*, was published. She dedicated the over 500-page tome to Franck, her beloved friend and mentor. The text was the first to explain how to interpret molecular spectra and gave the field a revolutionary, comprehensive overview of all known molecular spectra.

Finally financially secure, Hertha set about helping other scientists flee Nazi Germany, offering assistance where she could both before and after their escape. Hertha made inquiries about jobs, wrote letters of recommendation, helped with funding or job applications, and reached out to others she thought could help, like Franck.

She did her best to aid Hedwig, Hildegard, and several male scholars. She even tried to find a spot for Lise in America. Hertha knew she was privileged to be in a position to help. And she knew intimately what it was like to need such assistance.

In addition to offering her time and emotional support, Hertha donated money to the cause. After receiving her first paycheck in America, Hertha donated to the German Scientists Relief Fund. Other funding organizations approached her for donations, but this small group specifically for scientists was nearest to her heart since it had offered her funds when she was in need.

Hertha tried to convince Duke to hire Jewish physicist Max Born—the former physics head at the University of Göttingen—to fill the vacant post of chair of the theoretical physics department. They told her they preferred to consider American

candidates first. Born was ultimately settled, though. He escaped
to the UK, to a job at Cambridge and then at the University of
Edinburgh.

The need for positions was only increasing. A list of displaced
German scholars published in autumn 1936 by the Notgemein-
schaft Deutscher Wissenschaftler in Ausland (Emergency Association of German Scholars in Exile), included names of 1,639
refugee academics. The list contained all types of scholars, from
professors and lecturers to assistants and researchers.

Most, but not all, were people of Jewish descent; the rest were
those deemed "unreliable" by the Nazis or those who lost their
jobs because they were women or refused to teach Nazi ideology.

The list did not capture everyone who was forced from academia by the Nazis. Some scholars had managed to find jobs in
the private sector, such as medical professors who now worked
at hospitals or researchers at corporations.

Interestingly, the document was not just a list of those actively
in need of job placement; it included three levels of job standing: permanent placement found, temporary placement found,
and unplaced.

This means it was not simply a catalog of desperation or need,
but documentation of where the process of displacement stood as
of 1936. You didn't drop off the list once a placement had been
found. You stayed, to show you had been displaced, you were
displaced, and in some cases, you might yet be displaced further.

There are what were considered "successful" displacements—
those who found a permanent position in a safer country—
but even these cases represent lives interrupted. Each displaced
scholar meant another family uprooted or separated, a new language or culture to learn, and the loss of an integral member of
what had been a productive research team.

The trauma of being forced out of not only your job, but
your country, simply for who you were—of watching your
colleagues fail to raise a single finger in protest or even having

them turn you in to the authorities; the stab in the back from someone you considered a friend—was unimaginable. None of this screams "success."

On the list, we find Lise, Hertha, Hedwig, Franck, and Einstein in addition to such notables as political theorist and philosopher Hannah Arendt. Hildegard isn't listed likely because she was in Switzerland when she was fired, not Germany.

Approximately seventy-two of the academics on the list are women. And half of those women are listed under the ominous abbreviation "unpl"—unplaced. Arendt is one of them, as are Lise and Hedwig.

At this point, only Hertha—the only non-Jewish woman of the three female physicists on the list—had secured a permanent position outside of Germany. In all, a further twenty-five women scholars are listed as being temporarily placed, and eleven are permanently placed. In contrast, only 48 percent of the men on the list are unplaced.

Even being listed as placed in a temporary position did not guarantee safety from Nazi violence. As of 1936, Hitler's invasion and annexation of neighboring nations was still a few years out. No one yet suspected countries other than Germany would end up being just as dangerous for Jewish people. As the Nazi empire spread, safety was a mutable state and could turn on a dime from one day to the next.

Jewish zoologist Leonore Brecher, for example, was only whisked as far as Austria. She was noted on the list as being temporarily placed in a position in Vienna. In the end, this wasn't far enough.

Complicating matters was the need for these coordinated efforts to remain under the radar, so to speak. The Nazis' retaliation against the scholars on the list, should they get their hands on it, would have been devastating. The need for secrecy made disseminating the list and procuring positions even more difficult.

The list was published in London, in English, its few select recipients asked to keep it secret. Scholars' home addresses were left off the list as a precaution in case it fell into the wrong hands. Not to mention the scholars' addresses often changed rapidly as they were shunted around Europe on temporary positions or forced to move out of accommodations they could no longer afford.

This meant institutions largely had to work through intermediary organizations to communicate with scholars about potential jobs. Though it was a less than ideal setup, for many German scientists, it might represent their only means of escape.

28

Lise Looks for a Way Out

Determined to take up Bohr's offer to join him in Denmark, Lise met with KWI president Carl Bosch to see if he had any ideas on what could be done to get her out of Germany. The annexation of Austria had rendered her passport useless. Bosch wrote to the Ministry of the Interior in May 1938 asking permission for Lise to leave the country and for a guarantee that she would be allowed reentry, asserting it was a problem only the ministry could solve:

"Frau Prof. Meitner is non-Aryan, but the Ministry of Culture has permitted her to work, as she possesses great scientific experience." Lise had solved many major scientific problems and was well-known in international science circles, Bosch chirped, hoping to swing things in her favor.

She was ready to take a scientific position in another country, but the problem, he explained, was that since Austria's annexation, she needed a guarantee from the government that she would be permitted to leave and later return.

"It is only a question of obtaining notice that she may return to Germany or be issued a German passport," Bosch pleaded, noting, "otherwise travel abroad for purposes of employment is impossible."[150]

The government had no reason to offer Lise a speedy answer, let alone a German passport or their blessing to seek employment in another country.

Word of Lise's predicament soon reached more international friends. Swiss physicist Paul Scherrer wrote from Zürich with an invitation. Her old friend Dirk Coster said she should spend the summer with him in the Netherlands, a home that had housed several Jewish Germans on the run from Nazis.

Lise told everyone who reached out that she would love to be able to accept their invitations if only she was permitted to leave the country. Without a valid passport, she was, for all intents and purposes, stuck in Germany.

That June, Bohr stopped to have lunch with Lise while he was in Berlin for a few days. While Lise likely tried to downplay her dire situation so that others would not worry too much, their meeting must have spooked Bohr into action, since it was upon his return to Denmark that he began a campaign to ensure Lise got safely out of Germany fast.

While Bohr's institute could only furnish a temporary gig for Lise, he was hopeful that while she was there, a more permanent job would be found elsewhere. He told a colleague to send out a call for help across the country.

The colleague in turn tasked Coster and another Netherlands-based scientist, Adriaan Fokker, with finding a permanent position for Lise. This was no easy task at this point, but one they would have to undertake as quickly as possible.

Coster knew their communications to Germany could potentially be intercepted and cautioned those he contacted not to write to Lise directly since the mail was often opened.

"I have given my word that if I should get the impression that there is nothing for L.M. in Holland I shall let Bohr know in a week so that he can seek help in Denmark or Sweden. But I would regret it very much if we couldn't get her to Holland,"[151] Coster told Fokker. Lise would be welcome at either Coster's University of Groningen physics lab or Fokker's University of Leiden physics lab, but as usual, there was the problem of money.

Pots put aside for funding refugee scholars were running dry on multiple fronts. By the time Lise applied, the International Federation of University Women (IFUW) had been already inundated with applications from Austrians because of the German annexation. From Austrians alone, the IFUW had thirty grant applications, but in its coffers, only £100 ($125). (The average annual income in America in 1938 was around $1,700.)

Private funders were feeling equally tapped out by the volume of people who had come calling for help in the past few years.

The response Bosch got from the German government, which took a month to receive, explained succinctly and uncaringly: "Political considerations prevent the issuance of a passport for Frau Prof. Meitner. It is considered undesirable that well-known Jews leave Germany to travel abroad where they [might] demonstrate their inner attitude against Germany. Surely the K.W.G. can find a way for Frau Prof. Meitner to remain in Germany even after she resigns."[152]

So there it was: Lise was expected to resign. What's more, yet another attempt to secure her future through official channels had done more harm than good.

Just as Otto had caused trouble for Lise by going to Hörlein, Bosch going to the Ministry of the Interior had started a chain reaction that rippled all the way to the top of the Nazis' terror-inflicting paramilitary state police: the Schutzstaffel, or SS for short.

The ministry's response noted that the decision had come from the leader of the SS himself, Reichsführer Heinrich Himmler. He had personally taken Lise's case under consideration.

This would only spell imminent danger for Lise. As overseer of the Nazis' genocidal programs, Himmler directed the murder of millions of Jewish people and others that were seen as opponents or inferiors.

Peter Debye, who was Hertha's thesis advisor at the University of Göttingen and later succeeded Einstein as the director of the KWI for Physics in 1934, wrote to Bohr about the perilous progression of Lise's situation. He was purposefully circumspect, never using her name or any identifying details about her case: "Circumstances have substantially changed. It would be good if something could happen as soon as possible. Even a very modest offer would be considered,"[153] Debye noted, hoping Bohr would sense the implied urgency. He made a point to emphasize that even a bad offer that came sooner would be better than a good offer that came later. Later would probably be too late.

Lise had many allies attempting to help her, and they were all in a panic, running around doing anything they could think of to save her.

Otto frantically tried to find someone who could forge a passport for Lise. Coster and Fokker appealed to the Netherlands Ministry of Education to allow her to enter the country. They asserted that it was of utmost importance that Lise be allowed into the Netherlands and pledged her their full financial support (even though they had only managed to raise enough funds to cover a year of her expenses).

They even managed to secure the necessary faculty approval for such an international appointment. (International scholars could only accept unpaid lecturing positions.)

Coster was so alarmed he decided to go to Berlin to see if he needed to whisk Lise out of the country right then and there.

"Don't panic! Don't let your presence in Berlin make L.M. leave too hastily," Fokker cautioned. "Let her calmly conclude her business and pack her suitcase; don't fall victim to the masculine protective instinct. You must let her calmly make the decision herself."[154]

Coster alerted Debye to his impending arrival with a coded note saying he would be in the country on the hunt for a new "assistant."

At the same time, one of Bohr's colleagues arrived in Berlin, meeting with Lise at Debye's house to alert her that they'd found her a firmer job offer: as a researcher at a nuclear physics lab being built in Stockholm, Sweden. It would be part of the Royal Swedish Academy of Sciences and headed by Manne Siegbahn, who'd previously invited Lise to speak at Lund University. He was now a Nobel laureate.

Lise accepted the offer and began making plans to travel to Sweden in August.

The reality of leaving Germany finally set in, unsettling Lise to her core. Hearing that she was seemingly all set, Coster put off his trip.

Unfortunately, on July 4, 1938, Bosch told Lise that a new policy forbidding scientists from leaving Germany was about to be enacted. Lise was trapped.

29

The Net Closes in on Lise

Through a collage of diary entries, regularly posted letters, carefully coded telegrams, and smuggled communications, Lise's final days in Germany come into focus.

Upon news of the change, Coster resumed his plan to go to Germany and attempt to whisk Lise to safety. He followed up with the immigration authorities on his request for Lise to be allowed into the Netherlands.

The moment word came through that Lise could cross the border he jumped on a train to Berlin (an approximately seven-hour journey) without so much as a telegram. Debye was again in a panic, messaging Fokker for information.

Fokker sent back, "DIRK WITH YOU THIS EVENING IN BEST CONDITION," hoping that Debye would understand this meant they'd achieved a positive outcome and earned permission for Lise to enter the Netherlands. There was no way Fokker could've spelled out any of this in those exact terms, though. He did the best he could.

Coster arrived at Debye's house on Monday night, July 11, 1938, and finalized their plan to sneak Lise out of Germany.

The next morning, Lise reported to work early so Otto could explain the plan to her.

On Wednesday, Lise was to head to the train station, where she would happen to bump into her old pal Coster. Coster would have to be careful not to be seen in the neighborhood around the physics institute earlier in the day.

Lise and Coster would then travel together, taking an unpopular train line across Germany to the Netherlands border. Lise would stay with Bohr in Groningen, Netherlands, while awaiting permission to enter Sweden and start her new job.

Otto would tell her colleagues at the institute that she had gone to Vienna to visit relatives. There would be no time to say goodbye to any of her friends in Berlin, not even Elisabeth Schiemann or Max's wife, Marga Planck.

"So as not to arouse suspicion, I spent the last day of my life in Germany in the institute until 8 at night correcting a paper to be published by a young associate," Lise explained.

Trying to act normal was incredibly nerve-wracking when literally nothing felt normal. She glanced over at the unopened mail on her desk and hung her lab coat on the hook in her office for the very last time. "Then I had exactly 1½ hours to pack a few necessary things into two small suitcases,"[155] Lise observed.

Otto escorted Lise home. He and Lise's old friend Paul Rosbaud helped her pack her suitcases. They had to be as quiet as possible since Kurt Hess, the KWI's own in-house Nazi, was right next door in his apartment. He wasn't yet finished with his plan to see Lise punished.

Her suitcases had to appear as if she was going on a short vacation, which included only packing her summer clothes. She couldn't risk taking anything valuable or suspicious, such as scientific instruments or paperwork, since border guards searched the luggage of Jewish individuals leaving the country, keeping anything they believed had value and heavily taxing everything else.

Apparently, their planning and packing had not been stealthy enough. Hess sensed something was up. Immediately, he was on the horn to the authorities to inform them that Lise was planning to flee.

Rosbaud drove them all back to Otto's house so Lise could sleep over. The trio agreed on a code word that could be used in a telegram to communicate whether the journey had been a success.

Rosbaud was a fellow Austrian whom Lise met when he was a physics student in Berlin in the 1920s. He now worked at the science publication *Naturwissenschaften* (*The Science of Nature*), Springer's flagship multidisciplinary science journal.

After seeing his Jewish wife and daughter safely secreted to the UK, Rosbaud chose to remain in Germany to help others escape and to undermine the Nazi regime by serving as an allied spy for the British. In other words, he was a good friend to have.

The next morning, July 13, 1938, Lise climbed in Rosbaud's car. "I left Germany forever—with 10 marks in my purse,"[156] Lise later remarked.

On the way to the train station, she suddenly became overcome with terror and pleaded with Rosbaud to turn the car around. A gentle, gregarious man, he managed to calm her down and assure her that Coster was waiting at the station to get on the train with her.

Coster would ensure she crossed the border safely; everything would be all right, he promised. Had Rosbaud not had such a soothing influence, she might not have had the resolve to go through with the plan.

The danger, she knew, lay in the repeated inspections by SS officers of trains leaving Germany. "Over and over again, people trying to get out of the country were arrested on the trains and taken back," Otto explained.[157]

Otto was on top of her potentially problematic financial situation. "In case things should get really bad, I handed over a nicely cut diamond ring that I had never worn, but as I had inherited it from my late mother, I had always kept it safe,"[158] Otto recalled.

Stunningly, the trip went off without incident. Coster met Lise and escorted her the rest of the way. He even helped reassure her when she grew agitated just before the border crossing, as well as instructing her to take off the ring and place it in her pocket so as not to catch the eye of any border guards or SS officers.

Lise had been saved. The "baby" had arrived, Coster telegrammed Otto. Luckily, Hess's attempt to rat her out was unsuccessful.

After hearing from Hess, the police dispatched another Nazi scientist, rather than an SS officer, to investigate. Nothing amiss was found, and the follow-up investigation had gotten tied up in government bureaucracy.

"The shot that was to bring you down in the last minute missed you,"[159] a former colleague told Lise triumphantly of Hess's futile flailings.

Quantum physics trailblazer Wolfgang Pauli told Coster he would now be "as famous for the abduction of Lise Meitner as for [discovering] hafnium."[160]

30

Lise in Limbo

Lise was now no longer at risk of experiencing professional ruin or bodily harm at the hands of the Nazis. But she was cut off from the life she had built, both professional and personal, the only life she had known for the past three decades. Her lab set up just so, her colleagues who had long since become friends and enjoyed nights of music and laughing, dinners filled with stimulating conversations, hiking vacations with family and friends. All of it, gone. Stolen by the Nazis.

Lise confided in Otto her terrible sadness for the "deep divide" now separating them. "Surely no day will pass in which I do not think with gratitude and longing of our friendship, our work together and about the institute. But I no longer belong there," Lise conceded.

Logically, she understood she would never be able to return to the KWI; emotionally, well, that was a trickier matter. "I myself have not yet really comprehended that what I have written here is a reality, but it *is* a reality."[161]

As her panic dissipated, the ennui descended. Surely, many cigarettes were stress-smoked. But now that she had reached relative safety, Lise hated to burden anyone. She rarely admitted how depressed she felt. But those who knew her well realized how much she was truly hurting.

"Her sense of being inwardly torn apart is much worse than we can imagine,"[162] Fokker lamented to Coster's wife, Miep, after a visit with Lise.

Back home at her old institute, things felt nearly as hollowed out as she did. Lise's former grad student advisee Arno (Arnold) Flammersfeld let her know as much: "After you left us, most of the scientific spirit in the physics department is gone."[163]

And Lise's situation was not yet peril-free. Formalities regarding her permission to enter Sweden were not fully in order. Unfortunately, Siegbahn, the director of the new nuclear physics institute who'd offered her a job, had not secured permission for Lise to enter Sweden. Siegbahn must not have fully understood the urgency.

Her stay with Coster in Groningen would have to extend a little longer than expected. She really felt adrift now. She occupied herself as best she could by spending her days in Coster's lab or playing with his children and socializing with his family and friends.

"My situation is not very pleasant, but there is no sense dwelling on it,"[164] Lise sighed.

Finally, word came through that Sweden would allow her to enter the country on her Austrian passport—but only if she had written permission stating she was permitted to reenter Germany. Of course she didn't have that!

While many foreign governments were beginning to see how badly Germany was behaving (given its annexation of Austria a few months prior, this was becoming harder and harder to disguise), unless war was declared, there was an expectation of basic international cooperation.

Fokker wrote to Siegbahn to reiterate that she neither had

nor was able to obtain such a statement. Yes, her passport was technically invalid, but they knew she would never be able to procure a German passport. All they could do now was hope against hope that Sweden would show some leniency, maybe even some compassion.

If Sweden refused her, they could easily order her to return to Germany, where a fate no one wanted to imagine likely awaited. A fate few people living outside Germany could truly fathom.

"You will understand that if the Swedish government is not willing to admit her without restriction, then she will be lost," Fokker fumed. He couldn't believe he had to explain this again. "Our guest is a brave woman; she lives under great stress and anxiety, and will only be relieved from it when she sets foot in Sweden."[165]

While Lise was ostensibly out of the country "visiting relatives," the Germany Ministry of Education began the process of officially terminating her from her position at the KWI. Several people were vying to oust Otto, too, since he had not joined the Nazi party.

When Otto finally told the employees of the institute where Lise really was, he didn't include the fact that she had been forced out of her position and out of the country. She was livid to hear that as a result, they believed she'd simply lost her nerve. Lise demanded Otto fill them in on the full story.

"My future is cut off; shall the past also be taken from me?" Lise raged to Otto. "I have done nothing wrong, why should I suddenly be treated like a nonperson or worse, someone who is buried alive? Everything is hard enough as it is."[166]

This was the first fissure of many to come in their otherwise relatively solid relationship. Otto wrote back accusing her of being unnecessarily bitter and underestimating how difficult things were becoming for him in Germany.

Lise replied, more diplomatically this time, that she was not bitter, only upset. "I have regarded this work together as the best and most beautiful part of my life, and it hurts me to think these people might now think I left them in the lurch."

She noted that she did, in fact, understand that Otto was not having an altogether easy time of it either (though, arguably, significantly easier than Lise as he was so far still allowed to stay in Germany).[167]

It's unfortunate, even a bit rage-inducing, that on top of everything, Lise was being made to placate and soothe a man because he had expressed hurt feelings and demanded consideration of his own, less dire situation.

Otto felt abandoned, and perhaps that hurt was causing him to lash out. Lise wanted to preserve this important friendship, but what a terrible waste of her precious energy.

If only Otto had simply explained that Lise had been backed into a corner and had no other option but to flee. She most certainly would not have abandoned her colleagues without a proper transition or goodbye unless it was absolutely necessary, and she wished her colleagues knew that.

At last, full permission came through for Lise to enter Sweden with only the identity papers she had. "May the difficult time that awaits you until you are settled not last long,"[168] Fokker told her before she left.

To take a train to Stockholm would mean traveling back through Germany, an ordeal she most certainly did not want to go through again. Instead, she would take a plane to Denmark.

For the first leg of her trip, Lise flew to Copenhagen, where she would stop for a brief visit with her friend Bohr and her nephew Otto Robert. She hid the money Coster had collected for her—the only funds to her name—and boarded the flight.

In Copenhagen, Otto Robert excitedly gave her a tour of the new cyclotron that was being constructed at the Institute for Theoretical Physics. They enjoyed a brief reprieve at Bohr's summer house by the sea. She enjoyed spending time with friends and family but wished it were under better circumstances.

The rest of the journey involved boat rides and train trips. Her old friend, physicist Eva von Bahr-Bergius, met her part of the way and escorted her to Eva's new home in Kungälv.

Lise and Eva first met when Eva applied to work at the University of Berlin back in 1912 and subsequently became a research assistant to Professor Heinrich Rubens. She had left Sweden because, at the time, no university there would hire a woman physics professor.

Eva was forced to return to Sweden in 1914 to care for her ill mother and was unable to resume her position in Berlin once World War I broke out. Sweden still wasn't ready for a woman physics professor, so Eva took a job teaching high school. Missing her friend, Lise stayed with Eva for a month after World War I ended.

Happy to be with her old, trusted friend again, Lise would spend the rest of the summer at Eva's home, attempting to relax and rejuvenate before her position at Siegbahn's nuclear physics lab in Stockholm officially began in September. She still had a good six or seven hours of travel time ahead, but at least she would have a bit of a break first.

31

Hedwig Hopes for a Miracle

Hedwig had been the first woman in Germany to earn a PhD in physics, and now that Hertha, Hildegard, and Lise had all fled by the autumn of 1938, she was the last woman left qualified to teach physics at the university level.

It must have stung to watch nearly all your former colleagues and associates be whisked away to safer shores one by one over the years. You were happy they found a way out, of course, but there was also that horrible feeling of being left behind. The dread and urgency blooming in the pit of your stomach, ballooning with each passing day.

Still, it was a relief to know the people she cared about would now be safe. No matter how much her panic about her own situation consumed her, she could always spare a thought for the plight of others.

As Hedwig watched people escape to safety, she also witnessed many more being hauled to death camps and endured yet further curtailing of her rights as a Jewish woman.

July 12, 1936: Sachsenhausen concentration camp opened
July 15, 1937: Buchenwald concentration camp opened
March 24, 1938: Jewish people forbidden from conducting research in public archives
June 1938: First official execution in a concentration camp
August 17, 1938: Jewish people required to carry identity cards indicating their heritage and add "Israel" or "Sara" to their name to distinguish them as Jewish if they had "non-Jewish" first names
November 9 and 10, 1938: Kristallnacht. An organized pogrom sees Nazis destroy 250 synagogues, wreck 7,000 Jewish businesses, and drag 30,000 Jewish men to concentration camps: the first mass arrest of Jewish people simply for being Jewish
November 15, 1938: Jewish children expelled from public schools
November 28, 1938: The Reich Ministry of the Interior restricts Jewish people's freedom of movement
December 8, 1938: Jewish students expelled from German universities

By 1939, the Nazis will have enacted more than 400 regulations that methodically drained away the freedom of Jewish people. Hedwig would remain in Germany through them all.

It was the Kristallnacht, or Night of Broken Glass, that exposed the Nazis' true agenda for the Jewish population: they wanted them all dead. On November 9 and 10, 1938, Nazis torched more than 250 synagogues, and vandalized thousands of Jewish homes, schools, and businesses, killing nearly 100 Jewish people. They also dragged 30,000 Jewish men to concentration camps across Germany and Austria.

In Hedwig's town of Breslau stood one of the largest synagogues in Germany. Come the Kristallnacht pogrom, the New Synagogue was burnt down. Within a few months, the Nazis had nearly halved the population of Breslau's bustling Jewish community; it was down to 10,309.

The violence bled into Austria, where, in Vienna, 42 synagogues were wrecked, 4,000 shops looted, and 8,000 Jewish men arrested.

After the Kristallnacht, Hedwig knew her life depended on getting out of Nazi Germany. But she wasn't alone. This racially targeted rioting made many people finally wake up to the reality that a quick escape from all German-occupied territories was now a life-or-death matter for those of Jewish descent. The number of people attempting to emigrate increased dramatically in 1938.

"The difficulty in accommodating immigrants is enormous at the present time,"[169] Franck confided in Lise from America. Resources were spread very thin; if it was difficult to find a way out before, it was next to impossible now.

Rudolf Ladenburg had been going to bat for Hedwig with American institutions and funding organizations for over four years. He grew more impatient as her situation became more precarious.

In January 1939, Rudolf personally traveled from Princeton to Washington DC to plead Hedwig's immigration case with the American Association of University Women (AAUW). He met with Esther Brunauer, whom Franck had previously contacted about funds for Hertha. Esther was a scholar herself, having earned a doctorate in sociology.

To survive the Nazis, Rudolf explained, Hedwig would need a European safe haven to escape to while she waited for her US visa to come through. Rudolf implored Esther to bring Hedwig's case to the attention of the International Federation of University Women (IFUW).

Rudolf sent Esther a letter detailing Hedwig's publications, experience, and expertise. To really hammer home Hedwig's ever-increasing desperation and her many feverish attempts to find a path out, he ended the letter with: "She tries everything to leave Germany as she has no way of earning her living there and she will be glad to accept any position anywhere."[170]

And so, the search for a place for Hedwig recommenced in earnest. Esther sprang into action. In addition to reaching out to universities, she also contacted Erica Holme and Erna Hollitscher of the International Federation of University Women (IFUW), who began looking for any possible opportunity for Hedwig outside of the US.

Unfortunately, the initial responses were incredibly disheartening. In March 1939, Erica heard back from A. Vibert Douglas at the physics department of McGill University in Canada with a grim pronouncement.

"It is almost impossible for a woman to get a post in this country and a woman of middle age even with a grand record stands no chance," Douglas explained. "I can do nothing to suggest a place for Miss Kohn here. It sounds heartless and terrible and it is terrible but not heartless."[171]

Hedwig wasn't even the only German woman physicist desperate for a job in America.

Charlotte Riefenstahl's education reads like a who's who of German science. She studied at the University of Göttingen under Franck, Max Born, Richard Courant, David Hilbert, and Emmy Noether. She earned her PhD in 1927, in the same graduating class as her soon-to-be husband Fritz Houtermans (and the soon-to-be-famous J. Robert Oppenheimer, who also courted her).

Charlotte insisted on fleeing Germany once Hitler seized power since Fritz was a communist and had Jewish heritage. Fritz found a position in the Soviet Union but was arrested during Joseph Stalin's Great Purge in 1937. He confessed to being a spy under torture after they threatened his family.

Charlotte and their two young children narrowly escaped to Denmark and then sailed to America. Despite having a physics doctorate, Charlotte's occupation was listed as "housewife" on the transatlantic ship's manifest.

Now Charlotte needed a job to support her family. In March

1940, Esther Brunauer of the AAUW told her that Bennington College was hiring a physics professor, but she was painfully blunt about her chances of getting the job given her gender.

"The college wants a man for the position but it would surely do no harm to try," Esther explained. "Your training at Göttingen might compensate for your being a woman."[172]

Indeed, the college never took Charlotte under consideration. If Bennington wouldn't even look at an impressive candidate like Charlotte, who was already in America, what chance did Hedwig have of securing an American job from afar?

With her funds dwindling, Hedwig feared destitution would ensnare her before the Gestapo did.

"As long as I could, I tried to fight it out by myself, but now it is no longer possible to do so," Hedwig explained to Esther. "I would be most grateful for any help you could render me."

Hedwig received no pension and owned no property. She highlighted her dire financial precarity to Esther.

"Till last autumn, I could earn a modest livelihood. Now the circumstances no longer allow such work," Hedwig noted. "My savings will probably be sufficient for my subsistence in the present year and for the costs of emigration (passage, luggage)."[173]

Erna Hollitscher of the IFUW—known among friends as Holly—had more luck with the feelers she put out in Scotland on Hedwig's behalf. She extracted the promise of a research assistant position for Hedwig at the University of Aberdeen from Scottish astrophysicist John Carroll, who had invented the high-resolution spectrometer.

She could begin as soon as the winter of 1939 and could work with Professor Carroll until America was ready for her.

A grant was also pulled together for Hedwig to help finance this trip, consisting of £50 each from the British Federation of University Women and a Dutch university women's committee, and $300 from Rudolf's German Scientists Relief Fund.

Together, the money and job would suffice for a visa.

May 19, 1939: Ravensbrück concentration camp for women opened

By mid-August 1939, Hedwig received notice that her UK visa had been granted. Finally, she could breathe a sigh of relief. Rudolf was also relieved that his friend now had a path to freedom mapped out. He wrote to Lise to update her on Hedwig's situation and tell her all about the Scottish job offer.

Sadly, her relief was incredibly short-lived. Two weeks after her UK visa was granted—just as Hedwig was preparing to leave the country—the UK declared war on Germany. Visas granted to any "enemy aliens" (meaning all Germans) were immediately canceled; the money that had been sent to the UK for her was now inaccessible.

September 1, 1939: Germany invades Poland, prompting declarations of war from the UK and France; World War II begins
September 2, 1939: Stutthof concentration camp opened
October 1939: Nazis begin mass deportation of Jewish people to impoverished, enclosed ghettos or extermination camps

The Gestapo took up her case and began pressuring her, letting her know she was on their radar and likely to be included in future deportations. Hedwig's quota number on the US immigration waiting list was far too high. She would likely be killed before her visa was granted. Things were looking bleak.

32

A Last-Ditch Rescue Effort for Hedwig

Hedwig wouldn't survive the wait for her US visa approval if she stayed in Germany, but she and her team of helpers were not ready to give up just yet. They decided to look in a new direction.

After assessing all available avenues—considering where they had contacts, the amenability of immigration laws, and the potential cooperation of women's academic organizations—they concluded that her best hope to escape Germany alive was fleeing to Sweden as soon as possible, where she could safely await her US visa.

To stay in Sweden temporarily, she wouldn't need an immediate job, just the promise of a future one, a travel visa, and funds to ensure she wouldn't be a financial burden on the country.

They knew just who to turn to: "I think the chief thing is to induce Professor Meitner to help Dr. Kohn,"[174] Holly at the IFUW observed.

Spearheaded by Rudolf, a last-ditch attempt to save Hedwig's life saw a flurry of upwards of seventy letters exchanged among Hedwig, the AAUW, the Swedish and British branches of the IFUW, numerous women's colleges and one university in America, and several fellow physicists who had already fled Germany, including Rudolph, Lise, Hertha, and Max Born.

Hedwig was incredibly lucky to have dozens of people on her side lobbying on her behalf. They were all united in their determination that there must be a place for her, somewhere.

In November 1939, Rudolf wrote to Lise to enlist her help. He hoped Lise could assist Hedwig in securing a temporary visa, explaining that she was seeking a safe haven in which to await her US visa approval.

"I would like to ask you, first, to mediate the correspondence between Miss Kohn and these committees," Rudolf explained, adding: "I will take care of the costs. I hope you do not hold it against me that I bother you with these things and take advantage of your time and work."[175]

He then wrote to *and* telephoned Esther to ask her to write to Lise as well. Then, to be absolutely, positively sure Lise was informed of Hedwig's dire plight as soon as possible, he also wrote a letter to Max Born in Scotland to ask him to write to Lise, too.

Since they'd set their sights on Sweden, Lise's assistance was seen as crucial to Hedwig's escape, and these many letters to her reflect the growing desperation of Hedwig's helpers.

When no one heard back from Lise right away, they got nervous. Max Born was asked to reach out to her again. By this point, Lise was being flooded with letters about Hedwig's situation.

It turns out that Lise wasn't being cold to these many requests; she had been staying in Denmark for two weeks when the letters arrived. Once she was back at home in Stockholm and had received all her messages, she was more than happy to assist a fellow woman physicist fleeing the Nazis.

Lise quickly commenced an investigation into how to convince the immigration authorities to allow Hedwig into Sweden. The answer, as always, was money. While Lise couldn't act as Hedwig's financial sponsor since she didn't earn enough herself, that didn't stop her from doing whatever else she could to help.

Lise wrote to relief organizations and even a few individuals—anyone she could think of who might be able to help.

In January 1940, Lise penned a note to Hedwig that she could use as a letter of recommendation when approaching hiring institutions, funding agencies, or immigration authorities.

"Dr. Hedwig Kohn is an excellent physicist who has written several very good papers in her field. As a student and later long-time collaborator of the famous spectroscopist Lummer, she received a very good experimental and theoretical education," Lise wrote. "Every problem she deals with has been carried out with great expertise, unusual experimental skill and the highest scientific reliability."

Lise showed she was already familiar with Hedwig's work, noting that her experiments—particularly those on the heat of sublimation of carbon—displayed Hedwig's extensive theoretical knowledge and "mastery of very complicated experimental methods."

Lise concluded this glowing reference by saying Hedwig's scientific achievements and teaching talent went far beyond the average.[176]

Yet another recommendation letter for Hedwig from an eminent physicist! She had developed quite a collection of these recently. Would Lise's words be enough to sway those with the power to help?

While waiting for permission to enter Sweden to materialize, Hedwig thought she might have found a helpful lead in the form of an offer to work in an experimental physics lab at Fribourg University in Switzerland. The problem with the offer was that it was "without pay, of course."

No income meant it would likely be impossible to convince Switzerland to issue her even a temporary visa. And as Hildegard had proven, Switzerland wasn't exactly welcoming German immigrants across their border.

Lise, meanwhile, had enlisted a local member of the IFUW. Karin Kock was an economics lecturer at Stockholm University who also happened to be vice president of the IFUW. (Karin would soon become the first female full professor of economics in Sweden.)

Hedwig's letters to Karin had to be translated by Lise since Karin was not fluent in written German. By March, Lise and Karin had finally coaxed the Swedish immigration authority to promise Hedwig a temporary visa if three conditions could be met. Hedwig would need:

1. Letters of recommendation from Swedish scientists
2. Proof that she had qualified for a permanent visa in another country
3. Enough money to support herself for a year (meaning she would not come calling for financial assistance from the government)

Lise took care of gathering recommendations for Hedwig. After jumping through various paperwork hoops, her team finally regained access to the money that had been put aside for her time in Aberdeen, Scotland. Lise had managed to scrounge up an additional £50 from a British women's group and $300 from an American physicist. In total, the funds would cover one year of living expenses.

Yet even after meeting all of Sweden's immigration demands, its authorities were balking. Hedwig's American quota number was too high—so far down on the list that it wasn't likely to be her turn for several years—which meant she would likely be stuck in Sweden for longer than anticipated.

If she ended up needing to stay longer than a year, she would need more money than her cobbled-together funds could offer.

"The current unsureness in the political situation makes every help measure extraordinarily difficult," Lise confided in Rudolf. "The Swedes have become very nervous."[177]

The Jewish Community of Stockholm offered to intercede on Hedwig's behalf if her helpers could promise to provide 150 kronor ($36) per month to cover Hedwig's expenses for the entirety of her stay in Sweden.

Holly knew this was unlikely since this "may be several years!" She asked Esther: "Do you think that Dr. Kohn's American friends will undertake to give the Jewish Community of Stockholm such a far-reaching guarantee?"[178]

Esther didn't even have time to answer before another, decidedly more urgent letter from Hedwig landed in Lise's mailbox. Since she last wrote to Lise and her other helpers, conditions had deteriorated significantly.

"It is no longer a question of my desire to be employed as a physicist," Hedwig explained to Lise, but rather, finding any job offer that would get her out of the country was now a matter of life or death. "People go to great lengths, for which I am heartily grateful, but everything is far too vague in view of the extremely urgent circumstances."[179]

At the beginning of April 1940, Hedwig told Lise that if she had nowhere to go by early June, it would be too late. The Gestapo had given Hedwig a deadline: she would be deported to a camp in Poland in mid-June unless she could produce travel papers for another country.

Karin telegrammed Rudolf at once, and he then related the contents of the note to Esther in no uncertain terms.

"She has to know definitely by the *middle of June* where to go, otherwise it is too late."[180]

And now we find ourselves back where our story began: May 1940. Walls closing in. The clock ticking down. Desperation.

33

Safety on the Horizon for Hedwig

After months of no word from Rudolf, Hedwig was more frazzled than ever. Then, all at once, her mailbox was suddenly overflowing. Hedwig's attempts to escape Nazi Germany were filled with many of these hurry-up-and-wait periods: quick, fill out all these forms and reach out to all these people, then sit on the edge of your seat waiting for responses.

Conditions in the US were now looking more promising, Hedwig learned. America eased the non-quota visa requirements: academics now just needed two years of teaching experience *at some point*, rather than being required to have been teaching for the preceding two years. This relaxation greatly increased her likelihood of getting visa approval. Still, she needed to show she would not be a long-term financial burden.

Rudolf formulated what he hoped was a foolproof plan. He knew he had been appealing to Esther for help for Hedwig for six months by this point, but he was determined to rescue her.

They should send out a copy of the same letter to multiple women's colleges simultaneously, Rudolf told Esther. "I suppose we have to offer to the prospective institution some hundred dollars for her salary. I am trying to find such an amount." Rudolf reiterated what they were up against: "I am sorry to bother you again in this matter, but it seems now really to be a question of life or death."[181]

Karin's latest cable agreed: if a teaching job could be arranged at an American university, Hedwig might have a chance of being awarded a non-quota US visa, which could then garner her a temporary visa to enter Sweden until her position began.

Rudolf's plan was novel, a creative departure from the way things normally worked for displaced scholars. As if there was anything "normal" about what was happening.

One way that his strategy was unique is that sending the same letter out to several colleges simultaneously was essentially unheard of at the time. Most refugee academics found their jobs through a few strategically targeted letters, sent to different educational institutions consecutively after receiving a rejection from the previous one, not all at once.

Conspicuously absent from Rudolf's plan were large research universities. It is very likely that Hedwig would have fit in better at such a university—both personally and professionally—and her research experience would have been a great asset to those programs, but right now, Rudolf was less concerned about finding a good match for her skills and interests and more focused on the types of educational institutions he believed would be most amenable to quickly hiring a female science professor from a foreign country.

Hedwig would have much less time to conduct her research at a smaller coed or women's college than she would at a larger university. What's more, students at these schools were less advanced than the ones she was used to working with at German universities.

That meant not only that Hedwig might find the job boring

or lacking challenge, but also that her high-level expertise in a very specialized area of physics was not the type of experience these colleges typically looked for in a professor.

May 10, 1940: Nazis invade the Low Countries and France
May 20, 1940: Auschwitz complex opens, including a concentration camp, extermination camp, and forced labor camp

When Rudolf didn't hear back from Esther quickly enough for his satisfaction, he wrote again on May 24, including another copy of Karin's cable to be sure Esther understood that time was of the essence: "DEPORTATION POLAND A MATTER OF WEEKS."

But sweet, empathetic Esther didn't need reminding. She knew they had to act quickly. She had, in fact, already responded to Rudolf's letter. It just hadn't reached him yet.

Esther didn't hold out much hope at this point, but she promised Rudolf she would write to "some of the college presidents whom I think would be most sympathetic." She had written them all before, but maybe this time one of them might "reconsider the problem in light of Dr. Kohn's pending deportation to Poland."[182]

Esther posted letters to seven of the best-known women's colleges in the US: Sweet Briar College, Goucher College, Connecticut College, New Jersey College for Women, Wellesley College, Vassar College, and Sarah Lawrence College.

She needed their help with an "urgent, if not desperate refugee problem," Esther pleaded. Hedwig needed a "letter of invitation for next June." Otherwise, she would be sent to a concentration camp. She, too, included a copy of Karin's cable to show just how urgent the situation was.

Esther didn't mince words: "Dr. Hedwig Kohn of Breslau is in imminent danger of being deported to Poland unless some way can be found to get her admitted to Sweden before the middle

of June. The difficulty is that Sweden will not let her come because the time when her quota number is reached is likely to
be too far away."

Sweden would be willing to admit her, Esther said, if she
could leave in about a year and had a good chance of securing
a non-quota visa. "If you do think that you could offer a position to Dr. Kohn beginning with the academic year 1941-42,
please let me know immediately as the time is very short."[183]

Esther also tried to improve her chances of a positive response
by appealing to each college president's pocketbook. She let
them know that Rudolf already had roughly $500 guaranteed
for her support for a year in Sweden, and planned to find additional money to help fund her first year's salary in America.

The nature of Esther's near-groveling was unusually unprofes-
sional for a representative of the AAUW. She was close to putting the organization's reputation on the line. But Esther would
rather regret begging and be successful than regret not doing so
and seeing Hedwig face such a dangerous fate.

All they needed was one yes—one college willing to take
a chance on hiring a sweet German lady physicist with a solid
record of research, teaching, and grad-student supervision who
had just celebrated her fifty-third birthday.

Not a man in his thirties. Not an internationally recognized
Nobel laureate. Just a highly intelligent, hardworking, and scientifically curious middle-aged woman with a wry smile and a
fabulous sense of humor. One who'd had to work twice as hard
as most men her age to get to the same level.

34

US Colleges Respond to Hedwig

As expected, not every college replied to Hedwig's cry for help. And most of the ones that did expressed only regret that they could not be of assistance. At least the ones who deigned to reply did so in a very timely fashion, answering Esther within just a few days.

On May 28, 1940, Esther heard from the president of Goucher College in Baltimore, Maryland. She regretted that while she was deeply sympathetic to Hedwig's situation, Goucher College was not in a position to hire new faculty members at the moment. In fact, the faculty was already too large given the number of students enrolled.

"I am under the sad necessity of finding ways to make adaptations which cannot, at this time, include an additional member of the Physics Department."[184]

Sarah Lawrence College, in Bronxville, New York, responded that while they wished they could help, "it would be utterly impossible for us to offer a position sight-unseen," explained Constance Warren, the college president. Since teaching at their school required "more ability to get on well with students than any other I know of," Warren said they never hired people they had not personally met with.[185]

So they wanted to help, but not so much that they would hire someone without interviewing with them first. That's not an entirely unreasonable request, of course, but these were incredibly extenuating circumstances. Perhaps this comment about getting on well with students was a reference to the fact that English was not Hedwig's first language, and they feared that the language barrier would translate to an inability to cultivate relationships with students.

From Meta Glass, the president of Sweet Briar College in Virginia—and a personal friend of Esther's—came a not altogether unexpected rationalization that Hedwig was too advanced, too specialized for a small women's college. Glass was nervous that Hedwig wouldn't be content at their small school: their physics department only had one professor and he didn't even have enough work to warrant an assistant.

Despite this, Glass said they would be willing to extend an invitation to teach at Sweet Briar for the 1941–42 school year as a last resort if no others came through. It was more than anywhere else had offered so far.

"What we have to offer is plainly a makeshift. She may, however, rather have this than deportation to Poland, and I stand ready to send the invitation if you cannot do better."[186]

Glass said they could only provide her with living expenses in exchange for occasional lecturing (rather than a full salary). Still, they would happily permit her to pursue her own research if their laboratory held any equipment useful to her specialty.

Sweet Briar College made good on their offer a few days later when Glass sent Hedwig an official offer letter. Glass had in fact sidestepped the usual hiring procedure to extend this invitation to Hedwig; the small college most certainly did not need two physics teachers.

"It is good to know that there are still people like that in the world,"[187] Esther observed when informing Rudolf about Glass's offer. As someone tasked with attempting to rescue those imperiled by the violent intolerance of the Nazis, only to be met with xenophobia, that was easy to forget. "In the years I have known Miss Glass I have appreciated increasingly her combination of wisdom and human sympathy,"

The last college response came on June 6 from Mildred McAfee, the president of Wellesley College, which was a private liberal arts school in an affluent suburb of Boston, Massachusetts. Wellesley was no stranger to offering solace to women academics fleeing the Nazis, but as war had enveloped Europe, Americans became increasingly suspicious of Germans.

"You will not be surprised that I ran into the anxiety of some of our men lest Dr. Kohn be 'a front' for propaganda purposes," McAfee told Esther. "If you can assure me Dr. Kohn is a bona fide refugee," she said, the college could invite her as a visiting researcher for the 1941–42 school year.

McAfee lamented her impotence in view of the painfully slow wheels of academia, noting that if it were merely up to her, she would have sent a cable immediately welcoming Hedwig on to the faculty. Regrettably, due to budgetary constraints, this position would have no stipend attached to it.[188]

The response was fear. Not for Hedwig's life, but for themselves. Fear that she was potentially an informant or propagandist of some kind. As if refugee academics were not already doing enough to try and prove their academic merit, research acumen, and teaching aptitude. Such defenses were their only lifeline. No, they must also prove they were "real" refugees who deserved to be saved. Many Americans couldn't adequately fathom just how much danger these people were in. And not only that, but they had no money to offer her.

Luckily for Hedwig, Rudolf stepped in to intervene with Wellesley. He convinced McAfee and her colleagues that Hedwig was a real refugee in real trouble.

Rudolf told McAfee plainly: "The Gestapo in Breslau has set the middle of June as the deadline for her deportation to Poland if she cannot prove that she will be able to emigrate into another country."[189] Perhaps the use of the term "Gestapo" would help emphasize the seriousness of Hedwig's situation.

His letter clearly helped assuage McAfee's fears. The school's trustees were now willing to authorize a research position for Hedwig—without a stipend, but with housing. McAfee asked Esther if she thought Hedwig's immediate safety would be helped if Wellesley sent her an invitation for a second year in America. Wellesley could welcome her after her year at Sweet Briar.

Esther responded with a resounding yes that reasserted the particular horrors potentially awaiting Hedwig: "Dr. Kohn seems in immediate danger of deportation to Poland which in present circumstances amounts to slavery, starvation, or both. It would be tremendously helpful if Wellesley would offer a second year."[190]

By this time, Jewish citizens knew threats of deportation should be taken seriously. Starting in October 1939, the Nazis began rounding up Jewish people and transporting them to enclosed, overcrowded ghettos. The list of the names of those slated for deportation from Breslau had been generated in the spring of 1940.

Still, there was a brief window when relocation of Jewish people to other countries was an accepted, even encouraged practice. But by the fall of 1941, the Nazis disallowed Jewish people from emigrating elsewhere.

McAfee cabled Hedwig on June 19 to offer her a research

position at Wellesley for the academic year 1942–1943. Rudolf
had sent McAfee $3 to cover the cost of the cable.

"The cable to Dr. Kohn cost $2.77. I therefore enclose twenty-
three cents in stamps and accompany it with an expression of
great appreciation of your personal generosity,"[191] she wrote
him back.

Hedwig accepted her two offers of subsequent one-year contracts, at Sweet Briar College and Wellesley. Now, there was just
the little problem of getting out of Germany.

35

Another Offer for Hedwig

Hertha wasn't satisfied with Hedwig's two current offers—contracts for academic years 1941 to 1942 at Sweet Briar and 1942 to 1943 at Wellesley—so she was working frantically to secure Hedwig another guaranteed year, one that started right away. Hertha wanted to guarantee Hedwig—and the immigration authorities—that Hedwig had a professional reason to hightail it out of Germany as soon as possible. Ideally, she wanted the University of North Carolina (UNC) to add an offer for the 1940 to 1941 school year.

A position that started in just a few months could go a long way in convincing Swedish immigration authorities that Hedwig would not be a long-term drain on public resources, as well as convincing US visa processors that her application needed to be approved sooner rather than later.

If it all worked out as she hoped, Hedwig would soon be a mere one-hour train ride from Hertha.

By this point, Hertha was well into establishing herself as a respected member of Duke University, having spent nearly four years proving herself to be not only an inspiring professor and dedicated researcher, but also an invigorating, supportive colleague. She was alerted to Hedwig's plight by Rudolf's continued fundraising for the German Scientists Relief Fund among fellow émigré scholars who had successfully landed jobs in America.

Now, remembering her own difficulty in trying to find a suitable position outside of Germany, Hertha was determined to help Hedwig. From her new life in Durham, North Carolina, she reached out to Frank Porter Graham, the president of UNC. The state school included a women's college in Greensboro.

On May 30, 1940, Hertha called Graham. That same day, she mailed him a packet of information about Hedwig: her curriculum vitae and a list of her scientific publications.

Hertha stressed to Graham that it didn't really matter what the position's job description actually involved. It just needed to have a title that governments and immigration offices would believe was real and sounded like something Hedwig was qualified for.

Hertha promised that she would handle finding full funding for her salary. Any leftover money from the funds already raised for Hedwig's stay in Sweden could go toward a stipend to cover a year at UNC.

Franck was so proud of Hertha's actions, telling Lise, "I find the efforts she is exerting for Hedwig deserve our highest recognition."[192]

When she set her mind to something, Hertha could be like a dog with a bone. She kept writing and calling Graham until she had an answer, preferably in the affirmative. Hertha was counting on the squeaky wheel getting the grease.

She was also banking on Graham's reputation as a humanitarian with a rare and truly exceptional outlook for a Southern American college administrator at the time: empathy for refugee academics.

The UNC Woman's College physics department formally took Hedwig under consideration. This involved a lot of back-and-forth. Several meetings were held to discuss whether Hedwig was needed at the university and whether their college could really use someone with her qualifications.

Unfortunately, Graham's liberal views were not shared by other UNC administrators. Just like Mildred McAfee at Wellesley College, UNC Chancellor William Carmichael was more concerned about potential spies than about the danger to Jewish people who remained in Germany.

Carmichael wrote Graham a letter detailing his reservations about Hedwig's potential employment. While it's odd that he chose to write, given the fact that his and Graham's offices were in the same building, the letter did end up serving the important purpose of saving for posterity a perfect example of the attitudes of many Americans at the time.

Carmichael's letter, heavy with quotation marks, advises prioritizing extreme caution over compassion and trust, citing Hedwig's potential as a "fifth column." This was a term that gained steam beginning in 1936, defined as someone who aimed to undermine national interests in cooperation with rival nations. Fear of such people saw increasing popularity in the mid-to-late 1930s.

Definitely we don't want to become a party to the rather panicky hysteria that is sweeping the country in the wake of the bugaboo "Fifth Columnitis"; but frankly I am gravely apprehensive and deeply concerned over the possibilities connected with the engagement of Miss Hedwig Kohn as an instructress at the Woman's College.

I am in full sympathy with a Christlike attitude towards many innocent and deserving people in Europe today; but as a matter of patriotic responsibility—not to mention our own institutional selfishness—we must exercise every precaution in our dealings with possible sabotageurs. In every country that has been invaded by the Nazis it has developed that people have been planted—so called "persecuted refugees"—who when the "zero hour" struck, opened the gates and were chiefly responsible for the ultimate downfall of several countries.

The disarming openness of the people who were planted in these various European countries and their very appealing "plight" has been one of the ingenious facets of the entire Nazi plan. I cannot too strongly urge you to weigh carefully the possibilities that our charity and tolerance might be played upon most disastrously.

The "military significance" of our chemistry department prompts me to warn that we make doubly sure![193]

A lot is going on here. It's a letter deserving of much deconstruction, annotation even: Carmichael's use of the term "instructress," for one, his declaration that he doesn't want to fall into the trap of presuming someone in need is a spy that he then clearly falls in, his assertion that he has a "Christlike" attitude while simultaneously insisting they turn away a refugee in need, lest they take advantage of the school's well-appointed chemistry lab. It's almost overwhelming. But it's also an opportunity for an illuminating peek into the mind of a typical American of the era, not to mention a highly educated one in a position of power in academia.

Hertha, blissfully unaware of the xenophobia being spewed at UNC's highest levels, continued pestering Graham. Her persistence did not go unnoticed.

"Here comes Professor Sponer again. I am sending you the 'dope,'" Graham's secretary wrote to the dean of the women's college, W.C. Jackson. "Will you please advise preferably by telephone or wire? I understand that there is no pressure from the President on this. It is entirely in your hands and the hands of the faculty committee from the physics department."[194]

By miraculous happenstance, though, the UNC Woman's College physics department was, in fact, short-staffed. Before Carmichael's nasty letter even reached Graham, Graham had cabled Hedwig an offer for the position of a physics instructor at the Woman's College for the academic year 1940 to 1941. Hedwig wrote back accepting a few days later.

Hedwig now boasted offers for three consecutive one-year positions, at the Woman's College of the University of North Carolina, Sweet Briar College, and Wellesley College. In all likelihood, these appointments would garner her a US visa and would surely address the reservations of Swedish immigration officials.

Lise, along with Karin Kock (economist at the University of Stockholm and vice president of the IFUW), saw to the procurement of a three-month temporary Swedish visa for Hedwig. She could now leave Germany at once.

36

Hedwig's Rescue

Now that Hedwig had a valid entry visa to Sweden, she and her helpers could all breathe a sigh of relief—possibly even celebrate—upon seeing their years of hard work and pleading pay off. German authorities granted Hedwig permission to leave for Sweden without any major hassle.

In this instance, her lack of national eminence was a blessing. Unlike Einstein or Lise, Hedwig wasn't a renowned enough scientist to gain extra attention. The German government would feel no need to bother with giving her grief about leaving.

Since she hadn't had to sneak around as much as Lise, she had the luxury of packing up all the things she wanted to take with her to start a new life, both as a woman and a scientist.

From clothes, jewelry, photos, and books to research journal reprints, papers, and even a few hand-wound high-ohmic resistors that were required for discharge experiments, Hedwig's baggage was of both personal and professional importance. It was also a testament to what she valued.

On July 9, 1940, Hedwig (and her many, *many* bags and cases) arrived safely in Stockholm, Sweden. She slowly made her way to the room in the boarding house that had been arranged for her.

Unfortunately, she was suffering from what she called "visa sickness." She was likely ill with worry about her US visa not coming through, and exhausted by the letdown that can come from finally allowing yourself to relax after spending months in a state of panic and fear.

"But this illness was basically an objective matter," Hedwig explained to Lise. "A tough test of patience that you tried to make easier for me."[195] She said she actually experienced very little in the way of physical discomfort. Both women did so often downplay their problems.

While in Stockholm, Hedwig got together with Lise at least once a week to discuss physics and other topics. Lise was starving for the companionship and stimulating German conversation, and with a fellow woman physicist no less.

"You so often dedicated beautiful Sunday evenings to me, in your cozy home or in nature, which I have hardly ever enjoyed as consciously as during these weeks in Sweden,"[196] Hedwig gushed to Lise.

It was a beautiful sentiment: recognizing how consciously you're enjoying simply conversing with a friend in a comfy home or on a walk. A newfound appreciation of the little things in life may be one of the only positives to come from nearly losing your freedom and possibly your life. It was also a heartwarming image to conjure amid such horrors: Lise and Hedwig relaxing freely.

On one of Hedwig's visits to Lise's home, Lise tenderly pulled out the thick folder she kept that contained all the letters relating to Hedwig's case. It was truly an incredible sight: the physical embodiment of care and hard work, proof that people all around the world—friends and strangers alike—did whatever they could to save her life.

Setting it out would help Hedwig comprehend just how far

they'd gone to see her rescued. Had they not kept pressing and pestering, her case would have more than likely fallen through the cracks, just as so many others did.

Lise understood what Hedwig was going through better than most. She had been on the other side of this experience herself exactly two years prior. Lise knew *exactly* what it was like to rely on the kindness of friends and strangers, to live in limbo—safe but anxiously awaiting the rest of the journey ahead.

Escaping the Nazis with your life and health, while involving a complex array of emotions, could also bestow a particular form of relief that led to a newfound sense of appreciation for your life. The two women surely realized how special it was not only that they were both still alive and safe from harm, but that they were able to connect and share each other's company.

For two Jewish women physicists who had been exiled from Germany to be enjoying this rare moment of communion and convalescence wasn't just charming and coincidental. It was radical.

But these women didn't happen to meet up and hang out; the Nazis had forced them into a position that required them to reach out to each other for help. Had Hitler never come to power, these two women would likely have spent long, happy lives continuing to work as professors and researchers of physics at their respective institutes, only seeing each other at the occasional science conference.

The Nazis ensured that all was taken away from them and that they were forced to flee in fear for their lives. Their meeting now was the result of years of highly coordinated efforts by numerous parties to forge a path out of Germany for both Hedwig and Lise.

Alongside those feelings of relief often came posttraumatic exhaustion and a hefty helping of survivor's guilt. Things in Germany were getting much, much worse, not better, and so many Jewish people were still left behind. How could they possibly be happy?

"Of course, you hear a lot of sad things, and how strangely perverted people's thought processes have become is shown by how often you hear that you should be very happy to be outside of all these difficult experiences," Lise told Hedwig. "As if one could feel 'happy' with the background, or rather foreground, of the misfortune of so many others."[197]

As Einstein wrote to Lise on her sixtieth birthday: "I myself am glad to be here [in America] and would be truly happy if the human suffering and vileness were not so depressing."[198]

While Hedwig and Lise were appreciating the fresh air, fellowship, and freedom in Scandinavia, the Nazis began their systematic, daily bombing raids on Great Britain—the Blitz had begun. Though the women experienced relative safety since Sweden officially remained neutral throughout the war, it was far from a joyous time.

With Lise and Karin's help, Hedwig's US visa was at last secured. It took three months longer than planned, and Rudolf had to supply yet another letter of endorsement to the American consulate, but the coveted non-quota visa was hers.

The final obstacle was yet to come, however: getting from Stockholm to Greensboro, North Carolina, amidst a war. While the Atlantic Ocean had already become a hazardous arena of battle and unsafe to travel through, it would thankfully be a year before the Pacific Ocean became similarly entrenched.

That meant Hedwig had to go the long way 'round; she got transit visas to travel through the Soviet Union. While the Soviets had begun invading neighboring countries, the Nazis had yet to invade the Soviet Union.

SECTION 3:
FLOURISHING OR FLOUNDERING
IN NEW LANDS

37

A Less Than Warm Welcome

Hedwig wasn't the only one who was increasingly desperate for a job, any job, no matter the industry. In their account of the story of the Emergency Committee in Aid of Displaced Foreign Scholars, chairman Stephen Duggan and executive secretary Betty Drury note that refugee scholars were often happy to take on any sort of job that presented itself. So long as they could earn a living safely away from the Nazis, they would say yes to any offer.

"Many former teachers and research workers courageously took any work they could find. One woman did housework and acted as a governess. Another made artificial flowers; a third worked in a doll factory. A summer camp offered a place to a woman who taught needlework, crafts, and pattern making. A specialist in Romance languages gladly took a position with a banking firm as a secretary," Duggan and Drury explained.

"An erstwhile teacher of mathematics and physics hired out as a domestic, became nursemaid to a six-year-old youngster and [later] sewed uniforms in a factory. Others became tutors, worked in summer camps, taught skiing, tennis, or horseback riding."[199]

If you weren't affiliated with a university before attempting to flee the Nazis, things were even more challenging. Duggan and Drury describe the cases of a musicologist who could only find employment as a day laborer, a legal historian forced to take a job at a bakery, and a classical scholar who now found themselves washing dishes and taking out the trash at a restaurant for $20 a week plus meals.

This pay was low compared to what they were used to, but enough to temporarily make ends meet in most cases. In the US in 1940, the average annual income was approximately $1,500, but many professionals could easily expect to earn double that, especially more seasoned ones. College professors, for instance, averaged $3,000 to $5,000 for a mere nine-month contract.[200]

Often, these temp jobs only lasted until the end of the war, but other times, displaced immigrants never regained employment in their chosen field.

Men were still favored over women in most professions, even as the 1940s dawned amidst a burgeoning world war. Misogyny trumped defense needs in many nations, where universities were actively discouraged from increasing the enrollment of female students in their science and engineering programs despite the urgent demand for expertly trained scientists.

Even displaced women scientists with impressive qualifications and backgrounds could not find work in their field or remained woefully underemployed due to nationalist fears.

Some women took out their own ads: "LADY CHEMIST. German Refugee, aged 37. PhD (Berlin), seeks a position. Some research experience in Rubber Chemistry and accustomed to conduct searches in libraries and translate from German and French." The ad appeared in the British science journal *Chemistry and Industry* in March 1941.

Wartime work served as the foundation for a successful life-long career for most men. For women, on the other hand, it typically only filled a brief interlude before they inevitably settled into full-time homemaking and child-rearing.

Often, as time went on and the more intense parts of raising children abated, women would take on "unpaid voluntary work or part-time paid employment, but rarely a permanent post," historian Horrocks notes. "And, although some [women] enjoyed long careers, few reached senior positions."[201]

As Hertha had discovered, what awaited displaced scholars when they took jobs abroad without first seeing the facilities could be a case of hit-and-miss. Women were particularly impacted.

Many workplaces didn't have restroom facilities for women or didn't allow women entry into the company canteen. And as the refugee crisis intensified, the quality of their new institute's library became the least of their worries.

Even if refugee women succeeded in overcoming the sexism and xenophobia of international hiring managers and secured positions that allowed them to flee the Nazis, that didn't necessarily safeguard against further exposure to prejudice, sexual discrimination, and anti-Semitism in their new countries.

Managing to resettle in another country didn't always mean persecuted people were walking into the welcoming arms of a new community. They could be discriminated against just as much as they had been in their home countries, but the scale and brutality of the threat were likely less extreme.

Anti-Semitism was already widespread in America when European Jewish people fled there to escape the First World War. First published around 1917, the *Jewish Vacation Guide* aimed to help them by detailing the hotels, boardinghouses, restaurants, and other facilities where Jewish people were welcome. (The book served as the inspiration for the better-known *Green Book* for Black travelers, which came out two decades later.)

While Hitler was sowing the seeds of rabid anti-Semitism in Germany in the 1920s, several powerful people in America were spouting the same vile hatred. Henry Ford, for instance—the founder of the Ford Motor Company who revolutionized car production—barred Jewish people from living in Dearborn, the suburb he had created outside of Detroit for his workers.

Worse still, Ford's newspaper republished selections and ideas from *The Protocols of the Elders of Zion*. First published in Russia in the early 1900s, the book was purported to be minutes from the secret meetings of Jewish leaders.

In 1921, the London *Times* debunked the text, revealing it as entirely fictional (and largely plagiarized); its sole purpose was to foster widespread hatred of Jewish people. Under the title "The International Jew: The World's Problems," Ford's newspaper published weekly front-page nonsense declaring that the Jewish community was secretly plotting world domination by controlling the media and the economy.

The paper was distributed at car dealerships across the country. Unfortunately, Ford's status as a widely respected business leader gave these harmful conspiracy theories more cachet and therefore made them more likely to spread.

And spread they did. All the way to Germany. A German publisher reprinted the paper's articles as a four-book series. The series is noted to have radicalized several prominent Nazis in the country. Leading Nazi Heinrich Himmler called Ford "one of our most valuable, important, and witty fighters" in 1924.

The following year, Adolf Hitler's personal manifesto, *Mein Kampf*, calls out Henry Ford by name, saying he is a great man (Ford is, in fact, the only American Hitler mentions in the text in a positive light). Later, once the pogroms had begun in Germany, Ford's newspaper blamed Jewish people for provoking Nazi violence against them.

America's economic depression of the 1930s led to a growing resentment of immigrants, particularly Jewish people and other groups perceived as ethnic or religious outsiders. They were coming here and stealing jobs from Americans. The same old tired, terrible bigotry against immigrants.

Then, as a new international war dawned, this narrow-mindedness coalesced into a fear of foreign people in general (and of those from Germany and other Axis nations in particular). They weren't to be trusted; they were more than likely enemy aliens.

These economic and social factors conspired to see Jewish refugees, particularly Jewish Germans, turned away from borders and turned down for jobs that would have garnered them visas for decades.

Even when they knew Jewish people were potentially at risk of physical harm, most Americans maintained an anti-immigrant stance.

A few weeks after the Kristallnacht, a Gallup poll was conducted asking, "Should we allow a larger number of Jewish exiles from Germany to come to the United States to live?" A resounding 72 percent of Americans responded no.

This is all to say that Germany did not have a monopoly on anti-Semitism and intolerance at the time. Nor were America and the UK the only hotbeds of xenophobia.

It was also difficult for refugees' new coworkers and neighbors to truly understand the trauma they had just gone through. While some surely tried to be empathetic and welcoming, others—having never learned of the true depths of horrors perpetrated by the Nazis thanks to press manipulation and suppression—wondered why these immigrants couldn't simply adjust to their new surroundings and embrace their new lives.

For immigrants, not meeting expectations to assimilate quicker could be yet another cause of anxiety and isolation heaped on top of the trauma of displacement.

In addition to being separated from country, culture, language, and everything they knew, refugees were potentially grappling with the loss of a chosen job/career or high-level position, separation from colleagues, friends, and family, or even the death of friends and family members.

While science is a universal language, that didn't mean it was easy for displaced scholars to jump in and begin teaching or researching in a new nation.

American education styles were especially different from those in Germany, as well as other areas of Europe. Refugee academics reported that America allowed students to ask questions of professors at any time during lectures, and were shocked by the close, collegial atmosphere among students and faculty.

38

Lise Tries to Adjust to Sweden

Lise had arrived safely at her final destination, but she felt as if she was at an emotional impasse: "One dare not look back. One cannot look forward,"[202] she admitted to Coster. Her dear friend Franck wrote to Lise while she was resting at her friend's house. He appeared to respond to the sentiments she had just expressed to Coster.

"You must not look back, but forward. Believe me, it was (and still is sometimes) difficult for us. But you shouldn't let it get you down because you happen to be living in a time of mass madness," Franck declared.

He also tried to improve Lise's outlook by offering eloquent words about their important role in the world as scientists, especially during evil regimes.

"It is precisely then that one has to show whether one deserves to have been able to become a natural scientist. Even the dictators cannot change the laws of nature and you can only feel sorry for them in their mental narrowness."[203]

Franck always did have a way with words.

After the flurry of communications surrounding the coordination of her escape, the number of letters from friends Lise received naturally dropped off. Thankfully, the correspondence did not die off completely. Some folks checked in to see how she was holding up.

After she had settled in a bit, Hertha sent Lise a letter. Speaking from a place of very recent personal experience, she offered gentle advice on adjusting to life in a new land. The women did their best to offer each other as much emotional solace as they could, even from afar. Hertha was so happy to hear that Lise had safely absconded to Sweden.

"Have you settled in somewhat? What is it like to work there?" Hertha inquired. "I'm afraid that you will never again have it as good as you had before." Hertha assured Lise that adjusting to a new country happened more quickly than you expected. At least in her experience.[204]

But Lise was having a terrible time adjusting. At the new physics institute in Stockholm, she had a lab, but no equipment, assistants, or keys of her own, and no real definition of what her position entailed.

What's more, her summer dresses were no match for the autumn weather in Sweden. The rest of her wardrobe—three additional suitcases worth, which Otto helped arrange the packing and shipping of—didn't get to Lise until well into October. And she had to use her meager spending money on the exorbitant customs fee on the cases.

Otto couldn't simply ship Lise whatever she needed. The Ministry of Education told him all her belongings had to stay in Germany.

When he appealed, they performed a full inventory of the contents of Lise's apartment. It listed four scientific award medals, two towels, one cigar cutter, and two toothbrush holders, among other sundries big and small. Anything acquired after January 1933 was noted on a separate list, since it was during Nazi rule, including hand towels and a radio. After the full inventory, Otto had to wait for explicit permission to ship every item Lise requested.

She calculated that she wouldn't be able to afford the fees to have her furniture and books sent over. Her stipend was closer to that of a first-year assistant than a seasoned professional, her pension was nowhere in sight, and she had no way to access her German bank account. At least she had Otto to pack up and insure her books.

"Things are not going very well,"[205] Lise confided in Otto a few weeks into September. "I feel so completely lost and helpless."[206]

From the end of August through October, Lise wrote Otto seemingly constantly, much like Hertha had done with Franck. Alone and with no one to turn to for advice and reassurance while attempting to transition to new lives, both women sought the solace and level-headedness of their dearest professional companions.

At first, Lise's letters concerned her precarious finances, the organization of her belongings in Berlin, and general frustrations. Gradually, the letters contained more and more about the research she was conducting.

All the while, things in Germany were deteriorating. A month after regaling Lise with a pep talk from afar, Franck's tone became much less optimistic. In his correspondence with Hertha, he expressed fear that another war was on the horizon.

He couldn't concentrate on work because he was so "worried about the great probability of a war," he lamented. "Let's hope that war will be avoided at the last moment. I hope so not only for personal reasons but because I know that a war will not better the situation of the world, and millions of people will die."[207]

Lise's new colleagues didn't understand why she was so with-drawn and depressed; they largely treated her like an outsider (perhaps if they stopped to consider these two things might be related, things might have been different). The lack of support compounded the hurt.

"I absolutely do not fit in here," Lise admitted to Franck. "Here just being a woman is half a crime and having one's own opinion is completely forbidden." Not to mention the general lack of courtesy she encountered as well as a lack of collegiality in scientific circles she would not have thought possible.

It all added up to mean "that little bit of self-confidence that the Berlin colleagues, above all you and Planck, worked so hard to instill in me, the Swedes have driven out."[208]

But Lise wasn't only depressed because she felt lonely in a foreign land, overlooked at her institution, and was enduring terrible sexism. She was also terrified for her family members still left behind in Germany, just like so many others who had managed to escape were.

Lise was part of a large family. She had two older sisters, Gisela and Auguste (who was known as Gusti), and four younger sib-lings, Moriz (Fritz), Carola (Lola), Frida, and Walter. Fritz had died years earlier while mountaineering, but her other siblings were also forced to flee Nazi Germany.

Even though Walter and his wife had already escaped to Eng-land, they were having money problems. Gisela and her hus-band were also headed to England; Lola and Frida were bound for America.

But Otto Robert's parents, Gusti and her husband Justinian (known as Jutz), were still stranded in Vienna, with Jutz having been fired from his job at a publisher due to his Jewish ances-try. The Gestapo in Vienna was in the middle of a campaign of violence: stripping Jewish people of their jobs, stealing their be-longings, and attacking, imprisoning, or even murdering them.

Now that she was out of reach of the Reich, Lise did what she could to help her family. Jutz had arranged a job in Stockholm with a publishing house whose Jewish owners had just relocated there, but needed to get a visa.

Lise applied for permission for Gusti and Jutz to enter Sweden, even though their Austrian passports were now just as invalid as hers had been.

Tragedy struck, however, when on the first night of the Kristallnacht, Jutz was arrested and carted off to the Dachau concentration camp. "One always thinks life in this world cannot get much harder, but one is mistaken,"[209] Lise lamented of her family's plight. She couldn't feel safe, even in Stockholm, with so many of her family members still in grave danger.

39

Hertha's New Life in North Carolina

Hertha adjusted to her new life abroad much more easily than many other displaced academics. One thing she had going for her was that she could effortlessly shift between German, English, and French. Plus, she had already spent time at an American university, so they were not altogether unfamiliar territory.

"Whenever I think about how many of my old friends and acquaintances have to struggle and improvise, it seems unfair that I'm doing so well," Hertha lamented. She was also enlivened by regular visits with her dear Franck.

The only hurdle she'd had to overcome so far was the rich American food. That's because Hertha wasn't just anywhere in the US; she was in the South. "My digestive tract wasn't right for a few days; Southern cooking is causing me trouble,"[210] she admitted to Franck.

The weather was another thing that took some getting used to. She described the summers as very hot, humid, and long: "In the beginning, the climate is not so very pleasant for a European."[211] Though Hertha appreciated the beautiful pine forest surrounding Duke, she realized she would need a car to get around.

Since the department was essentially in its infancy, it was a sort of blank slate for Hertha to help mold and shape. It was a lot of responsibility, but also an awesome opportunity to tip funds toward her own research interests. Much of the focus at Duke thus far had been on teaching and little had been done to bolster the university's research efforts.

"But recently, an earnest effort has been made to raise the level of scientific research. All sorts of things are being purchased; the library is being expanded even though it is already good when it comes to scholarly journals,"[212] Hertha claimed a few months after arriving in America.

The number of advanced students was small at first, but she was confident about its development potential. Within a few years, Hertha was already at work on building a laboratory for spectroscopic absorption research in a room in the university basement that was forty meters long.

"I do believe our Physics Department will develop vigorously because we acquired four new research people during the last three years and sizable funds for new equipment has been approved," Hertha told Lise.[213] Her department's main areas of concentration were cosmic radiation, nuclear physics, spectroscopy, and magnetism.

Happily, Hertha was also able to reconnect with her former collaborator, Edward Teller. George Washington University in Washington, DC, was more than happy to welcome Teller onto their faculty in 1935 after he fled the Nazis.

Hertha and Teller resumed their research on the vibrational excitation of polyatomic molecules by electron collisions. Molecular vibration is the occasional motion of atoms within a molecule relative to each other. The distance between atoms isn't fixed, so this vibration is sort of like atoms dancing with each other on either end of a spring.

Their newly resumed partnership proved both stimulating and fruitful. They published numerous joint papers, the first of which was particularly significant. It was the first publication to focus on the spectrum of benzene molecules. Highly symmetric, the molecule was known as a six-sided carbon ring with a hydrogen atom attached to each carbon atom.

This 1939 paper offered the first "explicit proof that benzene should be represented by the two Kekulé formulae, differing in distribution of the double bonds," Teller said, adding that he considered it "an interesting example of the wave nature of the bonding electrons as applied to chemistry."[214]

Due to its significance, and being coauthored by a more prominent scientist, the paper also helped solidify Hertha as a legitimate researcher and significantly heightened her reputation in the US. She was truly a scientific mind worthy of note, as more and more people were realizing.

For another major paper, Teller and Hertha met at the US Bureau of Fisheries biological station in Beaufort, North Carolina, to collaborate free from disturbance or distraction.

Their final joint paper, "Electronic Spectra of Polyatomic Molecules," published in 1941, was a ninety-six-page behemoth that included some of the findings Hertha had made in the course of researching her book.

This was the first time these findings had appeared in English. The joint text would be referenced well into the next two decades. Their collaboration ended once Teller joined the Manhattan Project.

The war caused research activities at Duke to be put on the back burner as professors taught nonstop to rush military members through accelerated degree programs in three years. Hertha understood the importance of this work, but it wasn't what she was used to, and the pace ran her off her feet. She would've preferred a better balance of lab research and teaching.

In 1940, Hertha was asked to serve as associate editor of *The Journal of Chemical Physics*. By the end of the year, she had published nearly a dozen papers in scientific journals since she had moved to America.

Her research focused on measuring the UV absorption spectra of benzene derivatives, with titles ranging from "Recent Developments in Volume Spectroscopy of Polyatomic Molecules" and "Near Ultraviolet Absorption System of Heavy Benzene" to "The Absorption Spectra of Gaseous Methylamine and Dimethylamine in the Photographic Infrared."

"I really have a good life here, and enough time for my scientific research," Hertha gushed to Lise. She even had a private research assistant funded by the Rockefeller Foundation and was able to get more equipment.

"We built a vacuum spectrograph," Hertha noted. She was so grateful for her position and its associated resources. "Our work is the greatest joy we have right now, and we can be glad that we can focus on it."[215]

Lise was happy to hear Hertha was building a life she loved in America, and even more happy to see she had finally spread her wings after leaving Franck's nest and had come into her own as an accomplished researcher and professor.

"I do believe that Hertha is a loyal soul, and I have been happy to see from her published papers that she has developed well scientifically," Lise told Franck. But she gave Franck credit for giving Hertha a solid foundation. "You have had a considerable hand in both; without the benefit of your influence, the good that is within her on a human and scientific level would likely not have found its expression in the same way."[216]

Soon Hertha moved into a newly constructed home with a lush yard. Her home and her lab would quickly become a haven for dozens of displaced scholars who visited over the coming years.

She also found a new hobby that she became increasingly passionate about. After adopting a Doberman pinscher, she began showing, breeding, and selling the dogs. What a lovely life of work and leisure she had built in this new land.

40

Hildegard Looks for a Change

While Hildegard knew she was fortunate to have gotten a job in America, she longed for a permanent contract. The constant worry that came with being on a yearly contract—of not knowing whether hers would be renewed every year—was much too stressful. Eventually, the stress brought her to her wit's end. She'd been waiting years for a professorship to open up at Mount Holyoke, but now that one was becoming available, it was in less-than-ideal circumstances.

It had only been a few years, but Hildegard was no longer "happy, happy, happy." Far from it.

"I am in a very difficult situation,"[217] Hildegard explained to Franck. Rogers Rusk, a man who, to Hildegard's knowledge, had never paid attention to physics, was taking over as head of the Mount Holyoke physics department and wanted to create a new physics institute. Hildegard said he had but one wish: to hire men for his institute.

Emma Carr managed, against Rusk's wishes, to create a professorship for Hildegard that would see her shared between the chemistry and physics departments. The dual position promised to be arduous, and Hildegard was certain it wouldn't last longer than a year.

She knew Emma was doing her a huge favor by going out on a limb advocating for her to be hired for this position, especially since it would give her more time for doing scientific research. The consequence of this free time, though, was a much lesser salary.

"I cannot endure the uncertainty any longer. For seven years, I put up with one-to-two-year contracts and questionable future prospects. I just cannot take it anymore," she admitted to Franck. "I would like to leave."[218]

Hildegard loved working with Emma, but she'd asked her for professional recommendations several times and never received them. Without them, she wouldn't be able to apply for other positions.

She had tried to resign herself to the situation. Again and again she talked herself down from the panic of feeling trapped in the chemistry department by convincing herself that soon, a position at the Mount Holyoke physics department would be offered to her. But no such position ever materialized.

Now she was ready to accept any job that offered security and opportunities for research and advancement. She was looking to Franck and Hertha for help since she didn't know how to go about applying for positions in America.

"I am very depressed because I never expected to be forced to fight in such a low-class manner for my position after so many years,"[219] Hildegard told Franck.

Even the position Carr had planned for her—teaching two courses and having time for scientific work—still wouldn't be permanent. "I would always be on the list of those who will be fired first. This is convenient for the college but makes me sick."[220]

Hildegard needed a change of scenery. Hertha invited her to come work with her at Duke, but Hildegard thought it might be easier to make connections at a larger university in California.

Hildegard sought a leave of absence for a semester in hopes of studying theoretical physics and chemistry with renowned chemist Linus Pauling in his lab at the California Institute of Technology (Caltech) in Pasadena for one semester. Hildegard and Pauling may have crossed paths when he, too, was at the University of Zürich in the late 1920s.

She was also interested in doing some experimental work in the University of California, Los Angeles (UCLA) physics department and hoped the university might be willing to offer her a job.

But how to go about looking for and securing a new permanent role, and likely funding for that position? Hildegard again sought Franck's input. He wrote back right away. The letter was coauthored by Hertha, who happened to be in Chicago on a lecture tour.

"We think you are very right in trying to get offers,"[221] the two fellow expat German physicists explained. Hildegard had three options, as they saw it:

1. Look for a position at a good university or college where she would have the opportunity to do decent research work alongside teaching classes. This would probably be a relatively small school, like the one she was at now, but there might be more room for advancement.
2. Move on to astrophysics and reach out to observatories to find research openings.
3. Go to a university or college to take what would essentially be only a teaching position, but use the long school holidays for scientific work, as many American scientists did.

Option one they called "pretty hopeless" given the current influx of refugee academics seeking these types of positions.

"Unfortunately, you can believe us both on this matter because so many people have reached out to us," they added. "Of course, you can always come across a lucky coincidence."[222]

These jobs were typically entry-level positions that went to very young scholars just starting out and might even be temporary. While Hertha and Franck said they knew of a few such posts, they believed they were beneath Hildegard. Though they offered to tell her more about them if she wished.

As to the second option, they said they believed California held the most possibilities in astronomy.

The third option seemed like the best chance for Hildegard to earn a better salary and rank, they noted. And these types of positions were likely more plentiful.

Hertha and Franck said they knew of several cases where such university professors collected experimental data during school breaks and then spent the rest of the year analyzing it in their spare time, as well as writing and publishing papers on it.

"Small universities and colleges really aren't the worst thing,"[223] they encouraged, since they could offer a secure future. She could conduct her spectroscopy research during the school holidays and use the rest of the year to evaluate her results. Places for such holiday work were easily found, and Hertha and Franck graciously offered to help with the search.

They suggested she might want to check out Mills College near Oakland, California, which they described as a "mediocre women's college." They were certain the school would be interested in a good female physicist. Though there came a big caveat about the school: the head of the German department was a staunch Nazi. Even in America, you couldn't escape Nazis!

For Hildegard, that would mean a position there would be a no-go.

Hertha alternatively suggested the university where she had spent some time during her younger years: UC Berkeley. She wholeheartedly recommended working in Francis Jenkins's molecular spectroscopy lab there if Hildegard could find an opening.

As for whether Hildegard should directly approach the chairman of UCLA's physics department about working for him, Franck offered to help her prep for such a talk when she came through Chicago: "We can talk about the way you talk to a man like that."[224]

Hildegard also needed Franck's help in approaching the Rockefeller Foundation to secure funds for a new position. For both the foundation and university administrators, Hildegard would need a letter of recommendation from an American scholar.

Hertha and Franck suggested Millikan at Caltech. He knew the most about Hildegard's current work with Pauling, and he was influential enough that his recommendation would certainly ensure her appointment at UCLA.

Franck cautioned, however, that if and when she approached Millikan, she should first make it clear that she was not looking for a position at his institute, but simply a recommendation for a position elsewhere.

Millikan—who had recently warned Duke University against hiring Hertha via a lengthy screed about how terrible women were at physics—helped ensure Caltech did not hire women for academic positions.

Additionally, Hertha promised that when she returned to Durham, she would inquire about an opportunity for Hildegard at the University of North Carolina Woman's College in Greensboro, just as she had done for Hedwig. And she would be sure it was a permanent job opportunity. Both Hertha and Franck promised to keep their ears open for opportunities at any scientific meetings they attended.

The following month, Hildegard sent Franck her letter of request to the Rockefeller Foundation, asking him to read through it, ensure she "hit the right tone," offer any notes, and send it back to her. Hildegard poured effusive thanks over Franck for all of his assistance, including for hosting her on her recent visit to Chicago.

Hildegard was really looking forward to spending a semester away from Mount Holyoke. She had just arrived in Los Angeles and was headed to Pasadena the next day. She enjoyed the drive there immensely, the terrain of the American West being vastly different from that of Germany and Switzerland.

"The Grand Canyon is fantastic and Los Angeles is one of the seven wonders of the world, with oranges, palm trees, and the deep blue sea,"[225] she enthused to Franck.

Franck was very glad to hear Hildegard was feeling a bit more relaxed and taking time to appreciate her surroundings. He encouraged her to use his name as a potential reference, but that her current supervisor at Mount Holyoke, Emma Carr, would know the most about her work and experience. He cautioned Hildegard that it was best not to disillusion Emma about her chances of staying at the college.

He suggested it would be best if she did not explicitly point out her age in her Rockefeller letter, but let them figure it out by looking at her CV. Franck was concerned she might make it sound as if she expected to be fired by Mount Holyoke College.

He said she should couch her request in softer terms, noting that she was only looking for a new job because her position at Mount Holyoke had little room for advancement. Not to mention that it saw her split between the chemistry department and physics department; she would prefer a position where her duties were more sharply connected with one department, preferably physics.

Franck believed she should explain that she was looking for an institution where she had a good chance of being promoted since this would show how driven she was to progress and advance in her career.

In the end, he suggested scrapping the entire thing and starting over by writing: "I would gladly accept a position in a smaller college with the idea that I will find a place in a greater university over the summer when I can do my research and maybe take one or two graduate students with me."[226]

Franck wanted her to stress that with such an arrangement,

she would be helping develop the spirit of scientific research at the college.

She should advocate for her teaching load during the academic year to allow adequate time to evaluate the spectroscopic observations she'd made during her "vacation" time, Franck asserted.

Hildegard adjusted her letter to reflect Franck's suggestions.

As for securing additional references, she had trouble pinning down UCLA's physics department chairman, and once she finally did, the interaction did not inspire much enthusiasm. The one time she found the chance to snatch a moment with him, he got her name wrong and then proceeded to tell her the semester was about to start so he didn't have time to meet with her. He asked her to come back and see him in a week.

Her other meetings didn't go much better. When she asked Millikan for a recommendation, she could easily sense his antipathy toward women academics.

"Millikan is such a terribly funny chicken that I'm afraid to ask him," she told Franck. "I could possibly write to Millikan if you think a recommendation from him might be useful."

Knowing how many men continued to reject women in science— whether advocating against their hiring or harassing them outright— made the fact that Franck not only accepted and celebrated them but also did all he could to help them find jobs all the more impressive.

Of the handful of people Hildegard felt comfortable approaching for references, she seriously doubted any of them truly knew enough about her to effectively recommend her.

"I haven't really gotten in touch with the folks at Pasadena or UCLA yet,"[227] she fretted, but she hoped the administrators would be more amenable to her entreaties after the first week of school was over.

She was also looking forward to Pauling returning. He was often away for research but was poised to return presently, and with a new experiment planned for Hildegard no less.

In the end, Hildegard was disappointed to find Pauling so

noticeably absent from his lab. During the many months she spent there, Pauling was only around for a few weeks in total.

Franck sang Hildegard's praises to the Rockefeller Foundation. When she heard back, though, the news wasn't very encouraging: they simply said they didn't really have a say in recruitment. So far, she had only collected an offer to teach summer school at the University of Southern California the following year.

While Franck was corresponding with Hildegard, a minor drama was unfolding in Copenhagen with his Nobel Prize medal. After the Nazis had prohibited citizens from accepting or keeping Nobel Prizes, Franck and Max von Laue had secreted their medals off to Niels Bohr for safekeeping at his Institute of Theoretical Physics in Copenhagen. Unfortunately, on April 9, 1940, Germany invaded Denmark.

Bohr raced to hide the medals yet again. Otherwise they would certainly be seized by the Nazis. Should he bury them? Bohr wondered.

He consulted a chemist at his lab, George de Hevesy, who offered an ingenious solution to ensure the medals ceased to exist but could also be restored. It was a magic trick only a master chemist could perform.

De Hevesy dissolved the twenty-three-karat gold medals in nitro-hydrochloric acid, which is commonly called aqua regia. The subsequent orange liquid was poured into a flask and placed on a shelf in the lab. The nondescript container would hopefully attract no attention from the Nazis and could be reconstituted at a safer moment.

It's likely Franck had no idea about his medal's liquefaction since notifying him would give away what they'd done if the letter was intercepted.

Anyway, he was focused on helping Hildegard find a job that she didn't have to worry about being funded year after year. And everyone was worried about the seemingly constant expansion of the war across the Atlantic.

41

Lise's Collaboration from Afar Bears Fruit

After her covert escape from Germany, Lise did her best to continue her scientific collaboration with Otto and Fritz, albeit remotely. They were determined to see the research they had begun to its conclusion, so they exchanged information via telephone, letters, and even secret meetings for several months. The Nazis may have separated the team, but they hadn't completely destroyed it.

It was not ideal; the postal service was not conducive to the speed of their work. Letters, of course, could never keep pace with the minds of brilliant scientists. Plus, Otto was often cagey about the results he and Fritz were getting in their experiments, fearful Lise would leak the findings and fiercely competitive about wanting to be the first to publish them.

Nevertheless, it was something to keep Lise busy, something to focus her energy on, and something comfortably familiar when everything else felt foreign and her own lab resources limited.

"We are now almost convinced that we are dealing with several—two or three—radium isotopes," Otto told Lise excitedly. "The finding—radium probably by way of an alpha-emitting thorium, perhaps also capable of being enhanced—is really so interesting and improbable that we would like to publish it before Curie gets to it."[228] (They were racing to beat Irène Joliot-Curie and Pavel Savitch's Paris lab to the punch.)

Toward the beginning of November, Otto and Fritz submitted a paper to *Naturwissenschaften* on their most recent findings in the uranium-bombarding research Lise had begun back at the KWI. They reported—for the first time ever—"a case of *α-particles being split off by slow neutrons*."[229]

These findings stumped Lise. If uranium was to turn into radium, its nucleus would have to eject two alpha particles. Lise's tests earlier in the year had already shown that only slow neutrons would be captured, so she was sure that if an alpha particle was being splintered from a thorium nucleus, the neutron initiating the reaction would be fast, not slow.

When she and Otto secretly met while they were both in Copenhagen visiting Bohr, Lise urged him to recheck his results.

"Fortunately, L. Meitner's opinion and judgment carried so much weight with us in Berlin that the necessary control experiments were immediately undertaken,"[230] Fritz later noted. He realized it was these secondary experiments that became key to their team finding the answer.

Lise's biographer, Ruth Lewin Sime, points out the gravity of what they were about to uncover. This was not just another interesting discovery about an element. They were shattering the basic presumptions in the field of nuclear physics.

At the time, physicists believed unswervingly in two prevailing principles, the first being "that in every known nuclear reaction, the changes were always minor: the product nucleus never differed from the original by more than a few protons or neutrons," Sime explains. "The thought that a uranium nucleus might shatter, split, or otherwise drastically change when hit by a neutron was never entertained by either experimentalists or theoreticians."[231]

The second principle was that elements beyond uranium were always higher homologues of third-row transition elements on the periodic table. Though they were separated across countries, Lise's team was about to blow up these assumptions.

Their breakthrough finally came in December. Otto was so excited by it he wrote to Lise from the lab at 11 p.m. on the eve of Christmas break:

"There is something about the 'radium isotopes' that is so remarkable that for now we are telling only you. All reactions are consistent. Only, our Ra [radium] isotopes act like *Ba* [barium]," Otto bubbled. "It could still be an extremely strange coincidence. Perhaps you can come up with some sort of fantastic explanation. We know ourselves that it *can't* actually burst apart into Ba."[232]

What Otto and Fritz discovered was that if they bombarded uranium 235 with neutrons, the result was an unexpected element that was not there before. The element was about half the atomic mass of uranium. They theorized that it could be barium, but could find no chemical explanation for its presence. Would physics hold the answer?

Three days after writing his late-night missive to Lise (and three days before Christmas), Otto called Paul Rosbaud at Springer Verlag publishers to tell him he had just finished writing a paper. And not just any paper. It outlined their experiments that proved new elements were created when a uranium atom was bombarded by a slow neutron.

Rosbaud knew this was big. Very big. He sped over to Otto's lab to pick up the paper. Then he called the editor of his publisher's main science journal, *Naturwissenschaften*, and convinced him that this article was so important they simply *had* to bump one of their planned pieces for the next issue (which was already being typeset) and replace it with this one.

Though Otto had stopped short of seeing that they had split the atom, Rosbaud nonetheless recognized its destructive potential. How easily could it be weaponized? As a vehement anti-Nazi, he wanted physicists and governments all over the world to have access to this potentially powerful science as soon as the Nazis did. Publishing their discovery as soon as possible would accomplish this. It might give the Allies a fighting chance.

While Otto and Fritz's paper was being prepared for publication, Lise traveled to Kungälv to spend the winter holidays with her only close friend in Sweden, Eva von Bahr-Bergius.

Otto Robert Frisch, Lise's nephew, traveled from Copenhagen to join them since he usually spent Christmas with her. When he arrived for breakfast at their tiny hotel the first morning, he found Lise puzzling over Otto's letter, which she insisted he read.

"Its content was indeed so startling that I was at first inclined to be skeptical,"[233] Otto Robert admitted. Given the basic principles of nuclear physics, the results simply didn't make any sense. He suggested Otto's conclusions were incorrect; Lise disagreed, demanding that Otto was a good chemist and would not have made a mistake.

Lise convinced Otto Robert that they should take advantage of the bright, sunny day and go for a walk while noodling over the issue. While trudging through the woods together, they wondered how bombarding a uranium atom might create a barium atom since a barium nucleus has approximately half the mass of one of uranium.

They walked in the snow, he on skis and she on foot "(she said and proved that she could get on just as fast that way)," Otto Robert recalled. They wondered: Was the nucleus being cleaved, as if by a chisel? It became clear that an atomic nucleus could not just be cut in half by the impact of a neutron. Their minds crackled with this potentiality.

"Gradually the idea took shape that this was no chipping nor cracking of the nucleus but rather a process to be explained by Bohr's idea that the nucleus was like a liquid drop; such a drop might elongate and divide itself," Otto Robert noted.[234]

Here they stopped and looked at each other. A true light bulb moment. They found a fallen tree to sit on and began to argue.

When they put their differing, complementary forms of expertise together, sparks ensued, Otto Robert explained. "I knew that the surface tension of a droplet was reduced by electric charge, and the uranium nucleus is very highly charged; a simple calculation made it seem possible that the slight disturbance of an incoming neutron might cause that almost unstable drop to wobble itself in two."[235]

Otto Robert began drawing diagrams since he was good at visualizations. If, after being hit with a neutron, a uranium nucleus elongated until it split in two, then those two drops would be electrically repulsed by each other. The split nuclei would contain less mass than the original nucleus.

Lise began furiously making calculations. She was sure the missing fifth of mass had been converted into energy. Lise, of course, knew the formula for computing the loss of mass and subsequent energy release of such a process by heart.

By her calculations, when plugged into $E = mc^2$, the reaction would release 200 million electron volts (MeV) of energy. Otto Robert then verified that by allowing for the mutual electric repulsion of the two newly formed nuclei, the same value could be computed for their kinetic energy.

This proved it: bombarding uranium with neutrons released energy. A lot of energy. (Of course, it would take several days and multiple rounds of correspondence between Otto and Lise before they all fully realized the gravity of their findings.) A snowy walk in the Swedish woods was about to change the course of history.

Lise and her nephew Otto Robert continued to collaborate

by telephone after returning to their respective institutes in the new year. At Bohr's lab, Otto Robert "immediately demonstrated the great release of energy which followed from this radiation,"[236] Lise said. Lise also continued her correspondence with Otto about their research and conclusions.

On January 6, Otto and Fritz's paper appeared in *Naturwissenschaften*; it did not acknowledge Lise or Otto Robert, nor did it mention their recent conclusions made over the holidays in Sweden. With the publication occurring so quickly, the information likely had not made it back to Otto in time to make it into the paper.

A few days later, Lise and Otto Robert sent *their* findings to the top international scientific journal *Nature*, proposing that the process they discovered be called "fission" after the term used by biologists to describe cell division, "binary fission." Their paper was published on February 11, 1939.

Issues of attribution aside, the scientific community was abuzz. Within a few short months, dozens of physicists had confirmed the process: uranium 235 atoms absorbed loose neutrons, causing them to become unstable and split. The fission of one pound of uranium would release the same amount of explosive energy as roughly 8,000 tons of TNT. It might even prompt a chain reaction.

The potential practical applications were numerous, and the discovery prompted a flurry of investigations into the possibilities, particularly looking at combat uses in light of the growing political instability in Europe.

Fritz freely admitted Lise's role in the discovery. He long maintained that it was Lise's initial objection to their findings and insistence they reassess the evidence that brought them to their conclusion.

"To this day I remain convinced that it was L. Meitner's critical demand that motivated us to test our findings once again, after which the results came to us,"[237] Fritz insisted.

Otto was more circumspect about Lise specifically since he could not allude to their secret meeting in Copenhagen, but he admitted their revelatory tests to confirm their findings had been performed at the urging of others.

"Only after several physicists expressed their astonishment that slow neutrons should initiate two successive α-processes in uranium, did Strassmann and I investigate the properties of radium-isotopes more carefully,"[238] Otto reported.

Otto told Lise he didn't want to confess that she was actually the one who had puzzled everything out immediately. He worried about Lise's safety, about the Nazis somehow getting to her, but he also wanted to hog the limelight a bit on this, such an incredible finding.

Ironically enough, Otto had in fact made a mistake in his paper by assessing mass instead of atomic charge. His proposal's atomic numbers didn't add up. It was an uncharacteristic slip-up that caused several eminent physicists to question their understanding of their own work, including Einstein.

Still, Otto, Lise, and Fritz could rejoice that not even the Nazis had stopped the team from seeing her years-long project to completion. But it was a sort of hollow victory.

"How beautiful and exciting it would be if we could have worked together as before,"[239] Otto conceded sadly.

By all accounts, this should have been the pinnacle of Lise's already storied career. But Hitler ensured she was unable to be there in the lab in person alongside Otto and Fritz to make this discovery.

Because Lise's forced displacement meant she could only contribute to the research from afar and her participation could not be disclosed, Otto alone was eventually awarded the Nobel Prize in Chemistry for the discovery of nuclear fission.

Yet during the First World War, when Otto had been away fighting and Lise had continued their research on her own and discovered the element protactinium, both Lise and Otto received credit for the finding. Yes, Otto had been on leave and able to help with the experiments for short bursts throughout the war.

And yes, this current political situation was a bit different—being away serving your nation at a time of war was ostensibly different from being a veritable enemy of the state—but in both cases, a temporary absence from a years-long project should not have negated the work either party had already put in.

In both situations, both scientists deserved the credit. But in the end, it was only the woman with Jewish heritage who was robbed of acclaim.

"What difference does it make that Lise Meitner was not present for the 'discovery of fission,'" Fritz fumed, noting that it was Lise's project from the beginning. "She was bound to us intellectually from Sweden," he insisted, raw on her behalf at the injustice. "The intellectual leader of our team."[240]

Another reason Lise did not share the Nobel was that the award committee didn't really know what to do with cases of interdisciplinary work. The chemistry Nobel judges didn't necessarily understand what a physicist could possibly have contributed to a chemistry finding, and they weren't about to ask for clarification since the world was in the middle of an intense war.

"Surely Hahn fully deserved the Nobel Prize for chemistry. There is really no doubt about it," Lise asserted. "But I believe that Frisch and I contributed something not insignificant. I found it a bit unjust that I was called a *Mitarbeiterin* of Hahn's in the same sense that Strassmann was."[241]

Mitarbeiterin refers to someone who acts as an aide to an important person; a collaborator, yes, but a subordinate one. While Fritz and Lise had both been Otto Hahn's assistants once upon a time, for Lise, that was several decades ago. This particular project was spearheaded by Lise, who in turn invited Otto and Fritz to be her collaborators as colleagues and equals. So for Lise to call this term used in connection with her only "a bit unjust" is incredibly generous.

In more private notes, Lise admitted that the snub hurt deeply, especially since it came from someone she considered a friend. Had Otto not been so reticent to acknowledge her participation, she, too, might have received a Nobel. She confided in Otto Robert that she felt Otto's "attitude" was a factor in the Nobel committee declining to see them all equally awarded.

Over the course of her life, Lise was nominated for the Nobel Prize in Chemistry nineteen times and for the Nobel Prize in Physics thirty times. Her brilliance was not and would never be recognized by the Nobel committee.

Later, it would become a sort of joke, a generous jest from her friends in the physics community: Lise Meitner's greatest accomplishment was winning a Nobel Prize for Otto Hahn. That she never won once for herself is a true travesty.

Would Lise have discovered fission more quickly had she been able to remain in Germany at the KWI-C? Or would she even have made the discovery at all? Was she only able to interpret what had occurred because she was now free to concentrate on science, no longer consumed with fears for her life and livelihood?

"Physics has brought light and fullness into my life," Lise observed. "What still gives ground for anxiety, of course, is what mankind will make of this newly won knowledge, which could come to be used for destruction on a tremendous scale."[242]

42

Lise, Unmoored

Finally, some good news came through for Lise. Her brother Jutz had gotten lucky. He and his wife had been granted visas allowing them to enter Sweden based on a job offer he received. Quite miraculously, he was allowed to leave the Dachau concentration camp.

Still, Lise continued to struggle in her attempts to acclimate to her new country. While the people of Stockholm were all perfectly amiable, it was difficult to make friends when you didn't speak the language.

"My past life does mean much more for me than my present life," Lise lamented to Franck. "There are, of course, quite a lot of Swedish people I am on good terms with, but we do not speak—so to say—the same language."[243]

She knew Franck would be able to commiserate since he, too, was now living in a land far away from home, with a new language, culture, and customs. But unlike Lise, Franck had his family to help stave off loneliness.

His son-in-law and former student Arthur R. von Hippel had secured a job at the Massachusetts Institute of Technology. Franck's other daughter, Lisa, married pathologist Hermann Lisco, and they also moved to the US, joining Franck in Baltimore at first, and later moving to Boston. Both of his children blessed Franck with multiple grandchildren.

Lise had her siblings and nephew to rely on, but apart from her friend Eva von Bahr-Bergius (who even then lived about a seven-hour train ride away), there was no one locally that she could lean on or confide in. She lived vicariously through Franck, asking him to keep her informed about his work as well as the minutiae of his everyday life. She had little to say about her own work.

"I am scientifically completely isolated, I can never discuss my experiments with anyone who understands them and I am completely dependent on my own criticism, which keeps you worried that you could do something but overlook the source of the error," she admitted to Hedwig. "I have to adapt my problems to the work possibilities and not proceed the other way around, which would be more scientific and satisfactory."[244]

"I don't fit in here at all,"[245] Lise moaned to her brother Walter. It didn't help that Otto was continuing the research project she'd begun without her now, and publishing papers that appeared to discredit or at least disparage her paper with Otto Robert. She had to sit back and watch her life's work carry on without her. It must have hurt terribly.

By this point, most of Lise's old friends were writing her fairly regularly. Lise and Laue continued to write to each other almost weekly since they could no longer meet for weekly chats in person.

Hertha was also uniquely able to commiserate. She, too, had experienced a lonely Scandinavian sojourn before moving to the United States, though Lise's was much more permanent. After the war broke out, Hertha expressed her hopes that Lise would remain untouched by violence in Sweden. She also sent good wishes for improved working conditions and a happier personal life.[246]

"We neither have colloquia nor other scientific activities. I do not talk a word of physics with someone for weeks on end. I am very much isolated," Lise complained to Hertha.

She hadn't even received her copy of *Physics Review* for five months. "No one here is interested in nuclear physics, and no one really understands it. As far as physics is concerned, I live here like Robinson on his island. Sometimes, I have the feeling my brain is cracking up because of calcification."[247]

Hertha and Franck were concerned by the many lonely letters they were regularly receiving from Lise, but Hertha was happy to hear that Lise's home was at the very least still cozy. "I am thinking about your place in Berlin with the winter garden, the magnificent rooms and the beautiful yard," Hertha mused to Lise.

Of course, Hertha understood that a home was only one part of the happiness equation as a woman scientist. She told Lise the most important thing was how she was doing where physics was concerned.

"I feel very sorry for you because of the little contact you have with other scientists," Hertha told Lise. "I admire what you have managed to do in spite of these circumstances."[248]

Slowly, Lise developed a rapport with her young colleagues, which certainly helped her situation. She was grateful that they began to see her as someone to turn to for insight and expertise, and she could also learn about new advances in physics from them.

"I am very happy that the young physicists have gradually gained some trust in me, tell me about their work and get advice here and there," Lise admitted. "This makes you feel less superfluous and less self-centered in your own work."[249]

Lise loved hiking and was dismayed to find Swedes far preferred biking. She did the best she could to get in hiking time whenever she went on vacation, which was not nearly as often as she would have liked.

The little vacation she had in the summer of 1938 after escaping Germany was the only one she had for the next three years. At least she found time to attend the lectures of her friend Karin Kock.

Back in Berlin, things continued deteriorating. Even if she was ever allowed to return to Germany in the future, the institute of her past no longer existed in the same way.

Soon, air strikes and the subsequent fires saw the KWI for Chemistry reduced to splinters and ash. Amidst the rubble of the city, the concert hall alone stood strong. The band played on, Brahms's haunting strains floating above the ruins.

43

Hedwig Finally Makes It to America

Hedwig's trip to America proved incredibly arduous. The harrowing, months-long journey took her through Leningrad, Moscow, Vladivostok, Yokohama, San Francisco, and Chicago. Her voyage could begin as soon as a seat on the Trans-Siberian Railway express opened up for booking. She left Stockholm on October 12, 1940, first traveling by ship to Leningrad, Russia. She was then hit with delay after delay.

Unfortunately, the trip did not go according to plan, Hedwig told Lise from Moscow six days later. "The steamer *Molotov*'s departure was delayed." It was very foggy, so they had to wait until Tuesday morning to leave, so they didn't arrive in Leningrad until they should have already been on an express train to Moscow.

This meant they would miss their connection and might have to wait in Vladivostok, Russia, for a week. "Things might not work out," she worried.

The quarters on the train from Leningrad to Moscow were abysmal, but at least her fellow travelers were pleasant. "We talked and helped each other as much as we could. Again, I found plenty of people who were helping me,"[250] she mused.

Another bright spot was that the delay meant they got to go on a beautiful tour of Leningrad and spend two and a half days sightseeing in Moscow. Plus, the hotel in Moscow was wonderful. (By the following June, Hitler would have besieged both these cities.)

Next, she traveled on the Trans-Siberian Railway express to Vladivostok, Russia, which was on the coast of the Sea of Japan. From there, she waited even longer than she had feared—it was three weeks before she secured a Japanese transit visa and boarded a ship to Yokohama.

Yet again, her "visa sickness" returned. "Of course, we all had such fears during the long wait in Vladivostok, and so it was no wonder that after all that even the best nerves failed,"[251] Hedwig explained.

Hedwig still had a lot of people worrying about her. Hertha was eager to hear how her journey was going. On October 20, she wrote to Lise to ask her to call and let her know when Hedwig departed.

"It makes me nervous because I have not heard from her in a long time,"[252] Hertha told Lise. She responded by describing Hedwig's recent missive about her difficulties with delays to Lise.

Finally, Hedwig was allowed into Japanese territory. But again, it seems she missed her connection. By the time she arrived, her scheduled ship across the Pacific Ocean to Seattle had already left.

Instead, she boarded the Japanese passenger and cargo ship *Hie Maru* alongside other fleeing refugees. She was listed on the manifest as a teacher. The ship left Japan on November 22, 1940, bound for San Francisco. By December, war will have spread to the Pacific Ocean, so these routes were soon cut off to passenger ships. (Three years after Hedwig's voyage, the USS *Drum* torpedoed and sank the *Hie Maru*.)

Hedwig arrived on American soil two months after leaving Stockholm. (Two months spent traveling on seemingly every form of transportation available, bar airplane.)

At long last, the final leg of her trip was in sight: a train to Chicago, to be welcomed by the friendly German face of one James Franck. The train trip would take about forty hours and would've cost about $100 at the time. The conditions on her ocean voyage had taken their toll, and Hedwig grew increasingly ill. The train staff generously took care of her day and night.

By the end of her journey, she had only $27 left in her purse.

As the train pulled into the Chicago station, Hedwig was beyond exhausted. The porters begged her to allow them to call a stretcher for her. Ever the proud, proper lady, she shooed them away. She took a moment to muster all her wherewithal and made her way gingerly toward the train doors.

Hedwig made it down the steps, only to collapse into Franck's arms on the platform. Franck had been waiting at the station for her train for two hours in the cold Chicago chill. He was shocked by her dismal condition.

"The state in which I fell into the arms of poor, unsuspecting Professor Franck can hardly be described," Hedwig declared. "With my last remaining energy, I stopped the train staff from dragging me off the train on a stretcher. I stood on my own two feet."[253]

Hedwig probably should have taken the stretcher option. She was quite sick, having developed a serious kidney infection and intestinal virus on her journey. Franck whisked Hedwig to his apartment. In addition to experiencing complete nervous exhaustion, she was suffering from constant, excessive pain and was unable to eat.

Her illness was likely picked up on her long, joyless sea voyage. As Hertha put it when explaining Hedwig's plight to Lise, "Traveling third class is no paradise."[254]

Franck already had his hands full with a terminally ill wife, but his caregiving abilities expanded with the need. He set Hedwig up in a small room in the hotel next door and arranged for the doctor to come.

Franck brought her every meal and refused to leave until she downed at least a few bites. The doctor visited Hedwig almost daily and discussed her condition with Franck either in person or by phone.

Franck covered the cost of medical care personally since her funding could not stretch that far. Hedwig hated to be such a burden, but she wasn't in any state to argue. She noted, though, that financial fretting inhibited the improvement of her illness. Once she realized she really needed to rest in order to recover, she finally acquiesced to Franck's assistance.

"I was so unhappy about this fatal beginning that I finally left all thinking and acting to poor Prof. Franck,"[255] Hedwig explained.

Gradually, Franck began bringing up physics topics during his visits with Hedwig, hoping it would help perk her up.

"This was an excellent cure, thanks to which I got better much faster than anyone thought," Hedwig told Lise. "I can hardly find words for how much he and his family have taken care of me."[256]

Once she was well enough, Hedwig's first order of business was to tell Franck all about how Lise was doing, and how she had been faring personally and professionally in the years since she left Germany. As her former colleague and enduring friend, Franck eagerly drank in this firsthand report.

After two weeks under the care of Franck and her doctor, Hedwig's doctor permitted her to travel. Her recuperation continued in Durham, North Carolina, at Hertha's home.

When Hedwig arrived in North Carolina, like Franck, Hertha also eagerly asked for a report on how Lise was doing. Hertha was sad that the war meant she hadn't been able to visit Lise in Stockholm yet.

Hedwig was worried that the rich local food might aggravate her intestinal issues, so as she worked back up to eating a normal diet, Hertha only cooked her light meals. Another week under her friend's care saw her nursed back to health and ready to report to work in Greensboro.

Her pain and some other symptoms lingered a little longer, accompanying her to Durham and even occasionally flaring up in Greensboro, Hedwig noted. "But the main thing was that my ability to work, which I needed from the first moment in Greensboro, was restored."[257]

By January 1941, she was finally well enough to report for work at the Woman's College in Greensboro. Hertha took her there to get settled in.

Lise, meanwhile, was eager to hear from Hertha about how Hedwig was holding up and what her new job entailed.

"She has to give two lectures which, because of the language problem, will be a lot of work, however, this situation will get better with each day," Hertha reported to Lise. Sadly, she "has her hands full and there is no time left for scientific projects."[258]

Hertha invited Hedwig to give a talk to her colleagues at Duke as well. Since they both specialized in spectroscopy, Hertha hoped to be able to help Hedwig scratch her research itch.

"I very much hope that she is able to come here for a while during the summer vacation in order to do scientific work. All in all, she is doing well, and the people in Greensboro are very nice to her, and I think she will do well here,"[259] Hertha enthused to Lise.

When Franck next wrote to Hertha, he enclosed a letter for Hedwig—"since she is your protegee,"[260] he teased. Though Hertha was younger and less experienced, she took Hedwig under her wing, so to speak. Since Hertha had arrived in America before Hedwig, she was eager to help her acclimate.

Franck was also very interested to hear how she was settling in in Greensboro. After seeing how ill she was off the train in Chicago, he had a vested interest in her continued well-being. He was so happy to hear she was thriving.

44

Lise and the Bomb

Lise's fission breakthrough set the stage for the new nuclear age. War was brewing, so the race was on to develop a nuclear weapon from her discovery. Had the discovery been made in a time of peace instead, would bombs have been the first thing on everyone's mind, or might their thoughts have gone straight to creating power plants and sources of energy?

As the patent-holder for the concept of the neutron-induced nuclear chain reaction, physicist Leo Szilard foresaw the terrible destructive potential of nuclear fission. Szilard knew both Lise and Franck from his visits to the weekly physics colloquia in Berlin. He fled Germany as soon as Hitler took power. From London, he helped establish the Academic Assistance Council to help refugee scholars find new jobs.

Now, he feared the worst and leapt into action. In August 1939, he crafted a letter to President Roosevelt urging caution.

Szilard told Roosevelt that with large amounts of uranium, it was possible to set off a nuclear chain reaction.

"It appears almost certain that this could be achieved in the immediate future. This would also lead to the construction of extremely powerful bombs. A single bomb of this type, carried by boat and exploded in a port, might very well destroy the whole port together with some of the surrounding territory."[261]

To lend even more credence to the letter's contents, he had Einstein sign it. What then followed geopolitically meant caution was the last thing on leaders' minds.

> September 1, 1939: Germany invades Poland, prompting declarations of war from the UK and France, the first two Allied powers. World War II begins
>
> October 1939: Nazis begin mass deportation of Jewish people to impoverished enclosed ghettos or forced labor camps
>
> October and November 1939: The Soviet Union invades Estonia, Latvia, Lithuania, and Finland
>
> April 1940: Germany invades Denmark and Norway
>
> June 1940: Italy invades France, entering the war on the side of Axis powers

Caution was for the weak. No one knew how fast German research in this area was going or how far they'd gotten. What if Germany beat the Allied powers to the bomb?

According to Franck, it was the certainty that the Germans were working on a nuclear bomb—and that they would have no scruples about using it—that "was the main motivation of the initiative American scientists took in urging the development of nuclear power for military purposes in this country."[262]

Nazi scientists got nowhere near creating a bomb, but the world wouldn't know that until much later.

If America had a chance for an advantage, it would take it. In

1941, Roosevelt signed an executive order creating the Office of Scientific Research and Development.

December 8, 1941: US enters the war, joining the Allied powers

In 1942, Roosevelt approved a proposed budget of $90 million for the atomic research program. Thus, the Manhattan Project was born, with theoretical physicist J. Robert Oppenheimer of the University of California at the helm.

Leo Szilard also participated in the project. Franck, who had recently transferred from Johns Hopkins University to the University of Chicago, worked for the Manhattan Project as director of the chemistry division at the university's metallurgical laboratory.

Franck and Szilard hoped to be able to encourage caution and restraint from within, rather than helplessly railing against the bomb from the outside. Lise's nephew, Otto Robert, joined the project as leader of the critical assemblies group.

Lise refused to play any part in the weaponization of her work. She remembered all too vividly the horrors of war, which she experienced up close during her stint as a nurse at a military hospital near the Russian front in World War I.

She didn't want to be involved in the creation of something that would only bring pain, suffering, and death, and refused to apply her magnificent mind to create such catastrophic weaponry.

"I will have nothing to do with a bomb," Lise demanded when she was invited to work on the Manhattan Project.

It was essentially unheard of for a scientist to refuse to help their side during wartime. But Lise didn't care. Just because a bomb could be created did not mean it should be, or that Lise had to be the one to hasten its naissance.

Her refusal didn't represent a lack of support for the Allied cause, but rather a rejection of such an extreme escalation that would surely lead to the suffering and death of innocent civilians.

Science should exemplify progress, not destruction. As a young researcher, Lise's work with Otto had been used to help develop cancer treatments. Why couldn't more discoveries be like that? They should be used for the good of humanity, not its collapse.

Many scientists who'd joined the project left when they realized that the government planned to use an atomic bomb on anyone but the Nazis.

In June 1945, scientists again urged caution about nuclear weapons. Chaired by Franck, a committee of concerned scientists pleaded with the US government not to engage in nuclear warfare. They described themselves as people privy to the grave danger for the safety of all nations that nuclear warfare posed. The group was hopeful the war would end soon without it.

They felt compelled to speak out because they believed nuclear weapons to be infinitely more dangerous than all the other inventions of the past. "The consequences of nuclear warfare must be as abhorrent to other nations as to the United States."

They believed public opinion would be on their side; that if enlightened about the effect of atomic explosives, Americans would be against their country utilizing such an indiscriminate method of destruction. "As soon as the potentialities of nuclear weapons are revealed to the American people, one can be sure that they will support all attempts to make the use of such weapons impossible."[263]

Again, the US administration did not heed the warning. The following month came the Trinity test, the first successful detonation of a nuclear device created by the Manhattan Project team. It exerted the equivalent of roughly twenty kilotons of TNT and formed a crater 250 feet wide.

The US military decided to use this new weapon in the war, even though Germany had surrendered in May.

The target was the one Axis country still at war with the US: Japan. The Allies asserted that bombing Japan was the only way to end the war, but many people in the Manhattan Project believed that a demonstrative use, such as detonating over the Pacific Ocean, would be a big enough show of force to prompt surrender. Still others believed that intelligence reports pointed to Japan already being on the verge of surrender.

On August 6, 1945, the Allies bombed Hiroshima. On August 9, they bombed Nagasaki. The result was devastating.

Determining the total number of people killed by the effects of the atomic bombings is tricky due to many complicating factors, though it's estimated at between 150,000 and 226,000 people, largely civilians. Those who were not vaporized by the explosion suffered slow, agonizing deaths resulting from burns, radiation sickness, malnutrition, or injuries.

The bombs were the second massive hit made on the country. A few months prior, the US military killed approximately 100,000 Japanese civilians by burning down most of Tokyo. These stand among the deadliest mass casualty events in history not attributable to natural causes.

After Lise heard news of the bombing of Hiroshima, she went for a five-hour walk. What had her science wrought? She was devastated by the fact that her discovery had led to such destructive weapons that had been used to kill hundreds of thousands of people. It was a dark day for physics and for the world.

Rumors flew about Lise's role in the nuclear project, despite her clear lack of participation. "A lot of nonsense will surely be printed. Everyone I talked to understood nothing about it,"[264] Lise lamented in her diary.

Even before the bomb's creation, Lise had been connected to it. In September 1940, the *Saturday Evening Post* published the article "The Atom Gives Up," which purported to tell the full story behind the steps that had led to the development of an atom bomb. It essentially said Lise escaped Germany with a bomb in her purse. (And that Otto Robert was her friend and Niels Bohr his father-in-law, all incorrect.)

The *Post* reprinted several hundred thousand copies of the article in August 1945 after the first bomb was dropped. Later, the FBI pulled the issue out of circulation and investigated anyone who requested it.

Such nonsense was likely published not to indict Lise, but simply to craft a dramatic narrative yarn around the events when the actual details of the story either weren't known or weren't deemed thrilling enough.

But the truth was that while Lise had discovered fission, she knew nothing of the atom bomb's creation since she refused to take part in the Manhattan Project. She deplored this sensationalized, largely false publicity.

After the bombings, Lise attempted to head off similar accounts by writing an article herself as the media requests began to pour in. It didn't work.

The Stockholm *Expressen* newspaper surmised that the bomb had only been created because a "fleeing Jewess"[265] scientist escaped Germany and passed her secrets along to the Allies. Why, Lise was a "pioneer contributor to the atomic bomb,"[266] *Time* magazine crowed, the "Jewish mother of the bomb."

Eleanor Roosevelt interviewed Lise on NBC Radio in the days after the bombings. It went better than you might imagine, given what was being printed about Lise.

Roosevelt introduced Lise by proclaiming that if a woman could discover this tremendous force, "certainly other women throughout the world have an obligation to see to it that it is used now to bring the war to a close and to save human lives, and that in the future it is used for the good of all mankind and not for destructive purposes."

"Women have a great responsibility and they are obliged to try, so far as they can, to prevent another war," Lise agreed. "I hope that the construction of the atom bomb not only will help to finish this awful war, but that we will be able, too, to use this great energy that has been released for peaceful work."

But how could we hope to control this new force? Roosevelt probed.

"I hope that by the cooperation of several nations, it will be possible to come to better relations between all the nations and to prevent such horrible things as we have had to go through in the last few years," Lise replied.

"We are proud of your contributions as a woman in science," Roosevelt told Lise. She said she hoped that someday, the US would see Lise "just as we saw Madame Curie."[267]

Lise felt the interview had gone terribly, that she sat too close to the microphone and was too stiff. Plus, she could only understand half of what Eleanor Roosevelt was saying. The following day, the *New York Times* reported on the radio interview with the disparaging headline "Woman Bomb Aide Sees Future Good."

"The woman who is listed among those who made the atomic bomb possible disclaims any knowledge of how to make the terrifying explosive dropped on Hiroshima last August," the *New York Times* reported in March 1946. "Public impression that she had anything 'actually' to do with the atomic bomb disturbs her."

The reporter also interviewed Lise and quoted her as saying: "I did not know that the Allies had succeeded in constructing the atomic bomb until the Hiroshima announcement. I was surprised that it had been perfected in so short a time. You know so much more in America about the atomic bomb than I."

"Dr. Meitner restricts her talk to splitting the atom, and lets it go at that,"[268] the *Times* reporter admitted, likely wishing to have pulled a juicier scoop out of her.

But Lise's continued damage control efforts largely failed. Once the press had developed this tantalizing tale—of the Jewish woman who narrowly slipped through the Nazis' grasp whilst concealing the recipe for building a nuclear bomb—they would never let go of it, even if it couldn't be farther from the truth.

Lise was also ill at ease about being embraced by the American Jewish community since she was not an active member of the Jewish faith. She told her sister Frida she felt like an imposter when they praised her. Regardless, her heritage had made her a target, and that was enough for the Jewish community to embrace her as their own.

45

Remembering Those Who
Didn't Make It Out

It is clear from these women's stories that getting out of Nazi Germany safely often involved large teams of people working together closely across several countries in a carefully orchestrated campaign effort. Not everyone had such teams, such vast connections of well-positioned friends that would fight for them. Most could only apply to aid agencies and hope.

Aid organizations did what they could with all the money, manpower, and means at their disposal, but of course, it was nowhere near enough. Of the over 6,000 applicants to America's Emergency Committee in Aid of Displaced Foreign Scholars, only 335 received funding.

Nearly all of them were men between the ages of thirty-five and fifty-five. (The organization would only work with refugees ages thirty to fifty-eight who had earned habilitation to prevent competition for positions meant for younger American scientists.) Of the eighty women scholars who applied, only four received grants.

The Rockefeller Foundation Special Research Aid Fund for Deposed Scholars helped roughly 200 people flee Germany.

Storied mathematician Emmy Noether was one of them. After she was fired by the Nazis in 1933 for being Jewish, Bryn Mawr College in Pennsylvania expressed interest in recruiting her. The Rockefeller Foundation furnished a grant for Noether to take a temporary position there in late 1933, so she escaped before most other women academics. (Sadly, she passed away unexpectedly in 1935 as a result of postsurgical complications.)

After war broke out and the danger to Jewish people intensified exponentially, the Rockefeller Foundation renamed this funding arm the Emergency Program for European Scholars, and tightened the eligibility criteria for assistance because of the sheer volume of those in need. Only 100 people earned grants under this revamped program.

However, it's important to note that grant awardees for this organization and the Emergency Committee significantly overlap and that the Rockefeller Foundation reported that six grantees failed to make it to America. Most likely because they'd been captured by the Nazis.

The New School's University in Exile sponsored over 180 scholars. The UK's Academic Assistance Council (AAC, later the Society for the Protection of Science and Learning or SPSL) helped 100 physicists and mathematicians settle in the UK. By the beginning of World War II, the SPSL had aided over 900 scholars.

Roughly 340,000 Jewish people escaped Germany and Austria between 1933 and 1945. France accepted 100,000, Portugal 80,000 (though many of these sailed to the US and elsewhere from the Lisbon port), Italy 68,000, the UK 65,000, Palestine over 60,000, Yugoslavia 55,000, the Netherlands 35,000, and Argentina, Belgium, and Spain approximately 30,000 each, while Brazil, Chile, and Bolivia took in a combined 41,000, and China 20,000. Switzerland took in around 30,000 but turned away another 30,000.[269] A long list of other nations took in a few thousand Jewish refugees.

Between December 1938 and the outbreak of the war, the *Kindertransport* program saw roughly 10,000 Jewish children rescued from Nazi-controlled territories and placed in foster families in the United Kingdom as well as the Netherlands, Belgium, France, Sweden, and Switzerland. And while these children survived because of the program, most were permanently separated from their families.

Even after successfully escaping Nazi territory, close to 100,000 people found they had not traveled far enough. The Nazis eventually occupied their new nations, and they faced mortal peril yet again.

The needs of people currently within a country's borders were always the first concern for government officials since outsiders were viewed as a potential drain on public resources at best, and suspect at worst. Government wheels turn slowly and often err on the side of conservatism rather than compassion.

In June 1939, a ship carrying just over 900 Jewish passengers trying to escape Nazi Germany was turned away from Cuba and then the US. It was forced to return to Europe. Of these passengers, 254 were subsequently killed in the Holocaust.

When it came to issuing visas, the US State Department officials' strategy was purportedly "postpone and postpone and postpone." The war meant the department began investigating the political backgrounds of potential immigrants, using any potentially problematic views and activities as a reason to turn them away.

In 1939 and 1940, the full quota of US visas was granted, but that still left nearly 302,000 Germans and Austrians languishing on the years-long visa waiting list. All told, between 1933 and 1941, roughly 110,000 Jewish refugees were allowed to immigrate to America from Nazi-occupied countries.

As for America's much-coveted, little-utilized non-quota visas, a grand total of 944 professors and clergy, 451 wives, and

348 children were granted them until immigration was largely halted because of the war. Only sixty-seven of these scholars were from Germany.

With statistics like these, it's truly unbelievable that Hertha, Hedwig, Hildegard, and Lise all managed to escape. Sadly, many other women scientists were not as fortunate.

Things became infinitely worse in Germany the longer time went on. Rations for Jewish people were increasingly reduced or stopped. Seemingly as quickly as they could think of them, the Nazis declared edicts restricting the rights and lives of Jewish people, ranging from utterly petty to absolutely life-threatening.

May 1, 1941: Natzweiler concentration camp opened

June 22, 1941: Nazis invade the Soviet Union

September 1, 1941: Jewish people aged six or older are required to wear a yellow Star of David patch on their outer garments in public, and are forbidden from leaving their homes without permission from local police

September 18, 1941: Jewish people are forbidden from boarding crowded trams, buses, or local trains, using sleeping cars or restaurants on long-haul transportation, are required to obtain police permission to use taxis, hired cars, or steamer trains, and are only permitted in third class on trains

October 1941: Lublin-Majdanek concentration camp opened

December 3: Nazis require Jewish people to contribute to the costs of their deportation; no less than 25 percent of liquid assets

December 11, 1941: Nazis declare war on the United States

December 12, 1941: Jewish people forbidden from using public telephones

January 20, 1942: Top Nazis convene to discuss the "Final Solution to the Jewish Problem"; completion of their mass deportation and extermination plan is coordinated

March 1, 1942: Auschwitz-Birkenau concentration camp opened

May 15, 1942: Nazis forbid Jewish people from owning pets

The Nazis established more than 44,000 camps and ghettos for detainment, forced labor, and mass murder. Throughout 1942, they began to carry out their "Final Solution," wherein millions of Jewish people from Nazi-occupied territories were systematically deported by train to concentration camps.

They were told their destination was a labor camp or a new settlement in the east—only to arrive at extermination centers. Many of those who'd survived the regime thus far knew what lay ahead and chose instead to die by suicide.

Among them was Lise and Max von Laue's friend Arnold Berliner, the eighty-year-old Jewish former editor of *Naturwissenschaften*. After being ordered to vacate his apartment, he ingested poison. Berliner's death shook Laue to his core; he was so upset by it that he began vomiting after sharing the news with Lise.

Like Lise, Marie Anna Schirmann had a physics PhD from the University of Vienna. Her specialty was in high-vacuum physics. She'd patented several inventions and discovered the existence of static electricity between gases and solids.

After a dozen fruitful years as a research scientist, Schirmann sought habilation at Vienna's Physical Institute in 1930. The committee rejected her application, saying she had not demonstrated "the level of general knowledge demanded by a lecturer."

Given her experience, she certainly possessed such knowledge, but had been denied habilitation purely because she was Jewish and a woman.

Despite her best efforts, Schirmann was not able to find a way out of Nazi territory. The Emergency Committee tried, unsuccessfully, to secure her a position at the University of the Philippines or Pennsylvania State University.

On March 5, 1941, Schirmann became prisoner number 107. She was one of the 1,000 Austrian Jews arrested, crowded into boxcars, and transported from Vienna to the Jewish ghetto in the small town of Modliborzyce, Poland, that day.

The Nazis cleared out that ghetto in October 1942: the old

and ill they murdered right away, and the rest they took to extermination camps. Out of the original thousand, only thirteen survived.

While it's clear that Nazi anti-Semitism is what killed Schirmann, other factors led to her inability to escape, misogyny being one of them. The reticence of international universities to hire women academics in general, and women scientists in particular, definitely contributed to her death.

What's more, if Schirmann had been granted habilitation and begun teaching at her home university when she first applied instead of being turned down because she was a woman, her teaching history would have been considerably longer. This experience would have made her look like a much better prospect for international hire and potentially life-saving relocation.

Stefanie Horovitz, a Jewish chemist, was born in Warsaw, Poland, but moved to Austria as a child. Her mind was so bright and promising that Lise Meitner recommended Horovitz for a research assistant position at the Institute for Radium Research in Vienna while she was still finishing up her doctorate in organic chemistry.

Through her research, Horovitz proved that ionium was actually an isotope of thorium, upending the conventional wisdom that ionium was itself an element.

In addition, Horovitz's gravimetric analysis—to the thousandth of a gram—showed that lead formed from the radioactive decay of uranium had a lower atomic weight than typical lead. This finding proved that elements could have different atomic weights depending on their source. It was named one of the most significant findings in the field of chemistry during the first half of the twentieth century.[270]

World War I brought disturbance to Horovitz's family life and career. She chose to leave chemistry and establish a foster home for children and young adults in need of psychological therapy.

In 1937, Horovitz and her sister returned to Warsaw. Within a few years, the Nazis converted the city into a Jewish ghetto.

At its height, more than 400,000 Jewish people lived in the ghetto in horrific conditions. Horovitz and her sister were transported to the Treblinka extermination camp in 1942 and murdered in the gas chamber.

Leonore Brecher, the butterfly zoologist, had sexism and anti-Semitism working against her for her entire career. Like so many others, her habilitation application was rejected based on her gender and Jewish ancestry. (She had applied for habilitation at the University of Vienna seven years before Schirmann.)

From the outside, it appeared that Brecher should have been in a good position to escape Nazi violence. Born in Romania, she earned an AAUW fellowship to Rostock University in Germany in 1923. She later joined the University of Berlin and then enjoyed a brief fellowship at Cambridge University's Girton College for women. Finally, she took a position at Kiel University in Germany.

When Brecher was fired for being Jewish in 1933, the Emergency Association of German Science helped her find a job in Vienna at the illustrious Austrian Academy of Sciences. But she hadn't fled far enough. When Hitler annexed Austria, she was fired once again.

Brecher frantically reached out to the Emergency Committee, the AAUW, the Woods Hole Marine Biological Laboratory in Massachusetts, the SPSL, the International Federation of University Women (IFUW), and the International Federation of Business and Professional Women—all to no avail.

The SPSL rejected her funding application because her field of research was too specialized and she was too old (she was forty-seven).

The US quotas allowed only 603 Romanians to immigrate per year. Her number on the US visa waiting list was 3,749. She was six years away from being called up. Esther Brunauer at the

American Association of University Women, as usual, did all that she could to save Brecher. The Emergency Committee secretary concluded that it was her difficult personality that made it so hard for Brecher to secure a permanent job offer.

On September 14, 1942, Brecher was deported to Maly Trostenets, a massive death camp in Belarus near Minsk. A few days later, Brecher, prisoner number 703, was among those escorted into the woods and shot into open pits.

Elisabeth Wollman had earned a degree in physics and mathematics at the University of Liège in Belgium. When her husband, Eugène, received a scholarship for a research assistantship at the Pasteur Institute in France, Elisabeth began working there as well: as a voluntary assistant. When he was promoted to head of a lab, Elisabeth began collaborating with her husband, still unpaid.

The Wollmans were trailblazers in molecular genetics. Their fruitful, decades-long collaboration built the foundation that would allow future scientists to understand the nature of viruses. The couple had three children, two girls and a boy, who all went into scientific careers.

But the Wollmans were also Jewish. After the Nazi occupation of France, police arrested Elisabeth, Eugène, and their daughter Nadine and imprisoned them in the Drancy detention camp. Nadine worked in Irène and Frédéric Joliot-Curie's lab, so they thankfully were able to organize her release.

The Wollmans' son, Élie, an active member of the French Resistance, unsuccessfully tried to get his parents released. Elisabeth and Eugène were deported to Auschwitz in a group of 900. They were among those sent to the gas chamber upon arrival. After the war, their son, Élie, and one of their students continued the couple's research project, culminating in a Nobel Prize.

Erwin Planck, Max's only surviving child from his first marriage, was executed by the Nazis in 1945 for his role in the failed assassination attempt on Hitler. Max's oldest son was killed in

World War I, and his twin daughters had both died in childbirth—one after marrying her sister's widower.

Hedwig, Lise, and Hildegard weren't the only scholars that Hertha and Franck attempted to assist in fleeing Nazi territory. They both continued to assist their fellow scientists who still needed to find a haven via a job offer.

Franck and Hertha were very worried about their former University of Göttingen colleague and friend, Jewish geochemist Victor Goldschmidt. He'd fled Germany early in Hitler's rule, but in 1940, he found himself ensnared yet again when the Nazis invaded Norway.

In early 1941, Franck contacted the New School about helping Goldschmidt come to America. They replied that they could pay the salary for a position for Goldschmidt lasting one to two years if there was a university willing to offer him a place.

The school "wished to know whether Purdue would offer such a possibility," Franck told Hertha. "I am therefore writing at once, but if you know of any possibility please let me know immediately."[271] But their efforts came to naught.

In October 1942, Goldschmidt was arrested by the Nazis and imprisoned in the Berg concentration camp. By November, he found himself on the Oslo pier alongside all the other Jewish people left in Norway, awaiting cargo ship transportation to Auschwitz. At the last minute, he was granted a reprieve: his colleagues had convinced the chief of police that his scientific expertise was too important to Norway. He quickly fled to the UK via Sweden.

For many others, the people they were trying to help escape were more than friends or colleagues. Hedwig and Hertha both had siblings stuck in Germany, still at risk. Hedwig's older brother, Kurt, was her only living immediate family and was unable to get out of Breslau.

Once Hedwig was settled in North Carolina, she renewed her efforts to try and get him to safety. She told Lise she hoped her job would allow her to vouch for him so he could join her, that she could provide her brother with a financial affidavit that could pluck him out of harm's way. All of Kurt's previous attempts at fleeing Nazi Germany had come to naught.

"He's still in Breslau, and his letters are getting sadder and more urgent. I read a lot between the lines," Hedwig acknowledged. "I must try everything for him."[272]

Four months after Hedwig wrote that letter, in November 1941, Kurt was deported to the Kovno concentration camp, where he was murdered. Between 1941 and 1943, nearly 2,000 of the remaining Jewish people in Breslau were deported to ghettos and camps in Poland; to Tormersdorf, Grüssau, and Riebnig. Those who didn't die there were later transported to Theresienstadt, Auschwitz, and other concentration camps to be murdered.

Hertha might not have realized at the time her younger sister Margot was so at risk. Their family was not of Jewish descent, so her relatives should not have been in such immediate danger.

But Margot was a brave member of the underground resistance movement. She had spent the past few years secretly helping Jewish people hide and escape. This made her an enemy of the Nazis, no matter her heritage. Margot was an academic like her sister, a professor of Spanish and philosophy. The SS murdered her in Berlin on April 27, 1945, because of her work in the resistance movement.

The full scope of the Nazis' genocide is difficult to quantify, but we know it was extremely vast and incredibly vicious. It's impossible to know exactly how many people were killed during Hitler's reign.

The most comprehensive estimates indicate that the Nazis murdered 6 million Jewish people, 5.7 million Soviet civilians, 3 million Soviet prisoners of war, 1.8 million Polish civilians, 312,000 Serbian civilians, 250,000 disabled people, between 250,000 and 500,000 Roma, 70,000 criminals, sex workers, and other so-called "asocials" (likely including gay people), 2,000 Jehovah's Witnesses, and an undetermined number of German political opponents and members of the resistance.[273]

So much brilliance wasted, so much potential allowed to go uncultivated thanks to ignorance and hatred. Who knows what cultural, technological, and scientific advancements would have been made in the absence of humanity-stifling intolerance?

It's heartbreaking to imagine how many great minds were unable to flee Nazi territory as its cancer spread throughout Europe, finding themselves caught in their clutches and sent to die in concentration camps or wither away in ghettos. That anyone, no matter their brilliance, was killed simply for their heritage is utterly monstrous.

46

Hedwig Finally Begins Anew

Hedwig was lucky to be a survivor. She knew that. She was determined to make the most of her second chance at life. She would never again take living for granted, and she dedicated the rest of her days to being the best professor, mentor, neighbor, and friend she could possibly be.

In the first line of the 4,000-word letter Hedwig wrote to Lise in July 1941, she laments not being able to find the time to write to all the people "who sacrificed so much time" to help her escape as soon as she arrived in Greensboro.

This speaks volumes about Hedwig's character: overwhelmed by work, but worried her helpers would think her ungrateful if she did not say thank you right away. But she had to hit the ground running in her new position, with work expected of her both day and night. Not to mention she was still not fully recovered from a serious illness.

Hedwig turned to her landlady for advice on handling the

dueling pressures of making a good impression at her new job and writing long thank-you letters to her many helpers. She advised Hedwig not to fret and to wait and write during the first school holiday; everyone would understand.

Hedwig complied because all her strength was being used up by the overwhelming amount of work demanded of her from the moment she'd arrived on campus. Such a busy new beginning required her to sever herself from thoughts of the life she'd just left behind.

"I was still half invalid at the beginning," Hedwig confided in Lise. "But I was saddened by the thought of appearing ungrateful, and had disconnected myself from 'what once was.'"

Of course, her letters to Lise, Rudolf, Esther, and the others had said "thank you" many times before, but she was glad to now have the time and energy to express how truly grateful she was. Hedwig's hefty, heartfelt missive to Lise ends with more profuse thanks: "What moves me every day is the deepest gratitude for everyone who helped me. You are at the top, dear Professor Meitner."[274]

Hedwig's delay in writing to thank Lise was likely not only a matter of not being able to find the time. She probably didn't know how to find the words, either.

How do you thank someone who saved your life? Someone who dedicated so much time and effort to writing letters of recommendation, negotiating with immigration authorities, and even offering their company and calming words after she first escaped? Words alone seemed inadequate, but what else did she have to offer?

To Esther, Hedwig wrote that she'd heard from Hertha and Rudolf how much she had done for her, even up until the very last minute. "I know it is especially to your help that I owe the positions at the Women's Colleges and only those positions enabled me to get out of Europe, to come to this country and to live here—in other words to find a new life in this difficult time."[275]

But it was Esther's job to help refugees—and of course, Hedwig was immensely grateful for her dedication, which had clearly gone above and beyond the call of duty—but Lise had also gone above and beyond even though she wasn't obligated. She helped even though she was a fellow refugee who was no longer well-off or well-positioned. But that's just it—Lise had just been through what Hedwig had.

Hedwig's biographer, Brenda P. Winnewisser, says Hedwig would forever feel awkward around Lise because of what she had done for her, and she felt deeply obliged to Lise and Hertha for their assistance.

"She was conscious of a very deep debt that she had to these people. She was very conscious of owing a debt she could never repay. That meant she couldn't have a relaxed relationship with them," Winnewisser says. "It was the women who got her out, and the women's colleges. Without them, she would not have gotten out."[276]

Hedwig, in turn, remained deeply concerned about what those still left behind were going through. "When I now read the reports of so many places through which I traveled last year, I get very anxious and anxious, and I think with horror who might have been on the same path this June,"[277] she recalled of her journey.

While Hedwig was settling in at Greensboro, her former colleague Fritz Reiche and his wife Bertha still lived in constant fear of arrest and deportation to a concentration camp. Otto and Lise, who also knew Fritz, sent Rudolf a panicked telegram explaining that several of his friends had been arrested.

Rudolf managed to secure Fritz a $1,000 grant from the Emergency Committee, and he and another scientist donated additional money to the family. Einstein invited them to stay at his home in Princeton, New Jersey. At the end of March 1941, the Reiche family finally boarded a ship from Portugal bound for New York.

Hedwig tried to bury herself in her new job. At UNC Greens-boro, she found that the cooperation and exchange of ideas among both colleagues and students was "as extensive and fruit-ful as one could wish for."

Greensboro had approximately 2,500 students. Hedwig found the campus extremely lively, its inhabitants interesting, and the faculty talented. "I am learning a lot myself,"[278] she quipped.

Hedwig undertook the responsibility for half the duties of a typical professorship at the school because one role had been chopped in half to give her a job. While the position was se-cure, the annual salary was also seemingly cut in half: $1,000.

Her department was brand-new; Hedwig called it a wonder-ful, functional building with an amazing array of state-of-the-art equipment. The equipment just needed to be put together.

Still, she wished there was a spectrograph so she could carry out "actual research work." Hedwig told Lise she hoped to some-day get back to a real university so she could continue doing the research she wanted.

She found North Carolina's summer heat "unbelievable," but the winter quite mild—not unlike early spring back home. Hedwig enjoyed the scenery in Greensboro and the low cost of living in the area. Even though her room on campus was tiny, Hedwig felt at home with her lovely landlady.

But being the only foreigner in a sea of Americans took some getting used to. There was at least one other German woman at the UNC Woman's College: Elizabeth Jastrow, an archaeol-ogist and art historian similarly robbed of job prospects by the Nazis' 1933 civil service law. She had arrived in America in the fall of 1938, thanks to a fellowship from the AAUW and started working at the Woman's College in 1941.

Understanding English was difficult enough for Hedwig, let alone understanding English with a Southern accent, she ad-mitted to Lise.

Still, she had already made several good friends in Greensboro. Lise surely appreciated knowing how well Hedwig was acclimating to her new life, but it must have stung, at least a bit, to hear about how happy she was when Lise herself continued to feel so lonely and isolated.

In May, Hedwig was elated by the opportunity to attend the American Physical Society conference in Washington, DC, as a member.

"What a great pleasure to see all my friends and acquaintances from old times again," she mused. "My boss took me by the hand and introduced me to everyone, reciting the same poem about my knowledge, skills, etc. over and over again."[279]

At the end of the school year came commencement and then inventory of the laboratory, which for most faculty members would be rote drudgery—additional work required of them in an already overworked, underpaid role—but for Hedwig, this work meant she was a part of something again; a member of a team where her presence was not only needed, but valued.

"You certainly understand that such things mean a lot to me, even if they are not actually science, because they express the 'belonging' that one has been missing for so long,"[280] Hedwig confided in Lise.

"It is no small feat to familiarize yourself with completely new tasks in such a short time and you must have obviously done it particularly well," Lise cheered Hedwig. "I hope that through these successes you have completely overcome the difficult times you previously went through."[281]

On the way to the American Physical Society conference, Hedwig stopped by Sweet Briar College in Virginia to introduce herself before she began teaching there the following year.

She was very disappointed to find the school only had about 500 students, which meant the physics department was very small. The college itself seemed like an anachronous institution. Hedwig said it reminded her of a noble European sanatorium or a posh girls' boarding school from "the old, old days."

Sweet Briar was nestled deep in the Virginia countryside, in beautiful natural surroundings, yes, but also notably—almost eerily—far away from other human life. It was pastoral and almost too perfect. From the moment she stepped onto campus, Hedwig got the sense that the school didn't really belong in the modern world.[282]

Even though she was grateful for this institute's generous employment offer, she was not exactly looking forward to working there. It made her even more thankful that Hertha had secured her a position at UNC first.

Hedwig spent her summer break working with Hertha in her Duke University lab, joining a small group of physicists who were conducting spectroscopic research. How lucky Hedwig must have felt, not only to have made it out of Germany but to have a fellow German woman physicist—a spectroscopist, no less!—a short trip away.

They could do research together as well as reminisce—in German—about their unique shared experience of developing a passion for physics at a time when women were largely unwelcome in such disciplines. They also had a terrible misfortune in common. Both women had a sibling who'd been murdered by the Nazis.

Hertha felt it was her duty not only to help Hedwig adjust but to see her become as successful as possible. She impressed upon Hedwig the importance of publishing a scientific paper in America if she was to make a name for herself here. Hedwig should return to actively publishing in her field, to regularly putting her name out there with notable findings.

Hertha was more ambitious than many other displaced scholars. Not being Jewish, Hertha's experience hadn't been quite as harrowing. Hedwig, however, had almost certainly escaped death when she fled to America, an experience that left its mark on her. She was ecstatic to have a job in her field and a roof over her head. Moving up in the ranks and achieving prominence were likely far from her mind.

But seeing Hertha's success—seeing how far one could go despite a career being interrupted, despite a move thousands of miles from home where everything seemed foreign—was inspirational.

Hertha had achieved enormous things at Duke in just a few years. "The excellent spectroscopic devices are almost all hers and, as you have certainly seen from the journals, have produced many beautiful works," Hedwig gushed to Lise.

Hedwig was in awe of how well Hertha had settled in to American life. "She is fabulously calm, resilient, and successful. I believe that it has already helped many physicists here, especially female physicists."[283]

Hedwig saw how it might be possible to rebuild a life she loved. Simply the fact that someone cared enough about her to take her under their wing—to make sure she was cared for and supported and knew how to navigate American academia and culture—was incredibly heartening.

47

Hedwig Spreads Her Wings in Massachusetts

Since Hertha was adamant Hedwig get published in an American journal, they got down to work investigating the spectrum of benzene trifluoride at her Duke lab in the summer of 1941. Derived from benzene, this man-made chemical compound is a colorless liquid with a pleasant odor that is useful in creating high-temperature solvents, dyes, fungicides, and pesticides.

The study wasn't quick to bear fruit, however; Hertha says they encountered "bad luck." They returned to their investigation over the next seven years, both in correspondence and whenever Hedwig returned to Duke during school breaks.

Hedwig ended up spending a year and a half at the UNC Woman's College, then bypassing her invitation to Sweet Briar to go directly to her prearranged position at Wellesley College in 1942. (Her visit to Sweet Briar proved the institution would not be a good fit for her, so she was happy to have been allowed to bow out of the offer.)

Moving from the Southern US up north to Massachusetts was another big transition for an older academic, but Hedwig, ever the optimist, was up to the challenge. At least she could now be rid of the hellish summers.

The physics department at Wellesley and the school's Whiting Observatory had been established by Sarah Frances Whiting in 1875. Whiting became an early experimenter on X-rays. It was a comfort of sorts to be at an institution that women had been a part of since the beginning, and not just in liberal arts, but in hard sciences.

Hedwig lived in the faculty apartment in Wellesley's Norumbega House dormitory. She loved that this gave her even more contact with students. The dorm was right in the center of the campus, opposite the Physics Department in Pendleton Hall, which housed both physics and chemistry.

She was joining a department populated by five women professors and instructors as well as three assistants. For the 1942–1943 school year, Hedwig helped teach two sections of elementary physics and, on her own, taught two three-credit-hour classes.

Hedwig's atomic physics class covered the kinetic theory of gases, the nature of radiant energy, the nuclear and extra-nuclear makeup of atoms, and the phenomena of cathode rays, photoelectricity, ionization, optical spectra, X-rays, cosmic rays, radioactivity, and isotopes.

Her class on light touched on quantum theory, showed students how to use optical instruments, and introduced the concepts of wave theory and wave mechanics and how they applied to diffraction, refraction, polarization, and dispersion.

"She was a remarkable woman who was a great influence on me," mused former Wellesley student Betsy Ancker-Johnson, who also lived in Norumbega House during her freshman year. The dorm was "really a ramshackle old big house," Betsy laughed.

"I had met her because she dined in the same place we did and was very friendly. She knew I was taking physics so she invited me, if I had problems, 'Knock on the door. I'll be glad to talk to you.' And, I took advantage of that frequently and got to know her quite well at that point, though she was not one of my professors at that stage."[284]

It wasn't until much later, when Betsy came across a biography of Lise, that she truly understood what these women had been through. They "were so terribly persecuted in what was just an unbelievable situation. And of course, the women already suffered from a tremendous amount of male chauvinism," Betsy lamented. "She escaped with virtually nothing,"[285] she said of Hedwig.

After a while, Hedwig's dedication and scientific acumen were rewarded when she was allowed to establish a small research laboratory for flame spectroscopy at Wellesley. It didn't produce much in the way of publications, but it was hers. All she wanted was to build students' interest and aptitude in her beloved specialty.

In 1946, Hedwig was elated to be granted US citizenship. She could now truly call America home. By 1948, she was awarded full professorship at Wellesley. In November 1950, she gave the Sigma XI all-college lecture.

"Research in optical radiation is important not only to the physicist, but to every scientist," Hedwig announced. "Measurements of the intensities of spectral lines lead to a knowledge of the structure and constants of the atom, such as its size." She explained that she interpreted these measurements based on "our classical conceptions of light and the quantum theory."[286]

In coverage of the event the following day, *The Wellesley News* highlighted the potential applications Hedwig's research had in the areas of commercial lighting, chemistry, and astrophysics. Throughout her time in America, Hedwig had a very thick German accent, but her openness, sense of humor, and friendly demeanor ensured her accent didn't scare students away.

48

Hildegard Lands in Virginia

With Franck and Hertha's help, Hildegard continued reaching out to anyone she felt might hire her for the type of position she really wanted: a full-time, permanent physics professor job. So many displaced scholars were having to make do with positions that saw them underemployed, outside their expertise, or unappreciated because of hurdles related to language differences.

Hildegard knew she was lucky. Displaced scholars who'd found paid employment in their field were expected to be only grateful, gracious. But for many, it must have felt like a sort of punch in the gut to be so professionally demoted and then expected to be thankful.

To want more was viewed as audacious. But women scholars in particular were accustomed to pushing harder to get closer to where they wanted to be. It was a thin tightrope to walk, needing to appear grateful while confidently asserting you were capable of much more, if only you were given the opportunity.

When she contacted Dr. C. H. Kunsman, chief of the United States Department of Agriculture's physicochemical and analytical division, she name-dropped both Franck and Hertha. "I was told here that he was looking for all sorts of physicists," Hildegard said. "I also wrote him that in all probability I would still become a citizen this year." She was already in the process of turning in her final paperwork for naturalization.

At the very least, she remained enthusiastic about staying in California. "Pasadena is nice and I like the chemical institute very much. Most importantly, I'm relieved of the pressure I was constantly under at Mt. Holyoke."[287]

Miraculously, Hildegard managed to spend a year teaching at Caltech, in Millikan's "lady-free" sanctuary, from around 1941 to 1942. (Notably, the institute didn't accept female undergraduate students until *1970*!)

Her research apparently impressed Millikan enough to allow her to teach, though not enough to offer her a permanent post.

This was the second incident in Hildegard's history where she was able to work under men who were notoriously against women science professors. Robert Pohl back at the University of Göttingen and now Millikan at Caltech.

She hoped to have luck finding a permanent position elsewhere, ideally without such prejudice. When her time at Caltech was over, she applied for a position as a physicist at the National Cancer Institute of the National Institutes of Health.

Luckily, she could at least count one prominent friend who wholeheartedly supported women scientists; she listed James Franck as a reference on her application.

The institute's chief reached out to Franck, explaining that the nature of the work required thorough knowledge of electronics and would likely later branch out into work in biological studies of the action of radioactive isotopes.

Franck responded with a glowing recommendation, explaining that Hildegard had published many papers in the field of spectroscopy in relation to both chemistry and physics. What's more, her name was well known among spectroscopists.

Franck said she had an "agreeable" personality and was adept at adapting to new surroundings, a skill which she displayed "first in Germany, then in Switzerland, and then here in the U.S.A.," Franck asserted. "I would be glad if you could offer her this position as I have a very good opinion of Dr. Stücklen."[288]

Unfortunately, this letter wasn't enough to get her hired, but like Hertha, she knew better than to put all her eggs in one basket. Sweet Briar College in Virginia offered her a faculty position teaching physics in 1943.

Hildegard Stücklen faculty photo at Sweet Briar College, 1955.

Yes, it was another small women's college where she would have few research opportunities—and Hedwig seemed to think it looked more like an old-fashioned girls prep school than a college—but the post of head of the physics department was vacant, and it was Hildegard's if she wanted it.

It was one thing to take a sabbatical from Mount Holyoke to visit Caltech for a year, but leaving for good was quite another matter. When they heard about her offer from Sweet Briar, Mount Holyoke said it could make her position permanent if she would only stay. But she had long since wanted to leave, so to Sweet Briar she went.

Hildegard moved into the Book Shop Apartments and taught four sections of general physics, nuclear physics, atomic physics, electronics, and "Outline of Astronomy." This last one was an advanced seminar course that introduced the classical concepts as well as new advances in our knowledge of the stars, which had been made possible by applying astrophysical investigation methods.

Students and colleagues alike appreciated Hildegard's subtle sense of humor, and she settled in perfectly. It was a relief to be assigned to only one department now, not pulled between two as she was at Mount Holyoke.

Better, for sure, but not quite perfect. The extensive class load left little time for Hildegard to delve into her research interests. But there was a way to fix that.

Durham was only about three hours away from Sweet Briar. Hertha also felt a sense of responsibility for Hildegard, both for her well-being and her professional progress, so Hertha invited Hildegard to scratch her research itch at her Duke lab.

49

A Union of Scientists

Since Hertha's arrival in the US, she and Franck had grown even closer. Despite the fact they no longer shared a lab—and were now nearly 800 miles apart—their relationship continued to blossom.

Franck's first wife, Ingrid, died in 1942 at age 59 after suffering from multiple sclerosis for many years. For a while, Franck felt very lost. Hertha offered solace and helped him work through his grief. Soon her love inspired him toward a much more positive outlook.

But Hertha also needed a comforting shoulder to cry on. For one thing, her book's final chapter had finally come to a close. After war broke out, the US government declared Hertha's book, *MolekulSpektren*, one of many texts that had been penned by enemies of the state and therefore had potentially dangerous content. It confiscated any German copies in America and republished the book. The original authors would receive no compensation.

But she had much bigger concerns. During and after the war, Hertha was very concerned about her family members who were still in Europe. In December 1945, formerly occupied European countries now faced the prospect of starvation and a frigid winter.

In response to a panicked letter Hertha sent him, Franck did his best to provide consolation in a letter written two days before Christmas.

"I understand only too well your anxiety and desperation about your family," Franck admitted to Hertha. He explained how the Nazis had murdered two of his cousins and their families. "Believe me, it is not a nice feeling to always ask oneself whether one could have saved them. You really do not help if every moment you are torturing yourself."[289]

Describing all the losses your extended family suffered at the hands of the Nazis doesn't exactly qualify as comforting, but what Franck likely intended was to commiserate with Hertha's deep feelings of fear and sadness. He was trying to show her she wasn't alone and that beating herself up about not having done more was not going to change anything that occurred.

Hertha wasn't the only one who confided in Franck about feelings of helplessness from afar. Lise also confessed to Franck that she felt "very uneasy" that she was so far away from Germany, unable to do anything useful. "What a relief if I could now do some helpful work! I hear so many distressing things and therefore my desire to help gets still stronger."[290]

After his letter of comfort, Franck sent Hertha a large box of chocolates for Christmas. He wished she would have joined him in Chicago over the holidays. The distance from Durham to Chicago seemed especially pronounced during the holidays.

Slowly, the pair began to understand that their feelings for each other had now grown beyond friendship.

In June 1946, Hertha and Franck got married. Hertha was fifty years old, and Franck was sixty-three. By that point in her life, Hertha likely believed she would never get married, that she would continue to live a life of solitude devoted to her dogs and her work.

But love had finally come for Hertha: "We are happy; no, we are very happy,"[291] she gushed to Lise.

"Whenever my thoughts go to you and your delightful house, it makes me very happy to know that your dogs (how many are there at the moment?) are now playing second fiddle,"[292] Lise joked with Hertha.

A lot of thought went into whether it was a good idea or not to marry at their age.

"Of course I was full of inhibitions, the memory of Ingrid, my own age, the general situation in the world, and other reasons seemed to speak against our marriage," Franck admitted.

Ultimately, however, it was the right decision. They were like a couple of lovesick teens. "These reasons could not prevent us from marrying, as soon as we both realized how much we needed each other. I am more than grateful that fate had still so much happiness in store for both of us."[293]

Lise, after visiting them both shortly before their marriage, told their friends that they were "happy as children"[294] together.

Franck told Lise that after careful contemplation, he and Hertha realized it was the right thing for them.

"We knew that before as well, but exactly how right it is and how much we both needed one another, that's what we are finding out only now," Franck gushed to Lise. "It is nice to feel in every moment that we belong together and fit together. Although we've known each other forever, everything is still new and wonderful."[295]

Otto Robert said that in Franck's later years, he would joke with Lise that he had fallen in love with her as well. "Spät!" Lise chuckled in response. ("Late!")

When asked why she never married, Lise once replied: "I just never had time for it!" She had received a marriage proposal from a Greek physician during World War I, but while she kept the beautiful letter, she did not accept the offer.

If she ever possessed romantic feelings toward Otto earlier in their collaboration, she never admitted it. Their work relationship was so unique for the time—a woman working closely with a man alone—Lise felt they had to be careful to avoid appearing that they had anything more than a professional relationship.

"There was no question of any closer relationship between us outside of the laboratory. Lise Meitner had had a strict ladylike upbringing and was very reserved,"[296] Otto explained.

He says they rarely dined together or even took walks together, even though these likely would have been socially acceptable ways for friends to socialize at the time.

But even though she remained single throughout her life, Lise didn't buy into the idea that all women had to choose between a career and a family. Later in life, Lise told a group of women college students that the dual demands of career and children could quickly become too heavy a load for many professional women.

She noted that while the decline in domestic service meant it was more difficult for women to manage both family and professional responsibilities, it wasn't impossible.

"Some women are sufficiently healthy and well-balanced to cope with the double task of profession and family, without detriment to either, and without damage to themselves," Lise noted. "Undoubtedly, women can see no ideal solution to their problem: profession and family."[297]

She suggested husbands could assist by helping out around the house, but this was only part of the solution. Her understanding of the balancing act undertaken by women who try to "have it all" is quite impressive given she did not have children herself.

As for Hertha and Franck, Lise not only wholeheartedly approved of their union, she found it came just in time for Hertha.

"For 'the Sponerin' it is not only a godsend, but a deliverance. She was well on the way to becoming misanthropic," Lise told her good friend Laue. "She has had many very painful experiences; her younger sister was murdered by the Nazis because she participated in the underground movement; the wife and child of a young nephew were killed by a bombing, and the nephew, who lost a leg and right arm, is a prisoner of war in France."[298]

Lise was shocked by Hertha's poor mental state when she visited her in Washington D.C. during Lise's speaking tour of the US. Lise was very happy, and relieved, to discover that after getting engaged, it was as if Hertha was a totally different person.

The newlywed couple continued teaching at their respective institutions, he at the University of Chicago and she at Duke. Until Franck retired, they could only spend school breaks together, but they made the most of every moment.

"During the time we are together, we try to capture as much happiness as we can,"[299] Franck remarked. It must have felt like a new lease on life for both of them; a spark of hope in a world that had seemed so utterly hopeless as of late.

Another bright spot for Franck was the conclusion of the saga of his Nobel prize medal. The chemist who'd dissolved the medals, de Hevesy, had been forced to flee Copenhagen in 1943 because he was descended from Hungarian Jewish nobility.

When he returned to Bohr's lab after the war, he found the flask of dissolved medals entirely undisturbed. De Hevesy proceeded to precipitate the gold out from the acid and sent it to the Nobel Society. Franck's and Laue's medals were then recast from their original gold. The reconstituted medals were re-presented to the two men in 1952.

It was yet another way scientists used their genius to outsmart the Nazis at their own game. Medals and awards might not seem that significant when discussing people's lives and livelihoods, but they are an important way to showcase our values as a society and elevate the people who espouse the epitome of excellence in their field and dedication to the betterment of humanity.

50

Lise Tours America

Lise's plane landed in New York on January 25, 1946—her first trip to America. The petite scientist stepped out into the cool winter air and was met with a horde of reporters. Cameras flashed; journalists shouted questions. Lise immediately turned around and went back into the plane to compose herself since she was not at all prepared for the onslaught. She hurried to the embrace of her sisters Frida and Lola, and her nephew, Otto Robert, who were waiting for her on the tarmac. Otto Robert was now living in America after he agreed to join the Manhattan Project.

Lise had accepted a visiting professorship at Catholic University in Washington, DC, for the spring semester. But that wasn't all she had planned.

Her American itinerary was packed: it included stops across the country to visit several colleges and give talks, as well as make long-overdue visits to catch up with old, cherished friends.

Though she shunned publicity, she surely appreciated being asked by so many leading schools to speak about nuclear physics, women in science, and other issues that were dear to her heart.

After one of her classes at Catholic University, a sexist *New York Times* reporter described Lise as a quiet, diminutive woman who discussed nuclear fission like a home economics teacher showing a class of housewives how to make strawberry preserves.

"She may employ a friendly, sympathetic smile that begins quickly about the mouth and fades slowly and reluctantly from her brown eyes,"[300] the reporter quipped. One wonders if this journalist ever subjected male scientists he was reporting on to such demeaning aesthetic evaluation.

A Women's National Press Club banquet was given in her honor, where she was awarded "Woman of the Year." Reports say Lise was "visibly moved" by the award. At the event, she was seated next to President Truman. They discussed the bomb, with both parties agreeing they wished for it to never be used again.

After lecturing at Princeton University, she got to catch up with Einstein and Rudolf. Then it was on to speak at Columbia, Harvard, MIT, Smith College, the American Association of University Women, and other professional women's groups, including the women of Congress.

Brown and Purdue Universities bestowed honorary degrees on Lise. Next came visits to Goucher and Pembroke Colleges, Carnegie Mellon University, the University of Illinois, an American Physical Society meeting, and a cocktail party with people from the Manhattan Project.

At Hedwig's request, Lise spoke at Wellesley as well. Lise bunked with Hedwig in her very tiny apartment. "They rattled away in German for two or three days," student Betsy Ancker-Johnson remembered. "They had been through similar experiences, of course."

It was a big deal for a scientist as famous as Lise to come visit such a small women's college, and it only happened because of the women's friendship. Betsy was very excited to hear Lise speak and to know her professor could count such a renowned scientist as a friend. "I was terribly impressed, of course, to even be in the same building with such a famous person,"[301] Betsy admitted.

Another Wellesley student at the time, Janet Jeppson (future wife of Isaac Asimov), also remembered Lise's talk on nuclear fission: "I understood not a word of what she said, but I did understand the intensity of how she was saying it, and that fission could change the world."[302]

In April, Lise gave a lecture at another small women's institution, Sweet Briar College, at Hildegard's invitation. The two women physicists had met in Zürich, and while Lise was not as close with her as she was with Hertha and Hedwig, they maintained a correspondence.

In preparation for the event, the school paper quoted from Lise's interview with Eleanor Roosevelt:

"Dr. Meitner believes that the women of the world have a special aptitude for building international peace. Pointing out that, because of the power and resources of this country, American women particularly are fitted to play a big role in establishing and maintaining peace."[303]

Lise then went on to speak on atomic energy at Duke University. While in Durham, she visited Hertha and Hedwig at Hertha's home, making time to stop and smell the beautiful blooms of dogwood and meadowsweets in the garden. (Hedwig had come down from Massachusetts for the talk.)

Hertha arranged an intimate dinner for them at her home, with no additional guests to bother them. Lise was taken aback when Hertha took the opportunity to tell her in person how much of an impact she had had on Hertha as a young researcher.

All these large events she'd been attending were likely a bit overwhelming for Lise. It was a lot, especially after spending so many years in veritable isolation in Sweden. Over the years, Lise had never shaken the feeling that she didn't belong in Sweden.

"My working conditions are as bad as they were from the

beginning, but it is of no use to talk about it,"[304] she confided in Franck.

June saw a long stay with Franck in Chicago. Franck, she noted, was "as lovable as ever, with an admirable, wise understanding for many things."[305]

Like Franck, Lise often made public pleas for help in saving German civilians from starving to death after the war. But she was dismayed to discover that most people couldn't differentiate between Nazis and other Germans. To most Americans, all Germans were evil, end of story. She was stumped by how they could be so reductionist as to believe any non-Jewish resident of Germany was the equivalent of a perpetrator.

As a scientist of celebrity status thanks to her well-publicized discovery of fission that led to the creation of the atomic bomb, Lise's trip to America also meant dealing with Hollywood. Metro-Goldwyn-Mayer asked Lise to approve of her depiction in *The Beginning or the End*, a film about the Manhattan Project.

Lise thought it was absurd; "nonsense from the first word to the last. It is based on the stupid newspaper story that I left Germany with the bomb in my purse," she told Otto Robert. "I answered that it was against my innermost convictions to be shown in a film, and pointed out the errors in their story."[306]

In regards to approving the movie, Otto Robert recalled Lise saying something along the lines of "I would rather walk naked down Broadway!"[307] MGM hoped a bigger payday might persuade her to reconsider. In response, Lise threatened to sue. She gave Franck and two other friends in America power of attorney for her, advising them to sue MGM if any woman scientist bearing even a passing resemblance to her appeared in the film.

Lise continued to refuse permission to use her name in films and plays. J. Robert Oppenheimer, on the other hand, approved of the use of his likeness in the movie and was even a narrator, though he too admitted he found the script ridiculous.

July saw her on a ship crossing the Atlantic to spend time with friends and family in England. It was truly a glorious year of re-union and reconnection. After so many years spent lacking social-ization and professional stimulation, it must've been rejuvenating.

Still, seeing so many old colleagues and family members now happily settled in new surroundings threw Lise's lonely life in Stockholm into even starker relief. It wasn't in her nature to be envious, but she might now have begun to regret not trying harder to find a job in America or England.

"I cannot understand myself, having had the opportunity to stay in England in July 1939 that I did not do it," Lise lamented.[308]

In 1947, Lise's old collaborator Fritz Strassmann invited her to resume her position as head of physics at the new KWI-C, which he was in the process of rebuilding out of the rubble in Berlin. She took her time to consider the prospect, but in the end felt she could not face returning to Germany. In particular, she was apprehensive about not being able to trust her employees.

Instead, she joined a new facility for atomic research, the Royal Institute of Technology in Stockholm. Lise was given three rooms, two assistants, and access to technicians to create a small department of nuclear physics.

The institute even had friendly colleagues, thank goodness. Here, she continued her research on nuclear reactions, seeing what good she could bring from her work. She found purpose in helping to create Sweden's first nuclear reactor. She remained true to her ideals and never used science for war or other de-structive purposes.

"There are still so many problems to be solved," she explained. "I have much research work to do. I am a scientist."[309]

While her professional life in Sweden was finally looking up, there was no denying that Lise's time in Sweden had stunted the progression of her scientific career. Separating Lise from her team at the KWI had certainly robbed the world of further world-changing breakthroughs, but the Nazi era also revealed her former colleagues' true colors.

51

The Displaced Feel Betrayed
by Those Who Stayed

How to move on after the Nazi defeat? Who should experience repercussions? Where should blame lie? Was revenge against the Nazis ethically justifiable? Prominent Jewish émigré scientists discussed whether it was best to advocate a position akin to "forgive and forget" for fear that Germans who'd escaped or were members of the resistance would get caught in the crossfire, or to instead call for Germans to be prosecuted and penalized to the full extent of international law.

Franck and Einstein, for example, held different views.

"I personally do not belong to those who are willing to forgive all sins and crimes," Franck admitted to Einstein. "I wish they had dealt with the Nazi scum in a very different way."[310]

Still, Franck hoped to rise above the urge for vengeance.

"The feeling of revenge is, of course, strong in Jewish circles. If that goes on, the Nazis will have won in their battle for the demoralization of the whole world,"[311] Franck declared.

He agreed that Nazis should be punished, but Franck still had plenty of people in Germany he considered friends and he feared such retribution would doom many German civilians who now faced starvation during a bleak winter.

Franck told Einstein he planned to never set foot in Germany again because he did not want to come into contact with those who said yes to Nazism. But he also wanted no part in punishing the innocent. He concluded that the only way to forge a brighter future for mankind was by elevating our morals and ethics: "if the Nazis have robbed people of supporting this, then they have simply won."[312]

For Einstein, the horrors perpetrated by the Nazis deserved all the vengeance the international community could muster. Some things truly are unforgivable.

"The Germans slaughtered millions of civilians according to a carefully conceived plan in order to steal their [jobs]. They would do it again if they could. The few white ravens among them changes absolutely nothing."[313]

Lise felt deeply betrayed by those who stayed in Germany. Otto Hahn and Max von Laue in particular—both of whom she had known since her arrival in Berlin—drew sharp criticism from her. Lise believed Otto and Laue should've left the country or sought different jobs since their work directly supported the Nazi Party.

After reuniting with Laue in London when she was there for a nuclear physics conference, Lise found that while he seemed to understand that "the disaster that Nazism brought to Germany did not happen by chance, but was the consequence of an ideology that developed for over a hundred years," he also believed most of the people now condemning Germans wouldn't have acted any differently if they had been in Germany at the time.

Otto had shown Lise exactly who he was when he threw her out of the KWI to save his own skin and that of the institute.

"If I am thinking back on the old friends as Otto or Max, I am afraid, we should not agree on very important points,"[314] Lise admitted to Franck sadly. At least she had Franck to confide in. He was one of her few close friends who had similar ideas and impulses about the Nazis, having been similarly exiled from his position and country.

When Max Planck (who also remained in Germany) planned a visit to see Lise in Sweden in June 1943, she was of two minds. "Of course, I am looking forward to Max's visit, yet at the same time I am anxious—will we understand each other when talking frankly?"[315] (This was still a few years before Max's last surviving child would be murdered by the Nazis.)

Her anxiety stemmed from another visit Lise had recently endured—from the student of another research colleague who had stayed at the KWI—that gave Lise pause about how openly she would be able to speak with any of her old friends who'd stayed in Germany.

"He was rather unhappy, expecting that I would feel much pity for him and the others. He seemed very disappointed when I emphasized that the main feeling I had towards him and the others was the feeling of perfect inability to understand them," Lise fumed to Franck. "And what a dreadful thing that I did feel suspicious the whole time I was talking with him and was on my guard not to say anything that might be misused."[316]

She needn't have worried about Planck, though. Her dear mentor expressed such solidarity and remorse on his visit: "Terrible things must happen to us. We have done the most horrible things," Planck admitted. Lise was so relieved to hear these words.

"This 85-year-old man was more courageous in his resistance than all the others,"[317] Lise insisted.

Lise's close friend Elisabeth Schiemann had also remained in Germany. She'd taken charge of the crop history department at the new KWI for Crop Plant Research and even become a full professor at the University of Berlin.

During Hitler's rule, Elisabeth openly spoke out against the Nazis and, as a geneticist, felt uniquely positioned to denounce their eugenics ideas and policies as ludicrous. She participated in the resistance movement, hiding fleeing Jewish people and encouraging church leaders and government ministers to similarly speak out in protest of the terrible treatment of the Jewish community.

These activities meant that in 1940, Elisabeth was also fired from her teaching position at the University of Berlin, her habilitation withdrawn.

Yet even these heroic activities did not prevent a rift from forming between Lise and Elisabeth. Lise's letters grew colder and fewer, and when they finally reconnected in person in 1947, Lise could sense that the friendship likely would never be what it once was. Lise felt Elisabeth's patriotism and belief in German superiority were notions she simply couldn't agree with.

"It takes half or even a whole lifetime to make a few friends, and then one loses them in the blink of an eye,"[318] Lise acknowledged.

While she felt specifically betrayed by Otto, she wasn't ready to lose his friendship so easily. She fought hard to keep it by trying to make him see her point of view. She cared enough about their friendship to speak her mind and try to patch things up.

Had she not cared about her relationship with him, she would have simply written him off, not bothered spending her energy on trying to make him see how his actions had been hurtful to her and other Jewish people.

Lise wrote an incredibly powerful letter to Otto to make him understand where she was coming from. She'd lost contact with Otto and Laue after Germany surrendered to the Allies on May 8, 1945, but an American secret agent who came to Sweden to pump Lise for information about the state of German nuclear fission research promised her he could hand-deliver a letter to Otto.

In the letter, she explained that she had spent a long time composing its contents in her head. These were going to be hard words to hear, she warned, words that would test their friendship but that were born out of love. Otto didn't "comprehend the reality of the situation," she told him.

She desperately needed him to understand that many of the people forced to flee the Nazis thought those who stayed behind had lost their standards of justice. Otto was aware as early as 1938 that the Nazis had "horrible things" planned for Jewish people, Lise reminded him, yet he did nothing.

How could Otto not see how this was such a slap in the face to her?

I have so much to say that weighs on my heart. You all worked for Nazi Germany and you did not even try to offer passive resistance. Granted, to absolve your consciences you helped a persecuted person here and there, but millions of innocent people were allowed to be murdered without any kind of protest being uttered. So much depends upon your understanding of what you have permitted to take place. You betrayed your friends. You betrayed Germany itself because you never once spoke out. In the last few days, we have heard of the unbelievably gruesome things in the concentration camps. When I heard a very detailed report on Belsen and Buchenwald, I began to cry out loud and lay awake all night. Perhaps you recall how while I was still in Germany (and now I know that it was not only stupid, but very wrong that I did not leave at once) I often said to you: "As long as only we have sleepless nights and not you, things will not be better in Germany." But you had no sleepless night; you did not want to see; it was too uncomfortable.[319]

The letter never made it to Otto. The American spy turned it over to his agency instead of delivering it. When Otto later told her he never got the letter, she wasn't sure whether to believe him. The next letter she sent definitely arrived.

It was particularly blunt, bleak even: "The question 'Why go on?' is one I asked myself often enough, especially in the early

years in Stockholm. And for millions of people with the same
question, a horrible death (gas, etc.) cut off any answer. I cannot ever forget it."[320]

Lise was trying to shake Otto with her words, desperate to
wrest some sort of emotion out of him at what had transpired
while he looked on—sorrow, anger, regret, anything. It was in-
furiating to feel such deep sadness and rage and yet have someone who meant so much to her feel nothing.

Her appeal to his humanity using both her own personal
hopelessness as well as the suffering of other Jewish people didn't
seem to make a dent in Otto's point of view. He believed it was
best to keep his head down and keep working, for the sake of
the KWI and his own professional and personal safety. He felt
no responsibility for Nazi transgressions.

After the war, the commissioner for science in the UK asked
Lise to help him convince Laue, who was the current direc-
tor of the KWI for Physics, to change the name of the Kaiser
Wilhelm Institute. The Allies felt it was an important gesture
for them to show they were cutting ties from the Nazi era. But
Otto was enraged at the suggestion.

"The fact that the name is so repellent to the U.S. does not,
in my opinion, speak for a great deal of generosity. I would almost doubt that the behavior of the occupying forces is so much
nobler than that of the Germans in the occupying countries,"[321]
Otto railed.

Despite his protests, the British declared the KWI was no
more. A new organization would be born amidst its literal ashes,
dubbed the Max Planck Institute.

Lise wrote Otto another lengthy, well-thought-out letter re-
sponding to his opposition to changing the name of the KWI.
This time she used statistics and hard data to frame her plea for
him to understand and acknowledge the extent of the horrors
perpetrated by Nazis. She also pointed out the wrongness of his
assertion that the Allies were just as bad as the Nazis:

The idea that Germans are the select people and have the right to subjugate "inferior" people by any means was constantly repeated by politicians, and finally the Nazis tried to carry it out. This unfortunate tradition, which has brought the whole world and Germany itself the greatest misfortune, must finally be broken. And a small token of this insight is to change the name of the KWI. That a thoughtful German could seriously say, "I would almost doubt that the behavior of the occupying powers today is so much nobler than that of the Germans in some of the occupied countries." 6 million Jews were murdered. If the best Germans do not understand what has happened and what must never happen again, who should instruct young people that the path that was tried was tragic for Germany and the world? The enormous problems that the Nazis have created do not permit one to look away.[322]

"Again you are fighting with each other," Otto's wife Edith harrumphed to Lise, in an offensive simplification of their disagreement. "That is such a pity, as basically we all agree, don't we?"[323]

Edith was growing weary of their clashes, so she wrote to Lise in hopes of smoothing things over. The Hahns would be in Stockholm for the Nobel Prize ceremony that autumn, and Edith wanted Otto and Lise to patch things up before the visit so they could have a stress-free reunion.

It already wasn't a great occasion for a constructive reunification. The reminder that she had been passed over for the Nobel due to Otto's actions would rub salt in the wound of betrayal for Lise.

Edith was really looking forward to visiting Stockholm, where there would be "no political arguments," she stressed. "Lise, we are so tired of them, and tired and worn out ourselves. It was 12 years, of which you experienced only the five easiest ones."[324]

What Edith neglects to acknowledge is that had Lise stayed

in Germany, those five "easiest" years would likely have been the last years of her life. Edith wasn't Jewish, so she would never truly understand what it was like for Lise.

In situations where one group is persecuted or harassed, the other group often makes calls akin to, "Why can't we all just get along?" especially if that person doesn't feel they personally participated in the persecuting.

Such calls show that these people value nonconfrontation over true understanding and empathy. They want to move on, but they don't want to do the work of understanding how everyone can be included in the actual act, since it would mean they had to experience the temporary discomfort of reckoning with their role in the persecution.

The reunion didn't go well. Lise swallowed her pride in an attempt at creating peace, but their interactions were stilted, stiff. She promised herself she wouldn't bring up any personal arguments—even though she had every right to—so Otto could enjoy his moment of fame.

Once the Hahns returned to Germany, Lise told a friend that Otto had been very unfriendly during the visit. Worse still, she felt he was entirely unaware that he was being rude.

In the years after the war, Otto continued to double down on his and Fritz's role in the discovery of fission, often repeating his version of the story. By this point, the story had essentially taken on a life of its own. Though he was not part of the Manhattan Project, he was attempting to ride on its coattails by insisting it was his brilliance that had made it all possible.

Even though it was no longer potentially dangerous for him to call attention to Lise's role in the discovery, he continued to maintain that Lise and physics had little to do with their finding.

Otto was hoping that now, in poverty-stricken postwar Germany, drumming up some glory for himself would empower him to call for the rebuilding of Germany and of the advanced science it was once known for. It was yet another blow to Otto and Lise's relationship.

It was also a blow to women in science. Diminishing her participation meant her role in the discovery of fission was often glossed over or even forgotten in retellings. It meant yet again, little girls visiting museums or reading history books would not see a woman scientist to emulate.

While Otto never really did come around, Laue eventually wrote to Lise to say he finally recognized that his actions were wrong, and was grateful to her for trying to gently show him and Otto just how wrong.

"We all knew that injustice was taking place, but we didn't want to see it, we deceived ourselves," Laue admitted. "Come the year 1933 I followed a flag that we should have torn down immediately. I did not do so, and now I must bear responsibility for it."[325]

Of all her Berlin colleagues and acquaintances who had remained in Germany, Lise referred to Laue as her only remaining true friend.

A much happier reunion came when Hertha arrived in Sweden for a guest professorship in Uppsala in 1952, funded by a Guggenheim Fellowship. Uppsala was only a little over an hour's train ride from Stockholm, so Hertha visited Lise frequently during this year-long appointment.

Hertha was especially excited to get to spend Lise's seventy-fourth birthday with her in person that November instead of merely commemorating the event with letter-writing as they usually did.

They must have reminisced about Lise's forty-second birthday party during those lean post–World War I years when Hertha had carved little potato figurines for her. Franck was very jealous not to be there to celebrate with them but planned to join them over the Christmas holidays.

The following year, Hertha and Franck chipped in with other friends to buy Lise a record player and some records for her birthday. Finally, the music had returned.

52

Together at Duke: Hertha's Collaborations with Hildegard and Hedwig

Before their exile, Hedwig, Hildegard, and Hertha had all been connected with large, well-appointed university labs in Europe, but now, in America, only Hertha was attached to a similarly well-funded institution. Duke offered more space for labs and more time for research than most women's colleges. Knowing these other German women physicists were eager to get their hands into some real research again, Hertha wasn't stingy with her resources. She invited both Hildegard and Hedwig to come work with her in her lab whenever they had time.

Hertha and Hildegard began investigating pyridine, a highly flammable organic compound structurally related to benzene. The compound has a foul fishy smell, so hopefully the research didn't take too long.

In the fall of 1945, they submitted the coauthored paper "The Near Ultraviolet Absorption of Pyridine Vapor" to *The Journal of Chemical Physics*. It was published the following February. This wasn't Hildegard's first paper in an American journal because she'd published findings with her Mount Holyoke colleagues Emma P. Carr and Lucy Pickett beginning in 1936.

Hedwig continued to join them at Duke during her school vacation periods. In July 1948, Hertha told Hedwig that publishing the findings from the research they'd begun back in 1941 was now "urgent" because several other labs had taken up this area of study.

Physicists at the University of Texas, Catholic University, and Brown University all had teams working on it. According to Hertha, this was great news not only because it meant there was plenty of work to go around, but because it meant they were clearly onto something.

"But when we suddenly get a letter from Oxford telling us they are studying benzene trifluoride there, then that means there will be certain problems with the publications," she told Hedwig. "In short, it seems like stepping up the pace is in order."[326]

The number of teams studying the electronic and vibrational spectra of these benzenes pointed to the importance of the research, but also to competition.

Finally, in September 1948, the duo submitted their coauthored paper "Absorption Spectrum of 1,2,4-Trichlorobenzene in the Near Ultraviolet" to the *Journal of the Optical Society of America*. It was published on January 1, 1949. At long last, an American publication for Hedwig.

In 1948, Franck and Hertha were able to publish another joint paper, this time as a married couple. It had been sixteen years since their last one.

"We both are writing papers all the time. I myself work only four or five hours a day and Hertha still has all the duties at the University, which are quite heavy at the end of the term,"[327] Franck explained to Lise.

At the end of 1949, Hertha's laboratory moved to Duke's new physics building (which remains the main physics department site at Duke to this day). The lab was built in the subbasement;

dark, yes, but also cool and quiet. Plus, it was very easy to maintain the temperature.

Hertha had the lab specially equipped for her needs. For her precious spectrometer, pedestals were installed on separate foundations and vibration-free mountings fitted for its main optical component.

Upon Hedwig's retirement from Wellesley in 1952, Hertha invited her to come work with her at Duke on a permanent basis. Hedwig jumped at the opportunity. She wasn't quite ready to relax just yet. She resumed full-time research, mentored graduate students, and recruited postdoctoral fellows into spectroscopy.

Hertha and Hedwig shepherded dozens of students through their lab to their physics degrees over the years. Hertha oversaw twenty students while they achieved their doctorates and a dozen students earning master's degrees. Of these, a handful were women. Hedwig personally oversaw three grad students.

Hedwig remained an accessible educator and colleague. When anyone came to her office, she would put down her pencil and ask them to sit, giving them her full attention. All staff respected her and enjoyed her sense of humor.

On the wall of her new office at Duke University, Hedwig hung a photo of the University of Breslau, its stately building lined by trees and overlooking the calm Odra River. Breslau was her home, the university there her home base for so much of her life; the place where she discovered a real love of science and scientific collaboration.

At Duke, she found a new kind of contentment.

"She was very happy. She was enjoying her retirement. She had a laboratory and was happily engaged and was able to be supportive to students, which she enjoyed very much," her former student Betsy observed when she visited Hedwig at Duke. "It gave me a warm feeling to see that she was ending up in a much more comfortable situation."[328]

Thanks to Hedwig's incredible mentorship and encouragement, Betsy went on to become the Assistant Secretary for Science and Technology at the US Department of Commerce—the first woman presidential appointee in the department's history. Later, she became the associate lab director for physics research at Argonne National Laboratory.

Hedwig had spent a decade at Wellesley, then twelve years at Duke University as a research associate. Over the course of her career, she published more than twenty research papers, with seven being from her time at Duke. Her work laid the foundation for the creation of the field of radiometry: the measuring of electromagnetic radiation.

Radiometry is key to radio astronomy and remote sensing technology. When scientists began experimenting with rockets and plasma in the 1960s, citations of Hedwig's work skyrocketed.

As for Hildegard, one of her final papers was a fascinating departure from her usual focus on gases. She was dipping her toes into her other research passion: astrophysics. Her 1950 publication examined the effect of cosmic radiation on meteorites. While in space, meteorites endure exceedingly strong cosmic radiation, which can create radioactive atoms.

Hildegard gathered an array of meteorites that had landed on Earth at various points in history: as old as 457 years and as recent as nine months. Her investigation found that the oldest meteorite was inactive, the next oldest only slightly active. The younger meteorites, by contrast, were "very active indeed."

Hildegard retired in 1956. "I always will remember Sweet Briar," she told the school newspaper, to which the reporter responded, "She can be well assured that Sweet Briar feels the same way about her, too."[329]

Hildegard continued to correspond with many of her students from Sweet Briar. Not quite ready to be done with work, she spent four years as chair of the physics faculty at Wilson College in Chambersburg, Pennsylvania.

While Hedwig and Hildegard both worked in Hertha's Duke

lab, the pair never coauthored any papers together. Among the three physicists, Hertha was one of the most prolific authors, with over eighty scientific papers to her name, as well as two books and two chapters in books.

Sometimes she published more than a paper a year; in 1960, for example, she published three papers, which was considered a significant amount for a single year for a researcher who was also responsible for teaching several classes and supervising students.

Hertha confirmed several quantum mechanical theories and made many important contributions to our knowledge of the absorption spectra of various chemicals. In her papers, she was adept at showing how findings fit into the broader picture of what was known about the topic at hand.

Hertha and Hildegard were also rather unique in their ability to act as a liaison of sorts between the disciplines of physics and chemistry because they spoke the language of both fields well.

After retiring yet again in 1960, Hildegard returned to Germany, where she died in 1963 at age 71. Hedwig died in 1964 at age 77. It was a life well-lived, to an age many of her fellow Jewish Germans never saw.

Despite what Franck claimed to Einstein, he did eventually return to Germany; he died on a visit to Göttingen, also in 1964, at age 81. Hertha did the same. In 1966, she retired from Duke and returned to Germany; she died two years later, aged 72.

53

Women in Science, Postwar

While these women scientists didn't live to see the full disman-
tling of sexism toward women in science—sexism that is still,
regrettably, alive and well today—they did help usher in an era
of greater acceptance.

Lise helped nurture the growth of many young scientists during her time in Sweden, as well as driving the nation's nuclear
power initiatives.

At Duke, Hertha provided an exceptional example for both
male and female students (and colleagues for that matter), so everyone could see that women could make fantastic physicists and
professors. It's just as important for men to see women in tradi-
tionally male-dominated fields and positions as it is for women.

By bringing advanced physics to America's women's colleges,
Hildegard and Hedwig played key roles in increasing the quality of women's science education in the US.

At each institution they worked for in America, Hedwig,

Hertha, and Hildegard sparked a passion for physics in countless students. They offered encouragement and mentorship, which was particularly vital for women students.

They cultivated camaraderie in their laboratories and class-rooms and were great role models who exuded not only exper-tise, but also a deep sense of curiosity. Sure, most professors offer the former, but it's the latter that draws in students and inspires them to do more, go farther, and dig deeper.

Forging and maintaining connections with each other after immigrating was pivotal to both their advancement as academ-ics and to their acclimation to America. Their success hinged on the cultivation of a scientific sisterhood of women physicists who had gone through the same ordeal of being displaced by the Nazis.

They passed on to their students not only their love of phys-ics, but also the importance of supporting each other. This was an especially valuable lesson for women students since they were trying to carve a space for themselves in what was still a male-dominated field.

By the mid-1900s, most US universities and grad schools had finally relented and begun accepting women students. Once the doors were open, women flooded through them.

Women's numbers in graduate-level science grew in both America and the UK throughout the 1940s and beyond. Still, a few schools remained steadfast.

Princeton University, for instance, only began accepting a small number of women graduate students as a trial in 1962. Princeton and Yale finally fully admitted women in 1969; Co-lumbia University did not admit women until 1983.

Lise maintained that to appreciate the state of women's rights as of 1960, it was important to first see how far they'd come.

"The gradual development of the professional and legal equal-ity of women can only be properly understood if one remem-bers how many accepted customs had to be overcome in the struggle for the emancipation of women,"[330] Lise proclaimed in a speech at Bryn Mawr women's college outside of Philadelphia.

Lise was telling the next generation of women scholars that while it might not feel like it sometimes, progress had been made in increasing their rights, progress which appeared to be continuing on a positive trajectory.

While not all of the equality that women desired had been achieved, at the very least, "nearly all male professions have become accessible to women," Lise declared.

There was still plenty of room for progress, but Lise felt what had been achieved in her lifetime was something she could be proud of—something she surely had a hand in bringing about given her notoriety.

Everyone could see that Lise was a brilliant scientist. Surely other women deserved the chance to become one, too.

"We can no longer doubt the value and indeed necessity of woman's intellectual education, for herself, for the family, and for mankind," she concluded.

Lise remained in charge of her Stockholm nuclear physics lab until she retired in 1960 and moved to England to be closer to her family. After retirement, she reflected on a life spent dedicated to science.

As a young woman, Lise dreamed of a life that "need not be easy provided only it was not empty." Her wish was granted, and while two world wars ensured life was far from easy at times, "for the fact that it has indeed been full, I have to thank the wonderful development of physics during my lifetime and the great and lovable personalities with whom my work in physics brought me in contact."[331]

Lise never once lost sight of the good that could come of the pursuit of scientific knowledge.

"Science makes people reach selflessly for truth and objectivity," she asserted. "It teaches people to accept reality, with wonder and admiration, not to mention the deep joy and awe that the natural order of things brings to the true scientist."[332]

Despite a lifetime spent chain-smoking, Lise lived the longest of any of them. She died just a few days shy of her ninetieth birthday in 1968. She's been awarded numerous posthumous honors. Element 109, an extremely radioactive synthetic chemical, was named meitnerium after her. A main-belt asteroid as well as craters on the Moon and Venus now bear her name.

For a woman of Jewish descent to reach such a ripe old age and become so celebrated is truly a glorious "screw you" to the Nazis and all they stood for.

CONCLUSION

Who deserves to be saved? Who gets to be remembered? Einstein, Bohr, Planck, Schrödinger—these men's names are used as shorthand for scientific genius and physics prowess. But what of the countless women who supported them in their labs, assisted them in their research, and helped advance their scientific theories?

We've all heard about the exceptions—Marie Curie and her daughter Irène, for example—but we don't realize what the rarity of these cases is telling us. Throughout history, women have been scarce in notable scientific positions because most of the time, they were prevented from achieving them.

Women were the uncredited coauthors, the unattributed assistants, and the wives who act as editors or illustrators. They did most of the grunt work for none of the glory.

And what of these few women who did eventually make it quite far in the field? Lise is the closest a woman physicist has come to fame, but her name is not nearly as well-known as Einstein's. Her expulsion from Germany meant she lost out on a Nobel, not that the prize necessarily comes with more notoriety.

Maria Goeppert Mayer was the second woman to win the Nobel in physics, and few know her name. Of Mayer's incredible accomplishment, local headlines read, "San Diego Mother Wins Nobel Prize."

Women scientists deserve so much better.

Hedwig, Lise, Hildegard, and Hertha were brilliant scientists. Hertha advanced our knowledge of the spectra of multiple chemical compounds. Hedwig's patent improved lighting, and her work led to the quantum interpretation of optical dispersion. Hildegard determined the effect of cosmic radiation on meteorites. Why, Lise discovered nuclear fission, for goodness' sake!

Their intellect was just as dazzling as any of the men they collaborated with or assisted. But they had to work twice as hard just to get where they were simply because of sexism (often combined with anti-Semitism).

Then, after all that, the Nazis tore it down. They forced them out of their jobs because of their gender or heritage, reversing years of progress in gender equality.

Thanks to the massive teams of people who would not quit until they were safely ushered out of Germany, these women survived. Much was lost—including family and friends—but at least they had each other to help them navigate life after the Nazis.

If we take anything away from these women's stories, it should be that the Nazis didn't win. The Nazis didn't rob the world of all its Jewish thinkers or women scholars, despite its determined efforts to do so. The Nazis could never rob their opponents of their indomitable spirit, their will to go on and help others do the same.

These women's stories show us the importance of maintaining hope in the face of despair, of persevering amidst desperation. They illustrate the power of fascism and institutionalized intolerance to rob the world of incredible minds and severely stunt scientific progress. But they also show us how sisterhood and scientific curiosity can transcend borders and persist, flourish even, in the face of seemingly insurmountable odds.

★ ★ ★ ★ ★

AUTHOR'S NOTE

I've spent years conducting primary and secondary research to bring to life the most well-rounded and accurate portrayal of this particular moment in history. I've done my best to craft a faithful depiction of these women's lives, one I hope they would feel does them justice. For quotations, I've chosen to largely forgo the use of ellipses in cases where I've removed text as I feel these can slow down the reader. In all cases, deletions do not alter the meaning of the statements, and are only meant to improve understanding. Many quotes and other information stem from translations and are therefore subject to minor differences in interpretation.

ACKNOWLEDGMENTS

While authors may feel like recluses, books don't come into being without the hard work and dedication of many people. I'd like to thank my dedicated agent, Zoe Sandler, for her continued guidance and advocacy; editors Gabriella Mongelli and Laura Brown for their keen insights and tireless efforts in helping me mold this text into a narrative I'm proud of; the entire team at Park Row Books, from the editorial and design folks to the marketing and promotions experts; Professor Brenda Winnewisser for generously speaking with me and sharing her insights; my incredibly skilled translator, Elke Hedstrom; my phenomenal sensitivity reader, Enid Kassner; my therapist, Carolyn McKamey; the archivists, librarians, and curators at the institutions I contacted (they are all utter angels), especially Jessica Saunders at the Churchill Archives Centre; the hotels and property hosts who housed me during the research and writing of this book.

Thanks, of course, to my family: my husband, Ian, for his

steadfast love and support; my children, Caleb, Xander, and Miles, for their inspiration (and continued need for braces); our cats, Rosalina and Luma, for their much-needed cuddles; all my extended family for their continued encouragement—love you, Dad, Mom, Laura, Papa, Ellen, Louisa, David, Chris, Matt, Cindy and Brad, and Teddy and Tricia. And to my amazing friends Lara, Jillian, Jean, Sarah G., Joel, Mary R.H., Margaret, Sarah S.T., Melody, Sheena, Mary F., Simone, Hannah, and Allison.

In memory of my writing professors MaryAnn Owens and David Everett, whose mentorship and insights made all the difference. And to the people behind *Mystery Science Theater 3000* and RiffTrax: thank you for helping me laugh amid writing about what was at times overwhelmingly heavy subject matter.

ARCHIVES ACCESSED

American Association of University Women, Washington, DC.

Archive of the Society for the Protection of Science and Learning, Bodleian Library, University of Oxford, Oxford, United Kingdom. Documents reproduced by kind permission of Cara (the Council for At-Risk Academics).

Churchill Archives Centre, Churchill College, University of Cambridge, United Kingdom.

Duke University Archives, David M. Rubenstein Rare Book & Manuscript Library, Durham, North Carolina.

Hanna Holborn Gray Special Collections Research Center, Joseph Regenstein Library, University of Chicago Library, Chicago, Illinois.

Mount Holyoke College Archives and Special Collections, South Hadley, Massachusetts.

New York Public Library, Manuscripts and Archives Division, New York, New York.

Niels Bohr Library & Archives, American Institute of Physics, College Park, Maryland.

Rockefeller Archive Center, Sleepy Hollow, New York.

Special Collections, Getty Research Institute, Los Angeles, California.

SELECTED BIBLIOGRAPHY

Albisetti, James C. "The Reform of Female Education in Prussia, 1899-1908: A Study in Compromise and Containment." *German Studies Review* 8, no. 1 (February 1985): 11–41. https://doi.org/10.2307/1429602.

Allgoewer, Elisabeth. "Women Economists and the Changes in the Discipline of Economics in Germany (1895-1961)." *Œconomia* 12, no. 3 (September 2022): 625–661. https://doi.org/10.4000/oeconomia.12734.

Anonymous. *Displaced German Scholars: A Guide to Academics in Peril in Nazi Germany During the 1930s.* London, 1936. Reprinted San Bernardino, CA: Borgo Press, 1993.

Ball, Philip. *Serving the Reich: The Struggle for the Soul of Physics under Hitler.* Chicago: University of Chicago Press, 2014.

Boak, Helen. *Women in the Weimar Republic*. Manchester: Manchester University Press, 2013.

Boissoneault, Lorraine. "The Forgotten Women Scientists Who Fled the Holocaust for the United States." *Smithsonian Magazine*, November 9, 2017. https://www.smithsonianmag.com/history/forgotten-women-scientists-who-fled-holocaust-united-states-180967166.

Cardona, Manuel, and Werner Marx. "The Disaster of the Nazi-Power in Science as Reflected by Some Leading Journals and Scientists in Physics: A Bibliometric Study." *Scientometrics* 64, no. 3 (August 2005): 313–324. https://www.doi.org/10.1007/s11192-005-0253-8.

Cohen, Susan. "The British Federation of University Women: Helping Academic Women Refugees in the 1930s and 1940s." *Board of International Affairs of the Royal College of Psychiatrists* 7, no. 2 (April 2010): 47–49. https://doi.org/10.1192/S1749367600005762.

Duggan, Stephen, and Betty Drury. *The Rescue of Science and Learning: The Story of the Emergency Committee in Aid of Displaced Foreign Scholars*. New York: Macmillan Company, 1948.

Grant, Andrew. "The Scientific Exodus from Nazi Germany," *Physics Today*, September 26, 2018. https://doi.org/10.1063/PT.6.4.20180926a.

Gruner, Wolf, ed. *German Reich 1933–1937*. Vol. 7, *The Persecution and Murder of the European Jews by Nazi Germany, 1933-1945*. Berlin and Boston: De Gruyter, 2019.

Grüttner, Michael. "The Expulsion of Academic Teaching Staff from German Universities, 1933–45." *Journal of*

Contemporary History 57, no. 3 (2022): 513–533. https://doi.org/10.1177/00220094211063074.

Harvard University. "Xenophobia: Closing the Door." Harvard University Pluralism Project, Historical Perspectives. https://pluralism.org/xenophobia-closing-the-door.

Herzenberg, Caroline L., and Ruth H. Howes. *After the War: US Women in Physics*. San Rafael, CA: Morgan & Claypool Publishers, 2015.

Hirsch, Luise. *From the Shtetl to the Lecture Hall: Jewish Women and Cultural Exchange*. Lanham, MD: University Press of America, 2013.

Holocaust Encyclopedia. United States Holocaust Memorial Museum. https://encyclopedia.ushmm.org.

Horrocks, Sally. "The Women Who Cracked Science's Glass Ceiling," *Nature* 575, no. 7781 (November 2019): 243–246. https://doi.org/10.1038/d41586-019-03362-1.

Interview of Betsy Ancker-Johnson by Orville Butler on December 8, 2008. Niels Bohr Library & Archives, American Institute of Physics, College Park, MD. www.aip.org/history-programs/niels-bohr-library/oral-histories/33363.

Interview of Hedwig Kohn by Thomas S. Kuhn on June 7, 1962. Niels Bohr Library & Archives, American Institute of Physics, College Park, MD. www.aip.org/history-programs/niels-bohr-library/oral-histories/4512.

Interview of James Franck and Hertha Sponer Franck by Thomas S. Kuhn and Maria Goeppert Mayer on July 9, 1962. Niels Bohr

Library & Archives, American Institute of Physics, College Park, MD. www.aip.org/history-programs/niels-bohr-library/oral-histories/4609-1.

James, Jeremiah, Thomas Steinhauser, Dieter Hoffmann, and Bretislav Friedrich. *One Hundred Years at the Intersection of Chemistry and Physics: The Fritz Haber Institute of the Max Planck Society 1911-2011.* Berlin and Boston: De Gruyter, 2011. https://doi.org/10.1515/9783110239546.

Knapp, Ulla. "Nullpunkt. Volkswirtinnen an deutschen Hochschulen vor 1965." In *Verfestigte Schieflagen. Ökonomische Analysen zum Geschlechterverhältnis*, edited by Friederike Maier and Angela Fiedler, 123–168. Berlin: Sigma, 2008.

Kohn, Hedwig. "Über das Wesen der Emission der in Flammen leuchtenden Metalldämpfe." *Annalen der Physik* 349, no. 13 (1914): 749–782. https://doi.org/10.1002/andp.19143491304.

Kuhn, H. G. "James Franck. 1882-1964." *Biographical Memoirs of Fellows of the Royal Society* 11 (November 1965): 53–74. http://www.jstor.org/stable/769261.

Leff, Laurel. *Well Worth Saving: American Universities' Life-and-Death Decisions on Refugees from Nazi Europe.* New Haven, CT: Yale University Press, 2019.

Lemmerich, Jost. *Science and Conscience: The Life of James Franck.* Stanford, CA: Stanford University Press, 2011.

Maushart, Marie-Ann. *Hertha Sponer: A Woman's Life as a Physicist in the 20th Century "So You Won't Forget Me."* With additional material by Annette Vogt. Translated by Ralph A. Morris. Edited by Brenda P. Winnewisser. Duke University Department of Physics, Durham, NC: Xlibris, 2011.

Meitner, Lise. "Looking Back." *Bulletin of the Atomic Scientists* 20, no. 9 (1964): 2–7. https://doi.org/10.1080/00963402.1964. 11454713.

————. "The Status of Women in the Professions." *Physics Today* 13, no. 8 (1960): 16–21. https://doi.org/10.1063/1.3057062.

Mouton, Michelle. "From Adventure and Advancement to Derailment and Demotion: Effects of Nazi Gender Policy on Women's Careers and Lives." *Journal of Social History* 43, no. 4 (2010): 945–71. www.jstor.org/stable/40802012.

Niederland, Doron. "The Emigration of Jewish Academics and Professionals from Germany in the First Years of Nazi Rule." *The Leo Baeck Institute Year Book* 33, no. 1 (January 1988): 285–300. https://doi.org/10.1093/leobaeck/33.1.285.

Northeastern University. "Rediscovering the Refugee Scholars of the Nazi Era." Northeastern University Research Project. https://www.northeastern.edu/refugeescholars/about.

Ohm, Britta. "The Chair: A Short History of Structural Unfreedom, Anti-Democracy, and Disenfranchisement in German Academia." In *Academic Freedom and Precarity in the Global North: Free as a Bird*, edited by Asli Vatansever and Aysuda Kölemen, 17–39. United Kingdom: Taylor & Francis, 2022.

Rossiter, Margaret W. *Women Scientists in America: Struggles and Strategies to 1940*. Baltimore: Johns Hopkins University Press, 1982.

Rühle-Gerstel, Alice. "Back to the Good Old Days?" In *The*

Weimar Republic Sourcebook, edited by Anton Kaes, Martin Jay, and Edward Dimendberg, 218–219. Berkeley: University of California Press, 1994.

Silverman, Alexa. "Einstein, AAUW, and Getting Jewish Women Scientists out of Nazi Germany," American Association of University Women, March 14, 2013.

Sime, Ruth Lewin. "From Exceptional Prominence to Prominent Exception: Lise Meitner at the Kaiser Wilhelm Institute for Chemistry." *Ergebnisse* 24 (2005).

———. "Lise Meitner: A 20th Century Life in Physics." *Endeavour* 26, no. 1 (March 2002): 27–31. https://doi.org/10.1016/S0160-9327(00)01397-1.

———. *Lise Meitner: A Life in Physics*. Berkeley: University of California Press, 1996.

———. "Lise Meitner and the Discovery of Nuclear Fission." *Scientific American* 278, no. 1 (January 1998): 80–85. www.jstor.org/stable/26057626.

———. "Lise Meitner in Sweden 1938-1960: Exile from Physics." *American Journal of Physics* 62, no. 8 (August 1994): 695–701. https://doi.org/10.1119/1.17498.

———. "Lise Meitner's Escape from Germany." *American Journal of Physics* 58, no. 3 (March 1990): 262–267. https://doi.org/10.1119/1.16196.

Stephenson, Jill. *Women in Nazi Germany*. Essex, England: Pearson Education Limited, 2001.

Taltavulla, Marta Jordi. "Rudolf Ladenburg and the First Quantum Interpretation of Optical Dispersion." *The European Physical Journal H* 45 (September 2020): 123–173. https://doi.org/10.1140/epjh/e2020-10027-6.

Tobies, Renate. *"Aller Männerkultur zum Trotz": Frauen in Mathematik und Naturwissenschaften.* Frankfurt, Germany: Campus, 1997.

Tobies, Renate, and Annette B. Vogt, eds. *Women in Industrial Research.* Stuttgart: Franz Steiner Verlag, 2014.

Universität Bielefeld. "Timeline History of Equality." https://www.uni-bielefeld.de/uni/profil/gleichstellung/nachgelesen/geschichte-gleichstellung/zeittafel.

University of Oregon. "Principal Acts of Anti-Jewish Legislation in Germany, 1933–1942." https://pages.uoregon.edu/dluebke/NaziGermany443/Judenpolitik.html.

Vincenz, Bettina. *Biederfrauen oder Vorkämpferinnen? Der Schweizerische Verband der Akademikerinnen (SVA) in der Zwischenkriegszeit.* Baden, Germany: Hier und Jetzt Verlag, 2011.

Von Oertzen, Christine. *Science, Gender, and Internationalism: Women's Academic Networks, 1917-1955.* New York: Palgrave Macmillan US, 2016.

Winnewisser, Brenda P. "The Emigration of Hedwig Kohn, Physicist, 1940." *Mitteilungen der Österreichische Gesellschaft für Wissenschaftgeschichte* (1998): 41–58. Courtesy of Bibliothek des Deutsches Museum von Meisterwerken der Naturwissenschaft und Technik, Munich, Germany.

———. "Hedwig Kohn 1887–1964." In *Shalvi/Hyman Encyclo-*

pedia of Jewish Women. Jewish Women's Archive, February 27, 2009. https://jwa.org/encyclopedia/article/kohn-hedwig.

————. "Hedwig Kohn—eine Physikerin des zwanzigsten Jahrhunderts." *Physik Journal* (November 2003): 51–57.

Wunderlich, Frieda. "Women's Work in Germany." *Social Research* 2, no. 3 (August 1935): 310–336. http://www.jstor.org/stable/40981451.

Yeager, Ashley. "From the Basement, Female Physicists Shaped Duke and German Science." *Duke Research Blog*, December 5, 2012. https://researchblog.duke.edu/2012/12/05/from-the-basement-female-physicists-shaped-duke-and-german-science.

ENDNOTES

1   Tollmien, Cordula. "Emmy Noether (1882-1935): 'Die größte Mathematikerin, die jemals gelebt hat.'" *Des Kennenlernens werth. Bedeutende Frauen Göttingens.* Traudel Weber-Reich, ed. Göttingen, 1993. pp. 234.

2   Allgoewer, Elisabeth. "Women Economists and the Changes in the Discipline of Economics in Germany (1895-1961)," *Œconomia* 12-13, September 1, 2022, pp. 625-661. https://doi.org/10.4000/oeconomia.12734.

3   Karin Kock to Rudolf Ladenburg, May 7, 1940. American Association of University Women (AAUW) Archives.

4   Rudolf Ladenburg to Esther Brunauer, May 7, 1940. AAUW Archives.

5   Gruner, Wolf, Götz Aly, Caroline Pearce, Dorothy Mas, and Susanne Heim. *German Reich 1933–1937. The Persecution and Murder of the European Jews by Nazi Germany, 1933-1945. Vol. 1.* Berlin and Boston: De Gruyter, 2019, pp. 218-219.

6   Rudolf Ladenburg to Edward R. Murrow, January 4, 1934. Emergency Committee Papers, NYPL. Quoted in *Well Worth Saving: American*

Universities' Life-and-Death Decisions on Refugees from Nazi Europe, by Laurel Leff. New Haven, CT: Yale University Press, 2019.

7   Robert Bosse to the House of Deputies, 30 April 1898, cited in Agnes von Zahn-Harnack, *Die Frauenbewegung* (Berlin, 1928), p. 179.

8   Interview of Hedwig Kohn by Thomas S. Kuhn on June 7, 1962. Niels Bohr Library & Archives, American Institute of Physics, College Park, MD, www.aip.org/history-programs/niels-bohr-library/oral-histories/4512.

9   Rossiter, Margaret W. *Women Scientists in America: Struggles and Strategies to 1940*. Baltimore: Johns Hopkins University Press, 1982, p. 92.

10   Rossiter, Margaret W. *Women Scientists in America: Struggles and Strategies to 1940*. Baltimore: Johns Hopkins University Press, 1982, introduction, p. xvi.

11   Wunderlich, Frieda. "Women's Work in Germany." *Social Research* 2, no. 3 (1935): 310-336. http://www.jstor.org/stable/40981451.

12   Boak, Helen. *Women in the Weimar Republic*. Manchester University Press, 2013. http://www.jstor.org/stable/j.ctt18mvkrj, p. 34.

13   Talbot, William Henry Fox, "Some Experiments on Coloured Flames," *Edinburgh Journal of Science* 5:1 (July 1826), pp. 77-81.

14   Kohn, Hedwig. "Über das Wesen der Emission der in Flammen leuchtenden Metalldämpfe." *Annalen der Physik*, 349: (1914), 749-782. https://doi.org/10.1002/andp.19143491304.

15   Kohn, Hedwig. "Über das Wesen der Emission der in Flammen leuchtenden Metalldämpfe." *Annalen der Physik*, 349: (1914), 749-782. https://doi.org/10.1002/andp.19143491304.

16   Kohn, Hedwig. "Über das Wesen der Emission der in Flammen leuchtenden Metalldämpfe." *Annalen der Physik*, 349: (1914), 749-782. https://doi.org/10.1002/andp.19143491304.

17   Winnewisser, Brenda. "Hedwig Kohn—eine Physikerin des zwanzigsten Jahrhunderts." *Physik Journal*. (2003): November, pp. 51-57.

18   Hedwig Kohn to Albert Einstein, January 2 1920, in *Einstein: The Collected Papers* (2004, 337-338, doc. 241). Quoted in *Establishing Quan-*

tum Physics in Berlin- Einstein and the Kaiser Wilhelm Institute for Physics, 1917–1922, by Goenner, Hubert, and Giuseppe Castagnetti. Springer Briefs in History of Science and Technology. (2020).

19 Interview of Hedwig Kohn by Thomas S. Kuhn on June 7, 1962. Niels Bohr Library & Archives, American Institute of Physics, College Park, MD, www.aip.org/history-programs/niels-bohr-library/oral-histories/4512.

20 Joliot-Curie, Irène and Paul Savitch. "Sur la nature du radioélément de periode 3.5 heures formé dans l'uranium irradié par les neutrons," *Comptes Rendus*, 206 (1938), pp. 1643-1644.

21 Sutton, Mike. "Hahn, Meitner and the Discovery of Nuclear Fission," *Chemistry World*, November 5, 2018. https://www.chemistryworld.com/features/hahn-meitner-and-the-discovery-of-nuclear-fission/3009604.article.

22 Meitner, Lise. "Looking Back." *Bulletin of the Atomic Scientists*, 20 (1964), p. 4.

23 Meitner, Lise. "Looking Back." *Bulletin of the Atomic Scientists*, 20 (1964), p. 4.

24 "Besondere Begabung" in *Die Akademische Frau*, Arthur Kirchhoff (ed.), Berlin 1897, pp. 256-257.

25 Meitner, Lise. "Looking Back." *Bulletin of the Atomic Scientists*, 20 (1964), p. 5.

26 Meitner, Lise. "Looking Back." *Bulletin of the Atomic Scientists*, 20 (1964), p. 5.

27 Lise Meitner to Hedwig Kohn, November 9, 1941. Churchill Archives Centre, Cambridge, Lise Meitner Papers, GBR/0014/MTNR.

28 Meitner, Lise. "Looking Back." *Bulletin of the Atomic Scientists*, 20 (1964), p. 5.

29 Meitner, Lise. "The Status of Women in the Professions," *Physics Today* 13, 16-21 (1960) https://doi.org/10.1063/1.3057062.

30 Lise Meitner to Elisabeth Schiemann, December 22, 1915. Churchill Archives Centre, Cambridge, Lise Meitner Papers, GBR/0014/MTNR.

31   Lise Meitner to Otto Hahn. January 17, 1918. Quoted in *Lise Meit-ner: A Life in Physics*, by Ruth Lewin Sime. Berkeley: University of California Press, 1996, p.70.

32   Hahn, Otto; Meitner, Lise. "Die Muttersubstanz des Actiniums, ein neues radio-aktives Element von langer Lebensdauer," *Physikalische Zeitschrift* 19 (1918), 208-218.

33   Meitner, Lise. "Looking Back." *Bulletin of the Atomic Scientists*, 20 (1964), p. 5.

34   Interview of James Franck and Hertha Sponer Franck by Thomas S. Kuhn and Maria Goeppert Mayer on July 9, 1962. Niels Bohr Library & Archives, American Institute of Physics, College Park, MD, www. aip.org/history-programs/niels-bohr-library/oral-histories/4609-1.

35   Meitner, Lise. "Looking Back." *Bulletin of the Atomic Scientists*, 20 (1964), p. 7.

36   Lise Meitner to Hertha Sponer, November 27, 1950. Churchill Ar-chives Centre, Cambridge, Lise Meitner Papers, GBR/0014/MTNR.

37   Hertha Sponer to Lise Meitner, December 2, 1951. Churchill Archives Centre, Cambridge, Lise Meitner Papers, GBR/0014/MTNR.

38   Interview of James Franck and Hertha Sponer Franck by Thomas S. Kuhn and Maria Goeppert Mayer on July 9, 1962. Niels Bohr Library & Archives, American Institute of Physics, College Park, MD, www. aip.org/history-programs/niels-bohr-library/oral-histories/4609-1.

39   Interview of James Franck and Hertha Sponer Franck by Thomas S. Kuhn and Maria Goeppert Mayer on July 9, 1962. Niels Bohr Library & Archives, American Institute of Physics, College Park, MD, www. aip.org/history-programs/niels-bohr-library/oral-histories/4609-1.

40   Murphy, James (translator), Planck, Max. *Where Is Science Going?* George Allan and Unwin, 1933, p. 217.

41   Lise Meitner to Otto Hahn, November 16, 1916. Reprinted in: *Lise Meitner and Otto Hahn Letters from the Years 1912-1924*, by Sabine Ernst, Stuttgart, 1992, p. 64.

42   Meitner, Lise. "Looking Back." *Bulletin of the Atomic Scientists*, 20 (1964), p. 7.

43   von Soden, Kristine. "Zur Geschichte des Frauenstudiums," in *70 Jahre Frauenstudium: Frauen in der Wissenschaft*, Kristine von Soden and Gaby Zipfel, eds., Cologne, 1979, 9-42. p. 26.

44   Stücklen, Hildegard. *Zur Frage nach der scheinbaren Gestalt des Himmelsgewölbes*. PhD dissertation, University of Göttingen. Germany: Dieterich, 1919.

45   Rathenau, Gerhart W. "James Franck," in *Göttinger Universitätsreden* 69 (1983) p. 15. Quoted in *Hertha Sponer: A Woman's Life as a Physicist in the 20th Century "So You Won't Forget Me,"* by Marie-Ann Maushart. United States, Xlibris, 2011, p. 21.

46   Interview of James Franck and Hertha Sponer Franck by Thomas S. Kuhn and Maria Goeppert Mayer on 1962 July 9, Niels Bohr Library & Archives, American Institute of Physics, College Park, MD, www.aip.org/history-programs/niels-bohr-library/oral-histories/4609-1.

47   Hermann, Armin. "Die Deutsche Physikalische Gesellschaft 1899-1945," *Physikalische Blätter*. Vol. 51, Issue 1 (1995): F-61—F105, p. F-82. Translated and reprinted in *Hertha Sponer: A Woman's Life as a Physicist in the 20th Century "So You Won't Forget Me"* by Marie-Ann Maushart, p. 17.

48   Maushart, Marie-Ann. *Hertha Sponer: A Woman's Life as a Physicist in the 20th Century "So You Won't Forget Me"*. p. 17.

49   "Studienreise einer Göttinger Privatdozentin nach Amerika," *Göttinger Zeitung*, October 29, 1925.

50   Birge, R.T.; Hopfield, J.J. "The Ultra-Violet Band Spectrum of Nitrogen," *Astrophysical Journal*, vol. 68, p. 259, 1928. https://adsabs.harvard.edu/full/1928ApJ....68.257B.

51   Sponer, Hertha. "Absorption Bands in Nitrogen," *Nature*, 118, p. 696. November 13, 1926.

52   Mock, Geoffrey. "The Hertha Sponer Story," *Duke Today*, November 1, 2007. https://today.duke.edu/2007/11/sponer.html.

53   Meitner, Lise. "The Status of Women in the Professions," *Physics Today* 13, 16-21 (1960). https://doi.org/10.1063/1.3057062.

54   Rühle-Gerstel, Alice. "Back to the Good Old Days?" First published in *Die literarische Welt*, January 27, 1933. Reprinted in *The Weimar Re-*

public Sourcebook, ed. Anton Kaes, Martin Jay, and Edward Dimendberg (University of California Press, 1994), pp. 218-219.

55   James, Jeremiah, Thomas Steinhauser, Dieter Hoffmann, and Bretislav Friedrich. *One Hundred Years at the Intersection of Chemistry and Physics: The Fritz Haber Institute of the Max Planck Society 1911-2011.* Berlin and Boston: De Gruyter, 2011.

56   Horrocks, Sally. "The Women Who Cracked Science's Glass Ceiling," *Nature* 575, no. 7781, November 6, 2019: 243-246. https://doi.org/10.1038/d41586-019-03362-1.

57   Horrocks, Sally. "The Women Who Cracked Science's Glass Ceiling," *Nature* 575, no. 7781, November 6, 2019: 243-246. https://doi.org/10.1038/d41586-019-03362-1.

58   Knapp, Ulla. "Nullpunkt. Volkswirtinnen an deutschen Hochschulen vor 1965." In *Verfestigte Schieflagen: Ökonomische Analysen zum Geschlechterverhältnis*, edited by Friederike Maier and Angela Fiedler, 123-168. Berlin: Sigma, 2008.

59   Rossiter, Margaret W. *Women Scientists in America: Struggles and Strategies to 1940.* Baltimore: Johns Hopkins University Press, 1982, introduction, p. xvi.

60   Boak, Helen. *Women in the Weimar Republic.* Manchester University Press, 2013. http://www.jstor.org/stable/j.ctt18mvkrj, Introduction.

61   Rincklake, Martha and Magdalene von Tiling. *Neue Wege zu deutscher Frauenbildung.* Langensalza, Germany, 1925, p. 11.

62   Carr, Emma P. Mount Holyoke Alumnae Bulletin. July 1925.

63   Hildegard Stücklen, curriculum vitae. University of Chicago Joseph Regenstein Library, Hanna Holborn Gray Special Collections Research Center, James Franck Papers.

64   Lise Meitner to James Franck, January 1929. University of Chicago Joseph Regenstein Library, Hanna Holborn Gray Special Collections Research Center, James Franck Papers.

65   Lise Meitner to Elisabeth Schiemann, October 1927. Quoted in "Der Fall Lise Meitner: Von den Möglichkeiten zur Umkehrung des Matilda-Effekts." "Schwerpunkt: Lise Meitner," *Wissenschaftlerinnen-*

Rundbrief No.3/2010, edited by Zentrale Frauenbeauftragte der Freie Universität Berlin, No. 3, 2010.

66   Meitner, Lise. "The Status of Women in the Professions," *Physics Today* 13, 16-21 (1960). https://doi.org/10.1063/1.3057062.

67   Lise Meitner to James Franck, January 1929, University of Chicago Joseph Regenstein Library, Hanna Holborn Gray Special Collections Research Center, James Franck Papers.

68   James Franck to Lise Meitner, February 2, 1929, University of Chicago Joseph Regenstein Library, Hanna Holborn Gray Special Collections Research Center, James Franck Papers.

69   Hertha Sponer to Ferdinand Springer, January 27, 1931. Quoted in *Hertha Sponer: A Woman's Life as a Physicist in the 20th Century "So You Won't Forget Me,"* by Maushart, p. 49.

70   Springer Verlag to Hertha Sponer, February 3, 1932. Quoted in *Hertha Sponer: A Woman's Life as a Physicist in the 20th Century "So You Won't Forget Me,"* by Maushart, p. 49.

71   Interview with Dame Stephanie Shirley, Voices of Science oral history project, The British Library. https://www.bl.uk/voices-of-science.

72   Lise Meitner to Otto Hahn, March 21, 1933. Otto Hahn Estate, Archives of the Max Planck Society.

73   James Franck to Lise Meitner, February 11, 1933. University of Chicago Joseph Regenstein Library, Hanna Holborn Gray Special Collections Research Center, James Franck Papers.

74   Hirsch, Luise. *From the Shtetl to the Lecture Hall: Jewish Women and Cultural Exchange.* Lanham, MD: University Press of America, 2013, p. 159.

75   Samuels, Sarah. "'An Outstanding and Unusual Contribution': The Emergency Committee in Aid of Displaced Foreign Scholars." *Penn History Review,* Volume 24, Issue 2, April 5, 2019.

76   Walters, Cyrill; Jansen, Jonathan D., eds. *Fault Lines: A Primer on Race, Science and Society.* South Africa: African Sun Media, 2020.

77   Lise Meitner to Otto Hahn, June 8, 1933. Otto Hahn Estate, Archives of the Max Planck Society.

78   Lise Meitner to Otto Hahn, June 8, 1933. Otto Hahn Estate, Archives of the Max Planck Society.

79   Franck, James. Statement printed in *Göttinger Zeitung*, April 18, 1933.

80   Lemmerich, Jost. *Science and Conscience: The Life of James Franck.* Stanford, CA: Stanford University Press, 2011.

81   Hertha Sponer to Werner Heisenberg, November 22, 1933. Max Planck Archive, Max-Planck Institute of Physics, Munich. Quoted in *Hertha Sponer: A Woman's Life as a Physicist in the 20th Century "So You Won't Forget Me,"* by Maushart, p. 65.

82   Edingshaus, Anne-Lydia. *Heinz Maier-Leibnitz—ein halbes Jahrhundert experimentalle Physik*, Munich, 1986, p. 45. Reprinted in *Hertha Sponer: A Woman's Life as a Physicist in the 20th Century "So You Won't Forget Me,"* by Maushart, p. 57.

83   Hertha Sponer personnel file, ca 1936. Reprinted in *Hertha Sponer: A Woman's Life as a Physicist in the 20th Century "So You Won't Forget Me,"* by Maushart, p. 66.

84   Hertha Sponer to James Franck, January 27, 1935. University of Chicago Joseph Regenstein Library, Hanna Holborn Gray Special Collections Research Center, James Franck Papers.

85   Mock, Geoffrey. "The Hertha Sponer Story," *Duke Today*, November 1, 2007. https://today.duke.edu/2007/11/sponer.html.

86   Ohm, Britta. "The Chair: A Short History of Structural Unfreedom, Anti-Democracy, and Disenfranchisement in German Academia." In: *Academic Freedom and Precarity in the Global North: Free as a Bird*, edited by Asli Vatansever and Aysuda Kölemen, Routledge, 2022, p. 22.

87   Mouton, Michelle. "From Adventure and Advancement to Derailment and Demotion: Effects of Nazi Gender Policy on Women's Careers and Lives." *Journal of Social History* 43, no. 4 (2010): 945-971. www.jstor.org/stable/40802012.

88   Hertha Sponer to James Franck, October 11, 1933. University of Chicago Joseph Regenstein Library, Hanna Holborn Gray Special Collections Research Center, James Franck Papers.

89   "History of Equal Rights in Germany 1789–2007," Universität Bielefeld. www.uni-bielefeld.de/gendertexte.

90   Baumer, Gertrud. "Die Frauen in der Volks- und Staatskrise," *Die Frau*,
      6 (1933), p. 322. Quoted in *Frauen im Kriegsdienst 1914-1945*, by Ursula
      von Gersdorff. Stuttgart: Deutsche Verlags-Anstalt, 1969, p. 40.

91   Jarausch, Konrad H. *The Unfree Professions. German Lawyers, Teachers
      and Engineers, 1900-1950*. New York and Oxford: Oxford University
      Press, 1990, p. 105.

92   Wunderlich, Frieda. "Women's Work in Germany." *Social Research* 2,
      no. 3 (1935): pp. 310-336. http://www.jstor.org/stable/40981451.

93   Letter from Leipzig University student body to Reich Office of Stu-
      dent Affairs, September 20, 1932. Quoted in *Hertha Sponer: A Wom-
      an's Life as a Physicist in the 20th Century "So You Won't Forget Me,"* by
      Maushart, p. 60.

94   Lauer, A. *Die Frau in der Auffassung des Nationalsozialismus*. Cologne,
      1932, p. 18.

95   Mouton, Michelle. "From Adventure and Advancement to Derail-
      ment and Demotion: Effects of Nazi Gender Policy on Women's Ca-
      reers and Lives." *Journal of Social History* 43, no. 4 (2010), pp. 945-971.
      www.jstor.org/stable/40802012.

96   Mouton, Michelle. "From Adventure and Advancement to Derail-
      ment and Demotion: Effects of Nazi Gender Policy on Women's Ca-
      reers and Lives." *Journal of Social History* 43, no. 4 (2010), pp. 945-971.
      www.jstor.org/stable/40802012.

97   Said, Erika. "Zur Situation der Lehrerinnen in der Zeit des Nation-
      alsozialismus" in Frauengruppe Faschismusforschung ed. Mutterkreu;
      und Arbeitsbuch. Hamburg, 1981, p. 110. Referenced in Mouton,
      Michelle. "From Adventure and Advancement to Derailment and
      Demotion: Effects of Nazi Gender Policy on Women's Careers and
      Lives." *Journal of Social History* 43, no. 4 (2010), pp. 945-971. www.
      jstor.org/stable/40802012.

98   Stephenson, Jill. *Women in Nazi Germany*. Essex, England: Pearson
      Education Limited, 2001, pp. 19-20.

99   Weisz, G.M.; Kwiet, K. "Managing Pregnancy in Nazi Concentra-
      tion Camps: The Role of Two Jewish Doctors." *Rambam Maimonides
      Medical Journal*. Jul 30, 2018; Vol 9, Issue 3: e0026. doi: 10.5041/
      RMMJ.10347.

100 Docking, Kate. "Who Worked at Ravensbrück?" *History Today*, July 31, 2018. https://www.historytoday.com/miscellanies/who-worked-ravensbrück.

101 Hentschel, K.; Tobies, R. "Friedrich Hund zum 100. Geburtstag." *NTM N.S.* 4, 1–18 (1996). https://doi.org/10.1007/BF02913775.

102 Maushart, Marie-Ann. *Hertha Sponer: A Woman's Life as a Physicist in the 20th Century "So You Won't Forget Me."* p. 65.

103 Hertha Sponer to James Franck, January 16, 1934. University of Chicago Joseph Regenstein Library, Hanna Holborn Gray Special Collections Research Center, James Franck Papers.

104 James Franck to Victor Henri, October 1, 1933. University of Chicago Joseph Regenstein Library, Hanna Holborn Gray Special Collections Research Center, James Franck Papers.

105 Hertha Sponer to Charles W. Edwards, undated. University of Chicago Joseph Regenstein Library, Hanna Holborn Gray Special Collections Research Center, James Franck Papers.

106 Robert A. Millikan to William Few, June 24, 1936. Quoted in *Hertha Sponer: A Woman's Life as a Physicist in the 20th Century "So You Won't Forget Me,"* by Maushart, pp. 109-110.

107 Lise Meitner to James Franck, October 3, 1933. University of Chicago Joseph Regenstein Library, Hanna Holborn Gray Special Collections Research Center, James Franck Papers.

108 Hertha Sponer to Ferdinand Springer, June 24, 1932. Quoted in *Hertha Sponer: A Woman's Life as a Physicist in the 20th Century "So You Won't Forget Me,"* by Maushart, p. 49.

109 Hertha Sponer to James Franck, July 13, 1934. University of Chicago Joseph Regenstein Library, Hanna Holborn Gray Special Collections Research Center, James Franck Papers.

110 Theodora Bosanquet to James Franck, April 3, 1934. University of Chicago Joseph Regenstein Library, Hanna Holborn Gray Special Collections Research Center, James Franck Papers.

111 Esther Caukin Brunauer to James Franck, May 9, 1934. University of Chicago Joseph Regenstein Library, Hanna Holborn Gray Special Collections Research Center, James Franck Papers.

112   Hertha Sponer to James Franck, June 25, 1934. University of Chicago
      Joseph Regenstein Library, Hanna Holborn Gray Special Collections
      Research Center, James Franck Papers.

113   Hertha Sponer to James Franck, July 13, 1934. University of Chicago
      Joseph Regenstein Library, Hanna Holborn Gray Special Collections
      Research Center, James Franck Papers.

114   Hertha Sponer to James Franck, July 14, 1934. University of Chicago
      Joseph Regenstein Library, Hanna Holborn Gray Special Collections
      Research Center, James Franck Papers.

115   Hertha Sponer to James Franck, June 24, 1934. University of Chicago
      Joseph Regenstein Library, Hanna Holborn Gray Special Collections
      Research Center, James Franck Papers.

116   Hertha Sponer to James Franck, June 29, 1934. University of Chicago
      Joseph Regenstein Library, Hanna Holborn Gray Special Collections
      Research Center, James Franck Papers.

117   Hertha Sponer to James Franck, July 14, 1934. University of Chicago
      Joseph Regenstein Library, Hanna Holborn Gray Special Collections
      Research Center, James Franck Papers.

118   Hertha Sponer to James Franck, September 21, 1934. University of
      Chicago Joseph Regenstein Library, Hanna Holborn Gray Special
      Collections Research Center, James Franck Papers.

119   Hertha Sponer to James Franck, September 22, 1934. University of
      Chicago Joseph Regenstein Library, Hanna Holborn Gray Special
      Collections Research Center, James Franck Papers.

120   Hertha Sponer to James Franck, September 22, 1934. University of
      Chicago Joseph Regenstein Library, Hanna Holborn Gray Special
      Collections Research Center, James Franck Papers; Hertha Sponer to
      Lise Meitner, November 5, 1934. Churchill Archives Centre, Cam-
      bridge, Lise Meitner Papers, GBR/0014/MTNR.

121   Hertha Sponer to James Franck, October 4, 1934. University of Chi-
      cago Joseph Regenstein Library, Hanna Holborn Gray Special Col-
      lections Research Center, James Franck Papers.

122   Hertha Sponer to James Franck, June 15, 1935. University of Chicago
      Joseph Regenstein Library, Hanna Holborn Gray Special Collections
      Research Center, James Franck Papers.

123 Hertha Sponer to Lise Meitner, November 5, 1934. Churchill Archives Centre, Cambridge, Lise Meitner Papers, GBR/0014/MTNR.

124 Hertha Sponer to Lise Meitner. November 5, 1934. Churchill Archives Centre, Cambridge, Lise Meitner Papers, GBR/0014/MTNR.

125 Hertha Sponer to James Franck, March 27, 1935. University of Chicago Joseph Regenstein Library, Hanna Holborn Gray Special Collections Research Center, James Franck Papers.

126 Leslie Dunn to Leonore Brecher, December 19, 1933. L.C. Dunn papers, American Philosophical Society. Quoted in *Well Worth Saving: American Universities' Life-and-Death Decisions on Refugees from Nazi Europe*, by Leff, p. 50.

127 Leslie Dunn to Leonore Brecher, May 7, 1934. L.C. Dunn papers, APS. Quoted in *Well Worth Saving: American Universities' Life-and-Death Decisions on Refugees from Nazi Europe*, by Leff, p. 51.

128 Franklin Edgerton of Yale University, undated, Bryn Mawr College Archives, reprinted in *Antike Erzähl- und Deutungsmuster: Zwischen Exemplarität und Transformation*. Anja Behrendt, Anke Walter, and Simone Finkmann, eds. Germany: De Gruyter, 2018, p. 658.

129 Niederland, Doron. "The Emigration of Jewish Academics and Professionals from Germany in the First Years of Nazi Rule." *Leo Baeck Institute Year Book*, Volume 33, Issue 1, January 1988, p. 288.

130 Alvin Johnson to Lewis Gannett, December 5, 1938. Quoted in *Well Worth Saving: American Universities' Life-and-Death Decisions on Refugees from Nazi Europe*, by Leff, p. 4.

131 Greenleaf, Walter J. College Salaries 1936. Bulletin 1937, No. 9. US Department of the Interior Office of Education. p. 2. https://files.eric.ed.gov/fulltext/ED542538.pdf.

132 Hildegard Stücklen, curriculum vitae. University of Chicago Joseph Regenstein Library, Hanna Holborn Gray Special Collections Research Center, James Franck Papers.

133 Emma P. Carr, Mount Holyoke College, November 7, 1935. AAUW Archives.

134 *Science-Supplement*, September 8, 1939, Vol. 90, No. 2332. https://www.science.org/doi/pdf/10.1126/science.90.2332.8.s.

135 Hildegard Stücklen to James Franck, January 2, 1940. University of Chicago Joseph Regenstein Library, Hanna Holborn Gray Special Collections Research Center, James Franck Papers.

136 Hixson, Susan. "History of Research in Chemistry—Mount Holyoke College," Department of Chemistry, Mount Holyoke College, January 1984, pp. 22-29. Quoting Emma. P. Carr writing in 1948.

137 Emma P. Carr to Dr. Frank Blair Hanson at the Rockefeller Foundation, January 31, 1937. Rockefeller Archive Center, Sleepy Hollow, NY.

138 Emma P. Carr to Dr. Frank Blair Hanson at the Rockefeller Foundation, March 17, 1937. Rockefeller Archive Center, Sleepy Hollow, NY.

139 Lise Meitner to Gerta von Ubisch, July 1, 1947. Churchill Archives Centre, Cambridge, Lise Meitner Papers, GBR/0014/MTNR.

140 Hahn, Dietrich, ed. *Otto Hahn, Erlebnisse und Erkenntnisse*. Düsseldorf, Econ Verlag, 1975. p. 54.

141 Hahn, Dietrich, ed. *Otto Hahn, Erlebnisse und Erkenntnisse*. Düsseldorf, Econ Verlag, 1975. p. 54.

142 Niels Bohr to Lise Meitner, April 21, 1938. Churchill Archives Centre, Cambridge, Lise Meitner Papers, GBR/0014/MTNR.

143 James Franck to American Consul in Berlin Germany, June 2, 1938. University of Chicago Joseph Regenstein Library, Hanna Holborn Gray Special Collections Research Center, James Franck Papers.

144 C.D. Ellis to W.B. Brander, September 9, 1938. Quoted in *Lise Meitner: A Life in Physics*, by Sime, p. 208.

145 Meitner, Lise. "Looking Back." *Bulletin of the Atomic Scientists*, 20 (1964), p. 6.

146 Ball, Philip. *Serving the Reich: The Struggle for the Soul of Physics under Hitler*. United States, University of Chicago Press, 2014. p. 82.

147 Anonymous, *Displaced German Scholars: A Guide to Academics in Peril in Nazi Germany during the 1930s*. London, Autumn 1936. Reprinted San Bernardino, CA: Borgo Press, 1993.

148 Bernard Sachs to Franz Boas, August 10, 1933. Emergency Committee in Aid of Displaced Foreign Scholars Papers, New York Public Library.

149 Garner, James Wilford. "The Nazi Proscription of German Professors of International Law." *The American Journal of International Law* 33, no. 1 (1939): 112–119. https://doi.org/10.2307/2190844.

150 Carl Bosch to Wilhelm Frick, May 20, 1938. Quoted in Krafft, Fritz. *Im Schatten der Sensation: Leben und Wirken von Fritz Strassmann*, Verlag der Chemie, Weinheim (1981), p. 173.

151 Dirk Coster to Adriaan Fokker, June 11, 1938. Churchill Archives Centre, Cambridge, Lise Meitner Papers, GBR/0014/MTNR.

152 Reichsministerium Wilhelm Frick to Carl Bosch, June 16, 1938. Quoted in *Lise Meitner: A Life in Physics*, by Sime, p. 195.

153 Peter Debye to Niels Bohr, June 16, 1938. Churchill Archives Centre, Cambridge, Lise Meitner Papers, GBR/0014/MTNR.

154 Adriaan Fokker to Coster, June 27, 1938. Churchill Archives Centre, Cambridge, Lise Meitner Papers, GBR/0014/MTNR.

155 Lise Meitner to Gerta von Ubisch, July 1, 1947. Churchill Archives Centre, Cambridge, Lise Meitner Papers, GBR/0014/MTNR.

156 Lise Meitner to Gerta von Ubisch, July 1, 1947. Churchill Archives Centre, Cambridge, Lise Meitner Papers, GBR/0014/MTNR.

157 Hahn, Otto. *Mein Leben. Die Erinnerungen des großen Atomforschers und Humanisten. Erweiterte Neuausgabe, herausgegeben von Dietrich Hahn.* München, p. 149. Reprinted in *Hertha Sponer: A Woman's Life as a Physicist in the 20th Century "So You Won't Forget Me,"* by Maushart, p. 133.

158 Hahn, Otto. *Mein Leben. Die Erinnerungen des großen Atomforschers und Humanisten. Erweiterte Neuausgabe, herausgegeben von Dietrich Hahn.* München, p. 149. Quoted in *Hertha Sponer: A Woman's Life as a Physicist in the 20th Century "So You Won't Forget Me,"* by Maushart, p. 133.

159 Max von Laue to Lise Meitner, November 1958. Churchill Archives Centre, Cambridge, Lise Meitner Papers, GBR/0014/MTNR.

160 Sime, Ruth Lewin. *Lise Meitner: A Life in Physics*, p. 205.

161 Lise Meitner to Otto Hahn, August 24, 1938. Churchill Archives Centre, Cambridge, Lise Meitner Papers, GBR/0014/MTNR.

162 Adriaan Fokker to Miep Coster, July 16, 1938. Adriaan Fokker Papers, Museum Boerhaave, Leiden.

163 Arno Flammersfeld to Lise Meitner, December 24, 1938. Churchill Archives Centre, Cambridge, Lise Meitner Papers, GBR/0014/MTNR.

164 Lise Meitner to Paul Scherrer, July 20, 1938. Churchill Archives Centre, Cambridge, Lise Meitner Papers, GBR/0014/MTNR.

165 Adriaan Fokker to Manne Siegbahn, July 22, 1938. Adriaan Fokker Papers, Museum Boerhaave, Leiden.

166 Lise Meitner to Otto Hahn, September 6, 1938. Churchill Archives Centre, Cambridge, Lise Meitner Papers, GBR/0014/MTNR.

167 Lise Meitner to Otto Hahn, September 10, 1938. Churchill Archives Centre, Cambridge, Lise Meitner Papers, GBR/0014/MTNR.

168 Adriaan Fokker to Lise Meitner, July 27, 1938. Churchill Archives Centre, Cambridge, Lise Meitner Papers, GBR/0014/MTNR.

169 James Franck to Lise Meitner, April 23, 1939. University of Chicago Joseph Regenstein Library, Hanna Holborn Gray Special Collections Research Center, James Franck Papers.

170 Rudolf Ladenburg to Esther Brunauer, January 1, 1939. AAUW Archives.

171 A. Vibert Douglas to Erica Holme, March 17, 1939. AAUW Archives.

172 Esther Brunauer to Charlotte Houtermans, March 11, 1940. War Relief Files 839, AAUW Archives.

173 Hedwig Kohn to Esther Brunauer, March 29, 1939. AAUW Archives.

174 Erna Hollitscher to Esther Brunauer, December 19, 1939. AAUW Archives.

175 Rudolf Ladenburg to Lise Meitner, November 7, 1939. Churchill Archives Centre, Cambridge, Lise Meitner Papers, GBR/0014/MTNR.

176 Lise Meitner to Hedwig Kohn, January 2, 1940. Churchill Archives Centre, Cambridge, Lise Meitner Papers, GBR/0014/MTNR.

177 Lise Meitner to Rudolf Ladenburg, March 9, 1940. Churchill Archives Centre, Cambridge, Lise Meitner Papers, GBR/0014/MTNR.

178 Erna Hollitscher to Esther Brunauer, April 3, 1940. AAUW Archives.

179 Hedwig Kohn to Lise Meitner, April 9, 1940. Churchill Archives Centre, Cambridge, Lise Meitner Papers, GBR/0014/MTNR.

180 Rudolf Ladenburg to Esther Brunauer, May 7, 1940. AAUW Archives.

181 Rudolf Ladenburg to Esther Brunauer, May 7, 1940. AAUW Archives.

182 Esther Brunauer to Rudolf Ladenburg, May 25, 1940. AAUW Archives.

183 Esther Brunauer to Meta Glass, et al. May 25, 1940. AAUW Archives.

184 David A. Robertson to Esther Brunauer, May 28, 1940. AAUW Archives.

185 Constance Warren to Esther Brunauer, May 30, 1940. AAUW Archives.

186 Meta Glass to Esther Brunauer, May 28, 1940. AAUW Archives.

187 Esther Brunauer to Rudolf Ladenburg, June 5, 1940. AAUW Archives.

188 Mildred McAfee to Esther Brunauer, June 6, 1940. AAUW Archives.

189 Rudolf Ladenburg to Mildred McAfee, June 14, 1940. Wellesley College Archives.

190 Esther Brunauer to Mildred McAfee, June 18, 1940. AAUW Archives.

191 Mildred McAfee to Rudolf Ladenburg, June 22, 1940. Wellesley College Archives.

192 James Franck to Lise Meitner, undated (likely 1941). University of Chicago Joseph Regenstein Library, Hanna Holborn Gray Special Collections Research Center, James Franck Papers.

193 William D. Carmichael, Jr. to Frank Porter Graham, June 26, 1940. Frank Porter Graham Papers #01819, Southern Historical Collection, The Wilson Library, University of North Carolina at Chapel Hill.

194 Katharine Lackey to W.C. Jackson, June 6, 1940. Frank Porter Graham Papers #01819, Southern Historical Collection, The Wilson Library, University of North Carolina at Chapel Hill.

195   Hedwig Kohn to Lise Meitner, July 23, 1941. Churchill Archives Centre, Cambridge, Lise Meitner Papers, GBR/0014/MTNR.

196   Hedwig Kohn to Lise Meitner, July 23, 1941. Churchill Archives Centre, Cambridge, Lise Meitner Papers, GBR/0014/MTNR.

197   Lise Meitner to Hedwig Kohn, November 9, 1941. Churchill Archives Centre, Cambridge, Lise Meitner Papers, GBR/0014/MTNR.

198   Albert Einstein to Lise Meitner, October 31, 1938. Churchill Archives Centre, Cambridge, Lise Meitner Papers, GBR/0014/MTNR.

199   Duggan, Stephen and Betty Drury. *The Rescue of Science and Learning: The Story of the Emergency Committee in Aid of Displaced Foreign Scholars.* New York: The Macmillan Company, 1948.

200   Bureau of Labor Statistics. *Monthly Labor Review.* February 1942, Vol. 54, No. 2, United States. "Salaries in Colleges and Universities, 1939-40," pp. 497-499.

201   Horrocks, Sally. "The Women Who Cracked Science's Glass Ceiling," *Nature* 575, no. 7781, November 6, 2019: 243-246. https://doi.org/10.1038/d41586-019-03362-1.

202   Lise Meitner to Dirk Coster, August 9, 1938. Quoted in *Lise Meitner: A Life in Physics*, by Sime, p. 209.

203   James Franck to Lise Meitner, August 21, 1938. Churchill Archives Centre, Cambridge, Lise Meitner Papers, GBR/0014/MTNR.

204   Hertha Sponer to Lise Meitner, January 8, 1939. Churchill Archives Centre, Cambridge, Lise Meitner Papers, GBR/0014/MTNR.

205   Lise Meitner to Otto Hahn, September 14, 1938. Churchill Archives Centre, Cambridge, Lise Meitner Papers, GBR/0014/MTNR.

206   Lise Meitner to Otto Hahn, September 21, 1938. Churchill Archives Centre, Cambridge, Lise Meitner Papers, GBR/0014/MTNR.

207   James Franck to Hertha Sponer, September 28, 1938. University of Chicago Joseph Regenstein Library, Hanna Holborn Gray Special Collections Research Center, James Franck Papers.

208   Lise Meitner to James Franck, July 14, 1957. University of Chicago Joseph Regenstein Library, Hanna Holborn Gray Special Collections Research Center, James Franck Papers.

209 Lise Meitner to Max von Laue, November 20, 1938. Churchill Archives Centre, Cambridge, Lise Meitner Papers, GBR/0014/MTNR.

210 Hertha Sponer to James Franck, February 11, 1936. University of Chicago Joseph Regenstein Library, Hanna Holborn Gray Special Collections Research Center, James Franck Papers.

211 Hertha Sponer to Max Born, May 26, 1936. Quoted in *Hertha Sponer: A Woman's Life as a Physicist in the 20th Century "So You Won't Forget Me,"* by Maushart, p. 107.

212 Hertha Sponer to Max Born, April 13, 1936. Quoted in *Hertha Sponer: A Woman's Life as a Physicist in the 20th Century "So You Won't Forget Me,"* by Maushart, p. 106.

213 Hertha Sponer to Lise Meitner, January 8, 1939. Churchill Archives Centre, Cambridge, Lise Meitner Papers, GBR/0014/MTNR.

214 Interview of Edward Teller by Marie-Ann Maushart, October 26, 1995. Quoted in *Hertha Sponer: A Woman's Life as a Physicist in the 20th Century "So You Won't Forget Me,"* by Maushart, p. 122.

215 Hertha Sponer to Lise Meitner, October 20, 1940. Churchill Archives Centre, Cambridge, Lise Meitner Papers, GBR/0014/MTNR.

216 Lise Meitner to James Franck, October 7, 1941. University of Chicago Joseph Regenstein Library, Hanna Holborn Gray Special Collections Research Center, James Franck Papers.

217 Hildegard Stücklen to James Franck, January 2, 1940. University of Chicago Joseph Regenstein Library, Hanna Holborn Gray Special Collections Research Center, James Franck Papers.

218 Hildegard Stücklen to James Franck, January 2, 1940. University of Chicago Joseph Regenstein Library, Hanna Holborn Gray Special Collections Research Center, James Franck Papers.

219 Hildegard Stücklen to James Franck, January 2, 1940. University of Chicago Joseph Regenstein Library, Hanna Holborn Gray Special Collections Research Center, James Franck Papers.

220 Hildegard Stücklen to James Franck, January 2, 1940. University of Chicago Joseph Regenstein Library, Hanna Holborn Gray Special Collections Research Center, James Franck Papers.

221 Hertha Sponer and James Franck to Hildegard Stücklen, January 9, 1940. University of Chicago Joseph Regenstein Library, Hanna Holborn Gray Special Collections Research Center, James Franck Papers.

222 Hertha Sponer and James Franck to Hildegard Stücklen, January 9, 1940. University of Chicago Joseph Regenstein Library, Hanna Holborn Gray Special Collections Research Center, James Franck Papers.

223 Hertha Sponer and James Franck to Hildegard Stücklen, January 9, 1940. University of Chicago Joseph Regenstein Library, Hanna Holborn Gray Special Collections Research Center, James Franck Papers.

224 Hertha Sponer and James Franck to Hildegard Stücklen, January 9, 1940. University of Chicago Joseph Regenstein Library, Hanna Holborn Gray Special Collections Research Center, James Franck Papers.

225 Hildegard Stücklen to James Franck, February 11, 1940. University of Chicago Joseph Regenstein Library, Hanna Holborn Gray Special Collections Research Center, James Franck Papers.

226 James Franck to Hildegard Stücklen, mid-February, 1940. University of Chicago Joseph Regenstein Library, Hanna Holborn Gray Special Collections Research Center, James Franck Papers.

227 Hildegard Stücklen to James Franck, February 18, 1940. University of Chicago Joseph Regenstein Library, Hanna Holborn Gray Special Collections Research Center, James Franck Papers.

228 Lise Meitner to Otto Hahn, November 2, 1938. Churchill Archives Centre, Cambridge, Lise Meitner Papers, GBR/0014/MTNR.

229 Hahn, Otto and Fritz Strassmann. "Uber die Entstehung von Radiumisotopen aus Uran durch Bestrahlen mit schnellen und verlangsamten Neutronen," *Naturwissenschaften*, 26 (1938), p. 755 (received Nov. 8, 1938, published Nov. 18, 1938).

230 Strassmann, Fritz. *Kernspaltung: Berlin, December 1938*. Mainz: 1978, pp. 18-20. Quoted in *Im Schatten der Sensation*, by Fritz Krafft, p. 208.

231 Sime, Ruth Lewin. *Lise Meitner: A Life in Physics*, p. 168.

232 Otto Hahn to Lise Meitner, December 19, 1938. Churchill Archives Centre, Cambridge, Lise Meitner Papers, GBR/0014/MTNR.

233 Frisch, Otto Robert. *What Little I Remember.* United Kingdom: Cambridge University Press, 1980. "The Interest is Focussing on the Atomic Nucleus." In: *Niels Bohr: His Life and Work as Seen by His Friends and Colleagues,* Stefan Rozental, ed. Amsterdam: Wiley (1967), pp. 137–148.

234 Frisch, Otto Robert. "The Discovery of Nuclear Fission: How It All Began," *Physics Today* 20, no. 11, November 1967, p. 47.

235 Frisch, Otto Robert. "A Walk in the Snow." *New Scientist,* December 20, 1973, Vol. 60, No. 877, p. 833.

236 Meitner, Lise. "Looking Back." *Bulletin of the Atomic Scientists,* 20 (1964), p. 7.

237 Strassmann, Fritz. *Kernspaltung: Berlin, December 1938.* Mainz: 1978, p. 20. Quoted in *Im Schatten der Sensation,* by Krafft, p. 210.

238 Otto Hahn to Norman Feather, June 2, 1939. Quoted in *Otto Hahn and the Rise of Nuclear Physics,* by W.R. Shea, Netherlands: Springer Netherlands, 2012, p. 110.

239 Otto Hahn to Lise Meitner, December 21, 1938. Churchill Archives Centre, Cambridge, Lise Meitner Papers, GBR/0014/MTNR.

240 Strassmann, Fritz. *Kernspaltung: Berlin, December 1938.* Mainz: 1978, p. 20. Quoted in *Im Schatten der Sensation,* by Krafft, p. 211.

241 Lise Meitner to Birgit Aminoff, November 20, 1945. Churchill Archives Centre, Cambridge, Lise Meitner Papers, GBR/0014/MTNR.

242 Meitner, Lise. "Looking Back." *Bulletin of the Atomic Scientists,* 20 (1964), p. 7.

243 Lise Meitner to James Franck, September 8, 1944. University of Chicago Joseph Regenstein Library, Hanna Holborn Gray Special Collections Research Center, James Franck Papers.

244 Lise Meitner to Hedwig Kohn, November 9, 1941. Churchill Archives Centre, Cambridge, Lise Meitner Papers, GBR/0014/MTNR.

245 Lise Meitner to Walter Meitner, February 6, 1939. Churchill Archives Centre, Cambridge, Lise Meitner Papers, GBR/0014/MTNR.

246 Hertha Sponer to Lise Meitner, October 20, 1940. Churchill Archives Centre, Cambridge, Lise Meitner Papers, GBR/0014/MTNR.

247 Lise Meitner to Hertha Sponer, November 23, 1940. Churchill Archives Centre, Cambridge, Lise Meitner Papers, GBR/0014/MTNR.

248 Hertha Sponer to Lise Meitner, March 2, 1941. Churchill Archives Centre, Cambridge, Lise Meitner Papers, GBR/0014/MTNR.

249 Lise Meitner to Hedwig Kohn, November 9, 1941. Churchill Archives Centre, Cambridge, Lise Meitner Papers, GBR/0014/MTNR.

250 Hedwig Kohn to Lise Meitner, October 18, 1940. Churchill Archives Centre, Cambridge, Lise Meitner Papers, GBR/0014/MTNR.

251 Hedwig Kohn to Lise Meitner, July 23, 1941. Churchill Archives Centre, Cambridge, Lise Meitner Papers, GBR/0014/MTNR.

252 Hertha Sponer to Lise Meitner, October 20, 1940. Churchill Archives Centre, Cambridge, Lise Meitner Papers, GBR/0014/MTNR.

253 Hedwig Kohn to Lise Meitner, July 23, 1941. Churchill Archives Centre, Cambridge, Lise Meitner Papers, GBR/0014/MTNR.

254 Hertha Sponer to Lise Meitner, March 2, 1941. Churchill Archives Centre, Cambridge, Lise Meitner Papers, GBR/0014/MTNR.

255 Hedwig Kohn to Lise Meitner, July 23, 1941. Churchill Archives Centre, Cambridge, Lise Meitner Papers, GBR/0014/MTNR.

256 Hedwig Kohn to Lise Meitner, July 23, 1941. Churchill Archives Centre, Cambridge, Lise Meitner Papers, GBR/0014/MTNR.

257 Hedwig Kohn to Lise Meitner, July 23, 1941. Churchill Archives Centre, Cambridge, Lise Meitner Papers, GBR/0014/MTNR.

258 Hertha Sponer to Lise Meitner, March 2, 1941. Churchill Archives Centre, Cambridge, Lise Meitner Papers, GBR/0014/MTNR.

259 Hertha Sponer to Lise Meitner, March 2, 1941. Churchill Archives Centre, Cambridge, Lise Meitner Papers, GBR/0014/MTNR.

260 James Franck to Hertha Sponer, February 12, 1941. University of Chicago Joseph Regenstein Library, Hanna Holborn Gray Special Collections Research Center, James Franck Papers.

261 University of Houston, Digital History, "The Atomic Bomb: Albert Einstein's Letter to President Franklin D. Roosevelt." https://www.digitalhistory.uh.edu/disp_textbook.cfm?smtID=3&psid=1184.

262 "The Franck Report," A Report to the Secretary of War, June 1945. Federation of American Scientists. https://sgp.fas.org/eprint/franck.html.

263 "The Franck Report," A Report to the Secretary of War, June 1945. Federation of American Scientists. https://sgp.fas.org/eprint/franck.html.

264 Lise Meitner diary, August 7, 1946. Churchill Archives Centre, Cambridge, Lise Meitner Papers, GBR/0014/MTNR.

265 Stockholm *Expressen*, "FLYENDE JUDINNA," August 7, 1945.

266 "People," *Time Magazine*, February 4, 1946. https://content.time.com/time/subscriber/article/0,33009,776611,00.html.

267 "Woman Bomb Aide Sees Future Good; Dr. Lise Meitner, Interviewed Via Radio by Mrs. Roosevelt, Urges World Cooperation," *New York Times*, August 10, 1945. https://www.nytimes.com/1945/08/10/archives/woman-bomb-aide-sees-future-good-dr-lise-meitner-interviewed-via.html.

268 Walz, Jay. "Her Specialty: Atoms," *New York Times*, March 10, 1946. https://timesmachine.nytimes.com/timesmachine/1946/03/10/113132982.html?pageNumber=132.

269 US Holocaust Memorial Museum, Holocaust Encyclopedia, "Refugees," https://encyclopedia.ushmm.org/content/en/article/refugees; Statista, "Number of German Jewish refugees who arrived in selected countries from 1933 until 1945," Statista Research Department, September 16, 2014. https://www.statista.com/statistics/1289780/transit-destination-countries-german-jewish-refugees-wwii.

270 Leicester, H.M., ed. *Source Book in Chemistry, 1900-1950*. United Kingdom: Harvard University Press, 1968.

271 James Franck to Hertha Sponer. March 4, 1941. University of Chicago Joseph Regenstein Library, Hanna Holborn Gray Special Collections Research Center, James Franck Papers.

272 Hedwig Kohn to Lise Meitner, July 23, 1941. Churchill Archives Centre, Cambridge, Lise Meitner Papers, GBR/0014/MTNR.

273 Holocaust Encyclopedia, United States Holocaust Memorial Museum, Washington, DC. "Documenting Numbers of Victims of the Holocaust and Nazi Persecution," Dec 8, 2020. https://encyclopedia.ushmm.org/content/en/article/documenting-numbers-of-victims-of-the-holocaust-and-nazi-persecution.

274 Hedwig Kohn to Lise Meitner, July 23, 1941. Churchill Archives Centre, Cambridge, Lise Meitner Papers, GBR/0014/MTNR.

275 Hedwig Kohn to Esther Brunauer, January 12, 1941. AAUW Archives.

276 Author phone interview with Brenda P. Winnewisser, July 8, 2022.

277 Hedwig Kohn to Lise Meitner, July 23, 1941. Churchill Archives Centre, Cambridge, Lise Meitner Papers, GBR/0014/MTNR.

278 Hedwig Kohn to Lise Meitner, July 23, 1941. Churchill Archives Centre, Cambridge, Lise Meitner Papers, GBR/0014/MTNR.

279 Hedwig Kohn to Lise Meitner, July 23, 1941. Churchill Archives Centre, Cambridge, Lise Meitner Papers, GBR/0014/MTNR.

280 Hedwig Kohn to Lise Meitner, July 23, 1941. Churchill Archives Centre, Cambridge, Lise Meitner Papers, GBR/0014/MTNR.

281 Lise Meitner to Hedwig Kohn, November 9, 1941. Churchill Archives Centre, Cambridge, Lise Meitner Papers, GBR/0014/MTNR.

282 Hedwig Kohn to Lise Meitner, July 23, 1941. Churchill Archives Centre, Cambridge, Lise Meitner Papers, GBR/0014/MTNR.

283 Hedwig Kohn to Lise Meitner, July 23, 1941. Churchill Archives Centre, Cambridge, Lise Meitner Papers, GBR/0014/MTNR.

284 Interview of Betsy Ancker-Johnson by Orville Butler on December 8, 2008. Niels Bohr Library & Archives, American Institute of Physics, College Park, MD. www.aip.org/history-programs/niels-bohr-library/oral-histories/33363.

285 Interview of Betsy Ancker-Johnson by Orville Butler on December 8, 2008. Niels Bohr Library & Archives, American Institute of Physics, College Park, MD. www.aip.org/history-programs/niels-bohr-library/oral-histories/33363.

286 *The Wellesley News*, November 2, 1950. https://repository.wellesley.edu/object/wellesley29895?search=hedwig%2520kohn.

287   Hildegard Stücklen to James Franck, April 19, 1940. University of Chicago Joseph Regenstein Library, Hanna Holborn Gray Special Collections Research Center, James Franck Papers.

288   James Franck to Carl Voegtlin, February 5, 1942. University of Chicago Joseph Regenstein Library, Hanna Holborn Gray Special Collections Research Center, James Franck Papers.

289   James Franck to Hertha Sponer, December 23, 1945. University of Chicago Joseph Regenstein Library, Hanna Holborn Gray Special Collections Research Center, James Franck Papers.

290   Lise Meitner to James Franck, January 1, 1943. University of Chicago Joseph Regenstein Library, Hanna Holborn Gray Special Collections Research Center, James Franck Papers.

291   Hertha Sponer to Lise Meitner, July 6, 1946. Churchill Archives Centre, Cambridge, Lise Meitner Papers, GBR/0014/MTNR.

292   Lise Meitner to Hertha Sponer, July 10, 1947. Churchill Archives Centre, Cambridge, Lise Meitner Papers, GBR/0014/MTNR.

293   James Franck to Niels Bohr, July 10, 1946. University of Chicago Joseph Regenstein Library, Hanna Holborn Gray Special Collections Research Center, James Franck Papers.

294   Lise Meitner to Margrethe Bohr, August 17, 1946. Churchill Archives Centre, Cambridge, Lise Meitner Papers, GBR/0014/MTNR.

295   James Franck to Lise Meitner, July 3, 1946. University of Chicago Joseph Regenstein Library, Hanna Holborn Gray Special Collections Research Center, James Franck Papers.

296   Hahn, Otto. *Otto Hahn: My Life.* New York: Herder and Herder, 1970, p. 88.

297   Meitner, Lise. "The Status of Women in the Professions," *Physics Today* 13, 16–21 (1960). https://doi.org/10.1063/1.3057062.

298   Lise Meitner to Max von Laue, June 28, 1946. Quoted in *Hertha Sponer: A Woman's Life as a Physicist in the 20th Century "So You Won't Forget Me,"* by Maushart, p. 139.

299   James Franck to Wilhelm Westphal, January 10, 1947. University of Chicago Joseph Regenstein Library, Hanna Holborn Gray Special Collections Research Center, James Franck Papers.

300   Walz, Jay. "Her Specialty: Atoms," *New York Times*, March 10, 1946.
      https://timesmachine.nytimes.com/timesmachine/1946/03/10/
      113132982.html?pageNumber=132.

301   Ancker-Johnson, AIP interview.

302   Asimov, Janet. "The Bomb: Reflections on the Anniversary of the
      Hiroshima Attack," *The Humanist*, August 6, 2015. https://thehuman-
      ist.com/commentary/the-bomb-reflections-on-the-anniversary-of-
      the-hiroshima-attack/.

303   "Dr. Meitner Visits Sweet Briar," *Sweet Briar News*, Volume 19, No.
      20, April 17, 1946.

304   Lise Meitner to James Franck, January 1, 1943. University of Chicago
      Joseph Regenstein Library, Hanna Holborn Gray Special Collections
      Research Center, James Franck Papers.

305   Lise Meitner to Margrethe Bohr, November 22, 1946. Churchill Ar-
      chives Centre, Cambridge, Lise Meitner Papers, GBR/0014/MTNR.

306   Lise Meitner to Otto Robert Frisch, February 19, 1946. Churchill Ar-
      chives Centre, Cambridge, Lise Meitner Papers, GBR/0014/MTNR.

307   Interview with Otto Robert Frisch by Ruth Lewin Sime, June 16,
      1975. Quoted in *Lise Meitner: A Life in Physics*, by Sime, p. 332.

308   Lise Meitner to James Franck, January 1, 1943. University of Chicago
      Joseph Regenstein Library, Hanna Holborn Gray Special Collections
      Research Center, James Franck Papers.

309   Walz, Jay. "Her Specialty: Atoms," *New York Times*, March 10, 1946.
      https://timesmachine.nytimes.com/timesmachine/1946/03/10/
      113132982.html?pageNumber=132.

310   James Franck to Albert Einstein, December 11, 1945. University of
      Chicago Joseph Regenstein Library, Hanna Holborn Gray Special
      Collections Research Center, James Franck Papers.

311   James Franck to Albert Einstein, December 3, 1945. University of
      Chicago Joseph Regenstein Library, Hanna Holborn Gray Special
      Collections Research Center, James Franck Papers.

312   James Franck to Albert Einstein, December 11, 1945. University of
      Chicago Joseph Regenstein Library, Hanna Holborn Gray Special
      Collections Research Center, James Franck Papers.

313 Albert Einstein to James Franck, December 30, 1945. University of Chicago Joseph Regenstein Library, Hanna Holborn Gray Special Collections Research Center, James Franck Papers.

314 Lise Meitner to James Franck, September 8, 1944. University of Chicago Joseph Regenstein Library, Hanna Holborn Gray Special Collections Research Center, James Franck Papers.

315 Lise Meitner to James Franck, January 1, 1943. University of Chicago Joseph Regenstein Library, Hanna Holborn Gray Special Collections Research Center, James Franck Papers.

316 Lise Meitner to James Franck, January 1, 1943. University of Chicago Joseph Regenstein Library, Hanna Holborn Gray Special Collections Research Center, James Franck Papers.

317 Lise Meitner to Max Born, October 22, 1944. Churchill Archives Centre, Cambridge, Lise Meitner Papers, GBR/0014/MTNR.

318 Lise Meitner to Otto Hahn, February 26, 1942. Churchill Archives Centre, Cambridge, Lise Meitner Papers, GBR/0014/MTNR.

319 Lise Meitner to Otto Hahn, June 27, 1945. Churchill Archives Centre, Cambridge, Lise Meitner Papers, GBR/0014/MTNR.

320 Lise Meitner to Otto Hahn, April 1, 1946. Churchill Archives Centre, Cambridge, Lise Meitner Papers, GBR/0014/MTNR.

321 Otto Hahn to Lise Meitner, September 17, 1946. Churchill Archives Centre, Cambridge, Lise Meitner Papers, GBR/0014/MTNR.

322 Lise Meitner to Otto Hahn, October 20, 1946. Churchill Archives Centre, Cambridge, Lise Meitner Papers, GBR/0014/MTNR.

323 Edith Hahn to Lise Meitner, November 10, 1946. Churchill Archives Centre, Cambridge, Lise Meitner Papers, GBR/0014/MTNR.

324 Edith Hahn to Lise Meitner, October 10, 1946. Quoted in *Im Schatten der Sensation*, by Krafft, p. 483.

325 Max von Laue to Lise Meitner, November 7, 1958. Churchill Archives Centre, Cambridge, Lise Meitner Papers, GBR/0014/MTNR.

326 Hertha Sponer to Hedwig Kohn, July 28, 1948. Quoted in *Hertha Sponer: A Woman's Life as a Physicist in the 20th Century "So You Won't Forget Me,"* by Maushart, p. 150.

327 James Franck to Lise Meitner, undated, possibly spring 1947. University of Chicago Joseph Regenstein Library, Hanna Holborn Gray Special Collections Research Center, James Franck Papers.

328 Ancker-Johnson, AIP interview.

329 Jackson, Trudi. "Dr. Stücklen Retires in September," *The Sweet Briar News*, May 16, 1956. https://virginiachronicle.com/?a=d&d=SBN19560516.1.1&e=-------en-20--1--txt-txIN--------.

330 Meitner, Lise. "The Status of Women in the Professions," *Physics Today* 13, 16-21 (1960). https://doi.org/10.1063/1.3057062.

331 Meitner, Lise. "Looking Back." *Bulletin of the Atomic Scientists*, 20 (1964), p. 2.

332 Lise Meitner lecture to the Austrian UNESCO Commission in 1953. Quoted in *Lise Meitner: A Life in Physics*, by Sime, p. 375.

INDEX

A

Academic Assistance Council (AAC), 149, 268, 277

Allgoewer, Elisabeth, 11

American Association of University Women (AAUW), 132, 135, 151, 200, 290

American Jewish Joint Distribution Committee (JDC), 148–49

Ancker-Johnson, Betsy, 295–96, 307–8, 322–23

anti-Semitism, 99, 227–28, 229. *See also* Jews and Nazi Germany

Arendt, Hannah, 20, 177

Austria, 162–63, 194–95

B

Ball, Philip, 171

Becquerel, Jean, 88

Benedict, Elizabeth, *35*

Berliner, Arnold, 280

Bethe, Hans, 104

Birge, Raymond T., 78

Bohr, Niels, *61*
  correspondence principle of, 60
  Franck and, 105, 122, 170
  Meitner and, 165, 168, 180
  Nobel Prize, 248
  quantum model of atom, 42
  structure of atom and, 170

Born, Max, 24, 71, 175–76

Bosch, Carl, 164, 179–80, 183

Brecher, Leonore, 150, 177, 282

British Federation of University Women (BFUW), 151–52

Brunauer, Esther, 135, 195–96, 197, 206–7, 282–83, 288–89

Buchwald, Eberhard, *35*

Bunsen, Robert, 32

C

Carmichael, William, 215–16

Carr, Emma P., 88

spectroscopy and, 158–59

Stücklen and, 88, 89, 133, 155, 158–60, 241–42, 246

at University of Zürich, 88

Carroll, John, 197

Chisholm, Grace Emily, 26

concentration and death camps

Kohn and, 15, 203, 285

mass deportations of Jews to, 48, 198, 280, 285

openings of, 48, 97, 194, 198, 279

pregnant women in, 118

release from, 258

scientists murdered in, 282, 283

women as perpetrators in, 118–19

women forced into sex work, 118

Coster, Dirk, 63, 166, 180–81, 182–85, 187, 189

Courant, Richard, 24, 196

D

Das Handbuch der Physik (The Handbook of Physics), 87

Debye, Peter, 65, 182

de Hevesy, George, 61, 248, 305

Dlugosch, Gertrud, 35

Douglas, A. Vibert, 196

Drury, Betty, 225–26

Duggan, Stephen, 225–26

Dunn, Leslie, 150

E

Eder-Schwyzer, Jeanne, 132, 156

education

in pre-Nazi Germany, 23, 24, 28, 51, 84, 111, 234

in US, 20, 26–27, 104, 109, 230

education in Nazi Germany

academic appointments of women, 20, 28, 41, 106, 110–11

intellectual pursuits as unhealthy for women, 116

Jewish students and, 137, 194

Jews fired from faculty positions, 18–19, 48, 99–100, 121

restrictions on Jews and women, 110–11, 112–13, 116–17

Edwards, Charles W., 123–24, 135–36

Einstein, Albert, 73

Berlin physics colloquium and, 59

correspondence principle and, 60

Kohn and, 39

KWI-P and, 38

Meitner and, 63, 221

move to US, 104

musical ability of, 62

Nobel Prize, 72

on Noether, 9, 10

nuclear bomb and, 269

Planck and, 51

Prussian Academy of Sciences and, 103–4

quantum theory and, 60

as target of anti-Semitism, 72

on vengeance against Nazis, 312

Eucken, Arnold, 35, 41

F

Fermi, Enrico, 45

Few, William P., 124

"Final Solution," 98, 279–86

Fischer, Emil, 53, 55

Fischer, Eugen, 99–100

Fokker, Adriaan, 180, 182–83, 184, 189–90

Ford, Henry, 228

Franck, James, 61, 69, 69–70, 71, 102, 166–67, 324

Berlin physics colloquium and, 59–60

Bohr and, 60, 105, 122, 170

Born and, 71

on emigration from Nazi
Germany, 195

family of, 70, 73, *73,* 75, 120–21,
258-59

Frisch and, 166

Goldschmidt and, 284

Kohn and, 265–66, 267

at KWI-PC, 58, 70, *73, 73–74*

Meitner and, 54, 61–62, 165–66,
231–32, 234, 258, 259, 302,
308–9, 313, 319

on Nazis, 97

Nobel Prize, 76, 248, 305

nuclear bomb and, 269, 270, 271

on probability of war, 233

publications by, 104, 321

quantum theory, 59–60

Rubens and, 67

Sponer and, 70–71, 73–74, 75, 79,
91, 93, 94, 105, 120–21, 122,
135, 141–42, 214, 239, 301,
302–3, 305

Stücklen and, 132, 242, 243–45,
246–47, 248, 298–99

at University of Göttingen, 71,
74, 102–3, 105

in US, 144, 258–59

on vengeance against Nazis, 311–
12

Frisch, Otto Robert

Franck and, 166

Manhattan Project and, 270, 306

Meitner and, 191, 252–54, 257,
259, 303, 309

G

Garner, James Wilford, 172–73

Geiger, Hans, 59, *61*

German Scientists Relief Fund, 20–21,
128, 134–35

Glass, Meta, 209–10

Goebbels, Josef, 115

Goldschmidt, Victor, 123, 141, 284

Goudsmit, Helena Esther, 119

Graham, Frank Porter, 214, 217

Grotrian, Walter, *73*

Guckel, Margarete, 35–36

H

Haber, Fritz, 59, 60, *73,* 91, 170

habilitation, 37

in Nazi Germany, 110, 113

sexism and, 109–10, 280

at University of Breslau, 38

women achieving, 10–11, 37, 40–
41, 63, 75–76, 89

Hahn, Otto, *35, 55, 61, 73*

basic facts about, 53, 55

as director of KWI-C, 45

on findings of Joliot-Curie and
Savitch, 47

at KWI-C, 56–57, 91

at KWI-PC, 58

Meitner and, 45, 46–47, 52–54,
56–57, 58–59, 100, 163–64,
182, 185, 186–87, 190–91,
232–33, 249–52, 255–57, 312,
314–19

name change for KWI-P, 316

Nazis and, 45

Nobel Prize, 255, 256

Sponer and, 91

Strassmann and, 46–47, 249–52

Heisenberg, Werner, 42, 105

Henri, Victor, 86–87, 88

Hertz, Gustav, 59, 60, *61, 73, 73*

Herzberg, Gerhard, 104

Hess, Kurt, 100, 101, 163, 185-86, 187

Hilbert, David, 9, 10, 172

Himmler, Heinrich, 181–82, 228

Hirsch, Luise, 99

Hitler, Adolf, 96, 97, 98, 228

Hollitscher, Erna "Holly," 151–52, 197, 199, 203

Hopfield, John Joseph, 77

Hörlein, Heinrich, 163, 164

Horovitz, Stefanie, 281–82

Horrocks, Sally, 82, 227

I

Immerwahr, Clara, 25

International Federation of University Women (IFUW), 132, 135, 151, 181, 195–96, 200

International Rescue Committee, 104–5

J

Jarausch, Konrad, 116

Jastrow, Elizabeth, 290

Jeppson, Janet, 308

Jews and Nazi Germany
  definition of Jew, 96
  escape of, 146–47, 156, 195, 277–78
  "Final Solution," 98, 279–86
  fired from positions, 16, 17, 18–19, 48, 99, 100, 112, 121, 156
  first ghetto established, 211
  in non-Nazi nations, 153, 174, 227–29
  pogroms against, 153–54, 194–95
  restrictions on, 11–12, 16, 17, 18–19, 48, 99–100, 121, 193–94, 279–80
  as scholars, 71–72, 111
  science journals and, 162
  as university students, 137

Joliot-Curie, Irene, 47

Josephson, Ingrid, 70

K

Kaiser Wilhelm Institute for Chemistry (KWI-C)
  atmosphere at, in pre-Nazi Germany, 64
  destroyed, 261
  leadership of, 90–91
  Meitner at, 58, 97, 101, 162, 163, 164–65
  Nazis and, 100

Kaiser Wilhelm Institute for Physical Chemistry (KWI-PC), 29, 56, 58, 70, 73, *73*

Kaiser Wilhelm Institute for Physics (KWI-P), 38–39, 44, 45, 316

Kirchhoff, Gustav, 32, 33, 34

Knapp, Ulla, 82

Knipping, Paul, *61*

Kohn, Hedwig, 22–24, *30, 35,* 102, 287, 290, 324, 325–26
  arc lamp patent, 36
  black bodies experiment by, 33–34
  deportation order for, 15, 203
  at Duke University, 322, 323
  Einstein and, 39
  escape from Germany, 15, 19, 195–219, 262–65
  family of, 22, 111–12, 284–85
  Franck and, 265–66, 267
  German Physical Society and, 68
  habilitation achieved by, 41
  job seeking by, 129
  Ladenburg and, 15, 19, 20, 21, 32–33, 41, 42, 195–96, 199–200, 203, 204, 211, 212, 221
  at Lichtklimatisches Observatorium, 128–29
  loss of teaching license, 17, 19
  Lummer and, 34, 39, 40
  Meitner and, 200–203, 217, 219–21, 288, 289, 290–91, 307, 308
  at OSRAM, 127–28, 129, 130
  publications by, 40, 43, 127, 323
  Schaefer and, 17–18

spectroscopy and, 17, 30–31, 32–34, 38–40, 296

Sponer and, 213, 266–67, 292, 293, 322

University of Breslau and, 11, 17, 41, 128

at Wellesley College, 294–96, 323

at Women's College, 288, 290–91

L

Ladenburg, Rudolf, 32, *35, 61*

at Cornell University, 104

correspondence principle and, 60

escape from Nazi Germany, 43

Kohn and, 15, 19, 20, 21, 32–33, 41, 42, 195–96, 199–200, 203, 204, 211, 212, 221

quantum interpretation, 42

Reiche and, 289

US Emergency Committee in Aid of Displaced German Scholars and, 20

Lathbury, Kathleen Culhane, 82

Lenz, Wilhelm, *61*

Lorenz, Egon, *35*

Lummer, Otto, 33, 34, 39, 40, 51

M

Maltby, Margaret Elizabeth, 26

Manhattan Project, 270–71, 306

Maushart, Marie-Ann, 72

Mayer, Maria Goeppert, 330

McAfee, Mildred, 210–12

Meitner, Lise (Elise), 44, 50, 55, *55, 61, 63*, 63, *73*, 325, 328

on appointment of Hitler, 97

on atmosphere at KWI-C in pre-Nazi Germany, 64

awards and honors, 63, 307, 328

in Berlin, 59–60, 61–62, 161–62

Bohr and, 165, 168, 180

correspondence principle and, 60

Einstein and, 63, 221

on equality of women, 226–27

escape from Nazi Germany by, 48, 165–68, 179–92

experiments with Hahn and Strassmann, 46–47, 249–52

family of, 234–35, 258, 306

fission and, 252–56

Franck and, 54, 61–62, 165–66, 231–32, 234, 258, 259, 302, 308–9, 313, 319

Frisch and, 191, 252–54, 257, 259, 303, 309

German Physical Society and, 68

habilitation achieved by, 63

Hahn and, 45, 46–47, 52–54, 56–57, 58–59, 100, 163–64, 182, 185, 186–87, 190–91, 232–33, 249-52, 255–57, 312, 314–19

on Kurt Hess, 101

Horovitz and, 281

Kohn and, 200–203, 217, 219–21, 288, 289, 290–91, 307, 308

at KWI-C, 44, 56–57, 58, 97, 101, 162, 163, 164–65

Laue and, 259, 312, 314, 319

love of physics, 57

at Lund University, 62

Nazis and firing of, 48, 100

neutron experiments of, 45

Nobel nominations, 257

nuclear bomb and, 270–71, 272–75

Planck and, 45, 50, 51–52, 62, 100, 313

portrayal in films, 309

publications by, 54–55, 58–59, 92, 162, 254

on pursuit of scientific knowledge, 327–28

Schiemann and, 314

sexism and, 91–92

Sponer and, 61, 68, 73, 91–93,

125, 142–43, 232, 237, 239, 259–60, 263, 265–66, 303, 304–5, 308, 319

Stücklen and, 87–88, 308

in Sweden, 231–33, 234–35, 258, 259–61, 308–9, 310

United Kingdom and, 310

at University of Berlin, 51, 55

in US, 306–8, 309

on women in workplace, 80

during World War I, 57–58

Meyer, Edgar, 87

Meyer, Horst, 107

Millikan, Robert A., 124–25, 245, 247, 298

Minkowski, Rudolph, *35*

molecular vibration, 237–38

Moser, Wilhelm, *35*

Mouton, Michelle, 111

N

National Coordinating Committee for Aid to Refugees and Emigrants Coming from Germany (NCC), 148–49

National Institutes of Health, 298–99

National Refugee Service (NRS), 149

Nazi Germany. *See also* concentration camps; education in Nazi Germany; Jews and Nazi Germany

Anschluss with Austria, 162–63

censorship of mail in, 48

childbearing in, 117–19

denial of habilitation to women, 110

displaced academic scholars from, 176–78, 225–26

employment in, 115–16, 117

Hitler, Adolf, 96, 97, 98, 228

influence of Ford in, 228

physics in, 171–73

restrictions on women in, 11–12,

16, 17, 18–19, 48, 99–100, 112–13, 121

rights and role of women in, 114–15

Sponer as Jewish sympathizer and, 123, 143–44

women as perpetrators in, 118–19

Nobel Prize, 72, 76, 248, 255, 256, 257, 305

Noether, Emily, 9–11, 37, 66, 277

O

Ohm, Britta, 110

"On the Influence of Water Vapor on the Spark Potential" (Stücklen), 87

On the Nature of the Emission of Metal Vapors that Glow in Flames (Kohn), 33–34

Oppenheimer, J. Robert, 270, 309

P

Pauli, Wolfgang, 187

Pauling, Linus, 243, 247–48

Payne-Gaposchkin, Cecilia, 82–83

physics. *See also* spectroscopy

alpha and beta emissions, 46

first woman PhD in Germany in, 26

fission, 252–56, 268, 318

German dominance of, 169–71

as male subject, 26–27

Nazis and, 171–73

nuclear bomb, 269–75

optical dispersion, 42

properties of electrons, 17, 70

quantum, 51, 59–60

radioactive substances, 46–47, 56–57, 250–51, 252–54

theoretical vs. experimental, 65–66

thermal radiation, 33, 34, 51

women's employment in, 28

Pickett, Lucy, 158

Planck, Erwin, 283–84

Planck, Max, 51
Berlin physics colloquium and, 59
firing of Jewish faculty and, 121
Meitner and, 45, 50, 51–52, 62, 100, 313
theory of thermal radiations, 51
women in science and, 52

Pohl, Robert, 67, 75, 105, 106-07

Pringsheim, Peter, *61, 73*

R

Rathenau, Walther, 72

Reiche, Fritz, 41, 42, 43, 289

Riecke, Eduard, 66, 67

Riefenstahl, Charlotte, 196–97

Rockefeller Foundation, 76, 135, 149, 150, 154, 156, 175, 248, 277

Roosevelt, Eleanor, 273–74

Roosevelt, Franklin D., 153, 154, 268–70, 273

Rosbaud, Paul, 185, 186, 251–52

Rossiter, Margaret W., 28, 83

Rühle-Gerstel, Alice, 80–81

Rusch, Martin, *35*

Rusk, Rogers, 241–42

S

Sachs, Bernard, 172

Savitch, Paul, 47

Schaefer, Clemens, 17–18, *35,* 127, 128

Scherrer, Paul, 180

Schiemann, Elisabeth, 62, 91, 313–14

Schirmann, Marie Anna, 280–81

Schrödinger, Erwin, 88, 104

Schubert, Martha, *35*

sexism
academic appointments and, 10–11, 20, 28, 41, 75, 82, 106, 110–11, 116, 197, 281, 297, 298
backlash to post-World War I openings for women, 83
belief that women were bad at physics, 124–25, 245, 247
in education in pre-Nazi Germany, 23, 24, 51
in education in US, 20, 27
effect of failure by one woman on other women, 95
"feminine" scientific disciplines, 27, 226
"gender-blind" publications, 54–55, 90
habilitation and, 280
Meitner and, 91–92
motherhood as proper role for women, 83–84
of Planck, 52
of Pohl, 67
post-World War I positions in sciences and, 82–83
in professional societies in sciences, 27–28
replacement of Franck at University of Göttingen and, 106
by reporters, 307
restrictions on education of women, 116–17
unknown women due to, 329–30
women as less-deserving of immigration aid, 150, 151
women credited as authors, 34

Sherrill, Mary, 158

Shirley, Stephanie, 95

Siegbahn, Manne, 62–63, 189–90

Sime, Ruth Lewin, 250–51

spectroscopy
Carr and, 88
described, 31–32
Hopfield and, 77
Kohn and, 17, 30–31, 32–34, 38–40, 129, 296

Sponer and, 71, 74–75, 77

Stücklen and, 88, 158, 299

Sponer, Hertha, 65, 66, *66, 71, 73, 78,*
93, 94, 124, 324, 325, 326

attempt to help other scientists,
175–76, 213–14

Birge and, 78

Debye and, 65

Duke University and, 144, 145,
174–76, 321–22

family of, 143, 285, 302

Franck and, 70–71, 73–74, 75, 79,
91, 93, 94, 105, 120–21, 122,
135, 141–42, 214, 239, 301,
302–3, 305

German Physical Society and, 68

Goldschmidt and, 123, 141

habilitation achieved by, 75–76

Jews and, 123, 143–44

job seeking by, 123–24, 135

Kohn and, 213, 266–67, 292, 293,
322

at KWI, 91–93

Meitner and, 61, 68, 73, 91–93,
125, 142–43, 232, 237, 239,
259–60, 263, 265–66, 303,
304–5, 308, 319

Millikan and, 124–25

notice about departure of,
for America as "display of
feminism," 76–77

Pohl and, 67, 105

publications by, 90, 94–95, 104,
107, 126, 136–37, 142, 175,
238, 239, 301, 320–21, 324

Rockefeller grant awarded to, 76

spectroscopy and, 71, 74–75, 77

Stücklen and, 68, 243–45, 320–21

Teller and, 237–38

at University of Göttingen, 65,
73, *74,* 74–77, 90, 106, 107,
137

at University of Oslo, 142–45

in US, 76, 77–78, 236–40

Stephenson, Jill, 117

Stern, Otto, *61,* 166

Stone, Isabelle, 27

Strassmann, Fritz, 45, 46–47, 249–52,
254, 256, 310

Stücklen, Hildegard, 65–66, 324, 326

Carr and, 88, 89, 133, 155, 158–
60, 241–42, 246

Franck and, 132, 242, 243–45,
246–47, 248, 298–99

German Physical Society and, 68

habilitation achieved by, 89

Henri and, 86–87

job seeking, 132–33

Meitner and, 87–88, 308

Meyer, Edgar and, 87

Pauling and, 243, 247–48

Pohl and, 67, 75

publications by, 87, 320–21, 323

Sponer and, 68, 243–45, 320–21

at University of Göttingen,
65–66

at University of Zürich, 86–88,
131–32, 155, 160

in US, 89, 155–59, 241–42, 298,
299–300, 300, 323

Sutton, Mike, 47

Sweden

Kohn and, 199, 200–203, 205–7,
218–19

Meitner and, 62–63, 166, 183,
189–91, 231–33, 234–35, 258,
259–61, 308–9, 310

von Bahr-Bergius and, 192

Switzerland, 128–32, 201–2

Szilard, Leo, 268–69, 270

T

Talbot, William Henry Fox, 31

Teller, Edward, 104–5, 237–38

Thilo, Guenter, *35*

U

United Kingdom, immigration to, 149, 151–52, 268, 277, 310

United States

academic salaries in, (1935-1936), 156

anti-Semitism in, 227–29

bigotry and, 229

education in, 20, 26–27, 104, 109, 230

employment of women in sciences post-World War I, 28, 82–83

fear of "fifth column," 215–16, 253

impediments to, 147–48, 150–51, 153

importance of, 278–79

nonprofit organizations aiding, 148–49, 151, 152

non-quota visas, 152–53, 204

Roosevelt and, 153, 154

US Emergency Committee in Aid of Displaced German Scholars, 20, 124, 133, 149, 150, 225, 276

V

von Baeyer, Otto, 61, 73

von Bahr-Bergius, Eva, 192, 252, 259

von Karman, Theodore, 104

von Laue, Max

Berlin physics colloquium and, 59–60

on Einstein as target of anti-Semitism, 72

"Final Solution" and, 280

KWI-P and, 316

Meitner and, 259, 312, 314, 319

Nobel Prize, 248, 305

von Neumann, John, 104

von Tiling, Magdalene, 84

von Traubenberg, Heinrich Rausch, 66

W

Waetzmann, Erich, 35

Wagner, Ernst, 61

Weimar Germany, 80, 81, 82, 85, 96–97

Westphal, Wilhelm, 61, 73

Whiting, Sarah Frances, 27–28, 295

Winnewisser, Brenda P., 289

Winston, Mary Frances, 26

Wollman, Elisabeth and family, 283

Women. See also sexism

in American Men of Science, 28

depictions of childless, 84

displaced academic scholars from Nazi Germany, 177

effect of failure by one on other, 95

Emergency Committee in Aid of Displaced German Scholars and, 276

employment of, during World War I in Germany, 28–29

employment of, in Nazi Germany, 115–16, 117

employment of, in physics in US, 28

employment of, in sciences post-World War I, 82–83

feminism in Weimar Germany, 81

first PhD in US, 27

first PhDs in Europe, 25, 26

habilitation achieved by, 10–11, 37, 40–41, 63, 66, 75–76, 89

increase in, in graduate-level science, 326

increase in professional and legal equality of, 326–27

intellectual pursuits as unhealthy for, in Nazi Germany, 116

loss of positions at end of World War I to men, 81

male mentorships for, in sciences, 111

Mount Holyoke College, 156–59

nationalism and, 83–84

notice about Sponer's departure for America as "display of feminism," 76–77

options for non-Jewish scholars in Nazi Germany, 122

as perpetrators in Nazi Germany, 118–19

pregnant, in concentration camps, 118

"racially pure," as breeders, 117

rights and role of, in Nazi Germany, 114–15

as students at University of Göttingen, 66

at University of Breslau's Physics Institute, 38

in Weimar Germany, 80, 81, 82, 85

World War I, 28–29, 35, 57–58

World War II, 198, 206, 221, 269, 270, 271–72

Wreschner, Marie, 81